# Progress in IS

More information about this series at http://www.springer.com/series/10440

Andreas Meier • Luis Terán

# eDemocracy & eGovernment

Stages of a Democratic Knowledge Society

**Second Edition**

 Springer

Andreas Meier
Department of Informatics
University of Fribourg
Fribourg, Switzerland

Luis Terán
Department of Computer Science
Universidad de las Fuerzas Armadas (ESPE)
Sangolquí, Ecuador

Department of Informatics
University of Fribourg
Fribourg, Switzerland

ISSN 2196-8705                        ISSN 2196-8713   (electronic)
Progress in IS
ISBN 978-3-030-17587-0          ISBN 978-3-030-17585-6   (eBook)
https://doi.org/10.1007/978-3-030-17585-6

This Springer imprint is published by the registered company Springer Nature Switzerland AG
The registered company address is: Gewerbestrasse 11, 6330 Cham, Switzerland

# Editorial

The challenges of modernizing the state and its administration have increased, especially with regard to the targeted application of Internet technologies. By means of eDemocracy, it is intended to support the exchange of information, as well as democratic processes of decision-making, voting, and elections. eGovernment aims to put digital public services at disposal for citizens, companies, and organizations. Some examples are electronic services in taxation, employment services and online job markets, public offering via Web platforms, or mobile health services. The reference book eDemocracy & eGovernment aims to review systematically the use of the Internet in administration and politics. A process-oriented layer model (eGovernment Framework) of the University of Fribourg allows us to define the options of exchange and participation for the claim groups and to concretize them by application examples. The following topics, each including a case study of industrial, administrative or research practice, are the key aspects:

- *eAssistance* explains the application of Internet technologies and eGovernment portals, while keeping an eye on quality assurance. A case study on barrier free access gives procedure recommendations.

- *eProcurement* describes the Web-based procurement process and discusses the public offering via Internet. Reverse auctions, used in electronic procurement, provide case examples.

- *eService* discusses electronic governmental services for citizens and companies, as well as a Capability Maturity Model for benchmarking in the eGovernment. Two case studies on electronic health records and interoperability are presented.

- *eContracting* defines the electronic negotiation process and explains digital signatures. The case example is about face recognition in the biometric passport.

- *eSettlement* shows the sub-steps of the supply chain, including ePayment, eDistribution and eSecurity. The case study deals with security measures in electronic data exchange.

- *eCollaboration* gives the groundwork for content management, wiki tools and Weblogs, collaborative working environment and virtual forms of collaboration. Two case studies on virtual campus and massive open online courses are presented.

- *eDemocracy* explains participation types, shows electronic elections (eElection), votes (eVoting) and steps towards public memory. Two case studies on voting advice applications and procedural mechanisms to enhance transparency and trust in Internet voting for the Swiss elections are presented.

- *eCommunity* discusses communication strategies in the multi-channel management, as well as a model for citizen relationship management. The case studies *Participa Inteligente* and the Swiss center for telemedicine are presented.

This reference book is mainly addressed to students of economic sciences at Technical Colleges and Universities, who want to gain a systematic and comprehensive overview of the state of the art in eDemocracy and eGovernment. Apart from them, it is dedicated to citizens, politicians and executives, project leaders and experts in administration, who are occupied with the digital forms of exchange and participation in the knowledge society.

The book was created in the course of a master class in eGovernment and during the development of the eGovernment Framework at the University of Fribourg. Furthermore, the contacts with the eGovernment expert group of Switzerland (www.ech.ch), the Swiss ICT (www.swissict.ch) and the specialist group eHealth of the Society for Computer Science ("Gesellschaft für Informatik," www.gi-ev.de) have contributed to a great extent to the choice of topics and the focal points. We would like to take this opportunity to express my gratitude toward my colleagues, for our inspiring discussions: To Peter Haas, Andreea Ionas, Bruno Jeitziner, Andreas Meer, Willy Müller, Sigfried Reich, Marco Savini, Henrik Stormer, Heiko Schuldt, and Walter Stüdeli.

Big thanks goes to the experts from industry, administration and research, who contributed interesting case studies: Andrea Pacheco, Universidad Internacional del Ecuador; Sandra Sanchez-Gordon, Escuela Politécnica Nacional; Sergio Luján, University of Alicante; Jonathan Wheatley, Fernando Mendez, and Uwe Serdült, Centre for Democracy Studies Aarau (ZDA); Heidi Rubi and Joachim Weiss of the Swiss Federal Railways; Wolfgang Dorda, Georg Duftschmid and Walter Gall of the Medical University of Vienna; Christoph Busch of the Fraunhofer Institute for Computer Graphics Research in Darmstadt; Siegfried Reich and Felix Strohmeier of the Salzburg Research Society; Luka Hamza and Christian Kunz of BitsaboutMe AG; Aigul Kaskina of the University of Fribourg; Birgit Feldmann of the University of Hagen; Bruno Jeitziner of the University of Fribourg; Reto Zurflüh of the Swiss Center for Telemedicine; Jordi Puiggalí-Allepúz and Adrià Rodríguez-Pérez, Scytl Secure Electronic Voting, S.A.; Edy Portmann, University of Fribourg; Simone Franzelli and Astrid Habenstein, University of Bern.

Furthermore, the authors would like to thank the staff of Springer, most of all to Christian Rauscher for the pleasant collaboration.

Fribourg, March, 2019                                    Andreas Meier and Luis Terán

# Contents

**1 eGovernment Framework**     **1**
    1.1    The Lisbon Declaration  .................... 2
    1.2    Definition of eDemocracy and eGovernment  ............ 3
    1.3    Components of the eGovernment Framework  ............ 5
    1.4    Differentiation from eBusiness and eCommerce  ........... 7
    1.5    Chapter Overview  ........................ 8
    1.6    Bibliographical Notes  ..................... 11

**2 eAssistance**     **13**
    2.1    Search and Web Services in the Internet  ............. 14
    2.2    Web Development  ........................ 15
         2.2.1    Web 1.0 – Static Web  .................. 16
         2.2.2    Web 2.0 – The Writing and Participating Web  ......... 16
         2.2.3    Web 3.0 – The Semantic Web  .............. 18
         2.2.4    Web 4.0 – Open, Linked, and Intelligent Web  ......... 18
    2.3    Catalog for Municipality Web Sites  ............... 19
    2.4    Design of eGovernment Portals  ................. 20
    2.5    Barrier-Free Web Access  .................... 22
    2.6    Quality Assurance in the Internet  ................ 24
    2.7    Bibliographical Notes  ..................... 26
    2.8    Case Study—Web Accessibility From a Systems Approach  ...... 27
         2.8.1    Background  ...................... 27
         2.8.2    About Social Dimensions and Ongoing Programs for
                 Inclusion  ....................... 27
         2.8.3    Case Study: Website of the Technical Secretariat for the
                 Inclusive Management on Disabilities  ............ 29
         2.8.4    Future Work and Conclusions  .............. 30
         2.8.5    References  ....................... 32

**3 eProcurement**     **35**
    3.1    Internet-Based Procurement Process  ............... 36
    3.2    Procurement Model Seller-Side  ................. 38
    3.3    Procurement Model Buyer-Side  ................. 39
    3.4    Marketplace Procurement  .................... 40

3.5   Public Offering via Internet . . . . . . . . . . . . . . . . . . . .   42
3.6   Conducting Auctions . . . . . . . . . . . . . . . . . . . . . . . .   43
3.7   Desktop Purchasing . . . . . . . . . . . . . . . . . . . . . . . .   45
3.8   Bibliographical Notes . . . . . . . . . . . . . . . . . . . . . . .   46
3.9   Case Study—Inverse Auctions at the Procurement Agency of Swiss
      Federal Railways . . . . . . . . . . . . . . . . . . . . . . . . . .   47
      3.9.1   Background . . . . . . . . . . . . . . . . . . . . . . . . .   47
      3.9.2   Case Studies of Inverse Auctions in the SBB . . . . . . . .   47
      3.9.3   Case Example A—Procurement of a Service . . . . . . . . .   48
      3.9.4   Case Example B—Procurement of Clothing . . . . . . . . .   49
      3.9.5   Case Example C—Procurement of Working Clothes . . . . .   50
      3.9.6   Case Example D—Procurement of a Service . . . . . . . . .   51
      3.9.7   Opportunities and Risks . . . . . . . . . . . . . . . . . .   51

**4   eService**                                                           **53**
4.1   Technical, Organizational, and Semantic Interoperability . . . . . .   54
4.2   Electronic Governmental Services for Citizens . . . . . . . . . . .   56
4.3   eGovernment Services for Businesses . . . . . . . . . . . . . . . .   57
4.4   Municipality Product Plan . . . . . . . . . . . . . . . . . . . . .   58
4.5   eHealth Architecture for Mobile Services . . . . . . . . . . . . .   60
4.6   Capability Maturity Model for the eGovernment Benchmarking . . . .   62
4.7   Bibliographical Notes . . . . . . . . . . . . . . . . . . . . . . .   64
4.8   Case Study—The Austrian Electronic Health Record System ELGA  .   66
      4.8.1   Background . . . . . . . . . . . . . . . . . . . . . . . . .   66
      4.8.2   Case Study . . . . . . . . . . . . . . . . . . . . . . . . .   66
      4.8.3   Opportunities and Risks . . . . . . . . . . . . . . . . . .   68

**5   eContracting**                                                       **73**
5.1   Electronic Contracts . . . . . . . . . . . . . . . . . . . . . . . .   74
5.2   Generic Services for the Negotiation Process . . . . . . . . . . . .   75
5.3   Identity Management . . . . . . . . . . . . . . . . . . . . . . . .   76
5.4   Asymmetric Encryption . . . . . . . . . . . . . . . . . . . . . . .   78
5.5   Sealing Electronic Documents with Digital Signatures . . . . . . .   80
5.6   Public Key Infrastructure . . . . . . . . . . . . . . . . . . . . .   81
5.7   Blockchain as a Distributed Ledger with Consensus . . . . . . . . .   83
      5.7.1   The Blockchain Data Structure . . . . . . . . . . . . . . .   84
      5.7.2   Solving a Cryptographic Task . . . . . . . . . . . . . . . .   85
      5.7.3   The Criterion of the Longest Block Chain . . . . . . . . . .   86
      5.7.4   Blockchain Options for eGovernment . . . . . . . . . . . .   87
5.8   Legal Aspects . . . . . . . . . . . . . . . . . . . . . . . . . . .   88
5.9   Bibliographical Notes . . . . . . . . . . . . . . . . . . . . . . .   90
5.10  Case Study—Face Recognition in the Biometric Passport . . . . . .   91
      5.10.1  Background . . . . . . . . . . . . . . . . . . . . . . . . .   91
      5.10.2  Case Study on Biometric Data in Passports . . . . . . . . .   91
      5.10.3  Opportunities . . . . . . . . . . . . . . . . . . . . . . .   93
      5.10.4  Risks . . . . . . . . . . . . . . . . . . . . . . . . . . .   95

5.10.5 Conclusion . . . . . . . . . . . . . . . . . . . . . . . . . . . . 96

**6 eSettlement** **99**
6.1 Sub-Steps of a Supply Chain . . . . . . . . . . . . . . . . . . . . 100
6.2 Classification of Web-Based Payment Systems . . . . . . . . . . . 101
6.3 Online Versus Offline Distribution . . . . . . . . . . . . . . . . . 104
6.4 Protection of Personal Data . . . . . . . . . . . . . . . . . . . . . 107
6.5 Protection of Copyright . . . . . . . . . . . . . . . . . . . . . . . 108
6.6 Security Management . . . . . . . . . . . . . . . . . . . . . . . . 110
6.7 General Data Protection Regulation . . . . . . . . . . . . . . . . . 111
6.8 Bibliographical Notes . . . . . . . . . . . . . . . . . . . . . . . . 112
6.9 Case Study—Safeguards on Data Exchange of Salzburg
Research . . . . . . . . . . . . . . . . . . . . . . . . . . . . . . . 114
6.9.1 Background . . . . . . . . . . . . . . . . . . . . . . . . . 114
6.9.2 Case Study—Disregarding of Data Protection and Defense
Measures . . . . . . . . . . . . . . . . . . . . . . . . . . 114
6.9.3 Opportunities and Risks . . . . . . . . . . . . . . . . . . 118
6.10 Case Study—Consent Management System: A Case Study of
BitsaboutMe Platform . . . . . . . . . . . . . . . . . . . . . . . . 121
6.10.1 Background . . . . . . . . . . . . . . . . . . . . . . . . . 121
6.10.2 EU Data Protection Regulation . . . . . . . . . . . . . . . 122
6.10.3 Case Study – BitsaboutMe Platform . . . . . . . . . . . . 123
6.10.4 Consent Management System . . . . . . . . . . . . . . . . 124
6.10.5 Lessons Learned . . . . . . . . . . . . . . . . . . . . . . 126

**7 eCollaboration** **129**
7.1 Document Management . . . . . . . . . . . . . . . . . . . . . . . 130
7.2 Content Management . . . . . . . . . . . . . . . . . . . . . . . . . 132
7.3 Wiki Tools . . . . . . . . . . . . . . . . . . . . . . . . . . . . . . 134
7.4 Use of Weblogs . . . . . . . . . . . . . . . . . . . . . . . . . . . 136
7.5 Collaborative Working Environment . . . . . . . . . . . . . . . . . 138
7.6 Virtual Organization and Forms of Cooperation . . . . . . . . . . . 140
7.7 Bibliographical Notes . . . . . . . . . . . . . . . . . . . . . . . . 142
7.8 Case Study—Learning Environment Virtual Campus at the University
of Hagen . . . . . . . . . . . . . . . . . . . . . . . . . . . . . . . 144
7.8.1 Background . . . . . . . . . . . . . . . . . . . . . . . . . 144
7.8.2 Case Study—Characteristics of a Virtual Campus . . . . . 144
7.8.3 Changes in Learning and Teaching . . . . . . . . . . . . . 145
7.8.4 Communication and Interaction . . . . . . . . . . . . . . . 145
7.8.5 Cooperation . . . . . . . . . . . . . . . . . . . . . . . . . 146
7.8.6 Exams and Examination Regulations . . . . . . . . . . . . 146
7.8.7 Supervision Relationship . . . . . . . . . . . . . . . . . . 147
7.8.8 Changes in the Organization . . . . . . . . . . . . . . . . 147
7.8.9 Opportunities and Risks . . . . . . . . . . . . . . . . . . . 148

7.9    Case Study—Implementing Accessibility in Massive Open Online
       Courses' Platforms for Teaching, Learning and Collaborating at Large
       Scale . . . . . . . . . . . . . . . . . . . . . . . . . . . . . . . . . . . 151
       7.9.1   Background . . . . . . . . . . . . . . . . . . . . . . . . . . 151
       7.9.2   Case Description . . . . . . . . . . . . . . . . . . . . . . . 153
       7.9.3   Barriers . . . . . . . . . . . . . . . . . . . . . . . . . . . . 154
       7.9.4   Discussion and Evaluation . . . . . . . . . . . . . . . . . 156
       7.9.5   Conclusions . . . . . . . . . . . . . . . . . . . . . . . . . 158

**8  eDemocracy                                                                  161**
8.1    Pyramid of Types of Participation . . . . . . . . . . . . . . . . . . 162
8.2    Variety of Electronic Voting and Elections . . . . . . . . . . . . . . 163
8.3    Process Steps for eVoting and eElection . . . . . . . . . . . . . . . 165
8.4    Operation of Electronic Voting and Elections . . . . . . . . . . . . 167
8.5    Blockchain-based eVoting Systems . . . . . . . . . . . . . . . . . . 168
8.6    Analysis and Visualization of Multidimensional
       Data . . . . . . . . . . . . . . . . . . . . . . . . . . . . . . . . . . . 170
8.7    Steps to Public Memory . . . . . . . . . . . . . . . . . . . . . . . . 172
8.8    Bibliographical Notes . . . . . . . . . . . . . . . . . . . . . . . . . 173
8.9    Case Study—What Voting Advice Applications can Tell us About Vot-
       ers . . . . . . . . . . . . . . . . . . . . . . . . . . . . . . . . . . . . 175
       8.9.1   Background . . . . . . . . . . . . . . . . . . . . . . . . . . 175
       8.9.2   State of the Art . . . . . . . . . . . . . . . . . . . . . . . . 177
       8.9.3   A Brief Look at Data from Ecuador . . . . . . . . . . . . . 178
       8.9.4   Summary . . . . . . . . . . . . . . . . . . . . . . . . . . . 180
8.10   Case Study—Technical and Procedural Mechanisms to Enhance Trans-
       parency and Trust in Internet Voting for Swiss Elections and Votes . . . 184
       8.10.1  Background – Internet Voting in Switzerland . . . . . . . . . 184
       8.10.2  Scytl and Swiss Post's Online Voting Solution for Swiss
               Elections . . . . . . . . . . . . . . . . . . . . . . . . . . . . 185
       8.10.3  Discussion and Evaluation . . . . . . . . . . . . . . . . . . 187

**9  eCommunity                                                                   193**
9.1    Push vs. Pull Communication Strategies . . . . . . . . . . . . . . . 194
9.2    Multi-Channel Management . . . . . . . . . . . . . . . . . . . . . . 195
9.3    Establishment of a Citizen Communication Center . . . . . . . . . . 197
9.4    Development Model for Online Citizen . . . . . . . . . . . . . . . . 199
9.5    Performance Review for Public Web Platforms and Portals . . . . . . 202
9.6    Tools for Community Building . . . . . . . . . . . . . . . . . . . . . 204
9.7    Impact of Social Networks in Public Administration . . . . . . . . . 206
9.8    Bibliographical Notes . . . . . . . . . . . . . . . . . . . . . . . . . 207
9.9    Case Study—Medical Communication Center . . . . . . . . . . . . . 209
       9.9.1   Background . . . . . . . . . . . . . . . . . . . . . . . . . . 209
       9.9.2   Case Medgate . . . . . . . . . . . . . . . . . . . . . . . . . 209
       9.9.3   Chances and Risks . . . . . . . . . . . . . . . . . . . . . . 212

9.10 Case Study—Participa Inteligente: A Social Network Platform for Citizens' Discussion and Participation . . . . . . . . . . . . . . . . . . . . 214
9.10.1 Background . . . . . . . . . . . . . . . . . . . . . . . . . . 214
9.10.2 Current State of Research in the Field . . . . . . . . . . . . 214
9.10.3 Impact Evaluation . . . . . . . . . . . . . . . . . . . . . 217
9.10.4 Outlook . . . . . . . . . . . . . . . . . . . . . . . . . . . 218

**10 Knowledge Society** **221**
10.1 Decentralization in the New Public Management . . . . . . . . . . . 222
10.2 Toward the Information and Knowledge Society . . . . . . . . . . . 223
10.3 Use of Knowledge-Based Databases . . . . . . . . . . . . . . . . . 226
10.4 Development of a Knowledge Society . . . . . . . . . . . . . . . . . 227
10.5 Dangers and Risks of a Knowledge Society . . . . . . . . . . . . . 229
10.6 Ethic Rules in the Knowledge Society . . . . . . . . . . . . . . . . 230
10.7 Bibliographical Notes . . . . . . . . . . . . . . . . . . . . . . . . 232
10.8 Case Study—Cognitive Cities . . . . . . . . . . . . . . . . . . . . 234
10.8.1 Today's City: Between "Smart" and "Cognitive" . . . . . . . 234
10.8.2 Cognitive Systems and Cognitive Computing . . . . . . . . . 236
10.8.3 From Cognitive Computing to Cognitive Cities . . . . . . . . 238

**Glossary** **243**

**Bibliography** **249**

**Index** **260**

# Chapter 1

# eGovernment Framework

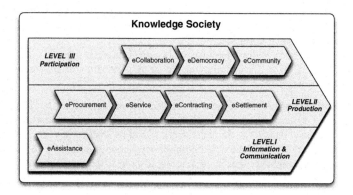

Chapter 1 introduces the topics eDemocracy and eGovernment. In Sect. 1.1, we will refer to the European eGovernment initiative, which is rooted in the Lisbon Strategy and includes the eGovernment Action Plan 2016-2020. The concepts of eDemocracy and eGovernment are defined in Sect. 1.2. In addition, we show different possibilities of interaction between administration and citizens on the one hand, and administration and companies on the other hand. The eGovernment Framework of the University of Fribourg consists of the three process levels, i.e., information and communication, production and participation (Sect. 1.3) and provides the structural concept for this book. Section 1.4 differentiates eGovernment from eBusiness and eCommerce. A topical overview of all chapters is given in Sect. 1.5. Bibliographical notes for eDemocracy, eGovernment, eBusiness, and eCommerce can be found in Sect. 1.6. The eight process areas eAssistance, eProcurement, eService, eContracting, eSettlement, eCollaboration, eDemocracy, and eCommunity make up the main chapters of this book and will each be complemented by a case study from either administration or investigation.

© Springer Nature Switzerland AG 2019
A. Meier, L. Terán, *eDemocracy & eGovernment*, Progress in IS,
https://doi.org/10.1007/978-3-030-17585-6_1

## 1.1   The Lisbon Declaration

*Strategic goals of the Lisbon Strategy*

The European Heads of State and Government met in Lisbon on March 23 and 24 of 2000 (Lisbon Strategy (2008)) and set out a strategy for the European Union in the current decade. The three strategic goals[1] that were passed are:

- Preparing the transition to a knowledge-based economy and society by better policies for the information society and R&D, as well as by stepping up the process of structural reform for competitiveness and innovation and by completing the internal market

- Modernizing the European social model, investing in people, and combating social exclusion

- Sustaining the healthy economic outlook and favorable growth prospects by applying an appropriate macro-economic policy mix

Subsequent to the strategy declaration, the eEurope Action Plan was developed in order to facilitate the transition from an information society to a knowledge society and to exploit the ePotential in Europe.

The eGovernment Action Plan, that was passed under the title "EU eGovernment Action Plan 2016-2020. Accelerating the digital transformation of government"[2] consists of the following key aspects:

*Avoiding the digital divide*

- **No citizen left behind:** It must be avoided that any citizens are left behind in the process of introducing Web-based technologies to the administration (see digital divide in Sect. 10.5). In particular, it has to be ensured that all eGovernment portals and electronic administration services are also accessible to people with handicaps, language, speech, or learning disorders (see Sect. 2.5 on barrier free Web access).

*Realizing regular benchmarking*

- **Making efficiency and effectiveness a reality:** Efficient and effective administration services for citizens, companies, and organizations strengthen the information and knowledge society. In order to measure the quality of governmental services, a benchmarking is carried out every year among the different countries (see agreement on administration services in Sects. 4.2 and 4.3 and the Capability Maturity Model for the benchmarking in Sect. 4.6).

*Importance of public offering*

- **Implementing impact key services:** Governmental services for citizens (Sect. 4.2) and companies (Sect. 4.3) are to be determined and carried out. There is a particular emphasis on eProcurement (see Chap. 3), in order to bring forward Public Offering via the Internet, among other things (see Sect. 3.5 and the case study on reverse auctions in administration in Chap. 3).

*Ensuring data privacy and security*

- **Putting key enablers in place:** The transition from an information society to a knowledge society demands the application of innovative technologies and procedures. For example, an electronic identification system (see identity management

---

[1] See Lisbon Strategy in bibliographical notes.
[2] EU eGovernment Action Plan 2016-2020 in bibliographical notes (European Comission (2016)).

in Sect. 5.3) has to be developed, in order to ensure electronic data interchange for the citizens that take data privacy and security into account (see digital signatures in Sect. 5.5 and public key infrastructure in Sect. 5.6).

- **Strengthening participation and democratic making:** A change in participation models (see participation types pyramid in Sect. 8.1) allows to give citizens extended information, discussion and participation rights. In addition to electronic voting (eVoting) and election (eElection), community formation has to be promoted in preceding and succeeding process steps (see Chap. 8 on eDemocracy). Merely then will it be possible to carry out a political controlling by the citizens in the long-term (see steps toward public memory in Sect. 8.7).

*Developing participation and community formation*

The eGovernment project of the European Union is an ambitious and sustainable program. By concretizing adequate action plans, it will be possible to measure, comment on and publish target achievement, accomplishment, and quality on a regular basis. After the Lisbon Strategy had passed, all European countries adapted on a national level their strategies for an information and knowledge society, generated the general legal conditions for implementation and are currently in the process of realizing partial projects (e.g., eHealth, see service oriented eHealth architecture for mobile services in Sect. 4.5 or the case study on electronic health record in Chap. 4).

## 1.2 Definition of eDemocracy and eGovernment

In the transformation process from an industrial society to an information and knowledge society, the factor "information" gains in importance over the factor "production." The application of information and communication technology is conceived as a chance for amplifying the capacity of the citizens to act, for strengthening cross-border contacts and relations and for developing an open society with cultural diversity.

*An important resource: information*

By Electronic Democracy or eDemocracy, we understand the support and enhancement of civil rights and duties in the information and knowledge society. In the center of attention stand options of participation, which, by the aid of information and communication technology, can be carried out time- and location-independently: Inclusion of the citizens even in early stages of clarification and planning by the public entities, improved information and discussion policy that is suited to the citizens' requirements, barrier-free Web access in electronic votes and elections, formation of communities in different public sectors and for different social concerns, practice of civil rights on all communal levels and improvement of political controlling by use of adequate archiving and documentation systems.

*What is eDemocracy?*

By means of eDemocracy and the possibilities of participation that come along with it, the information society is to develop into a knowledge society. The primary target of this is not the creation of new rights and duties for the citizens, but an extended information policy, activation of citizens, community formation, and creation of transparency (see public memory in Sect. 8.7). Apart from that, it is a goal of the European eGovernment initiative to maintain the cultural autonomy and diversity and to promote the mutual understanding and the interchange beyond language boundaries and country borders.

*Amplify possibilities of participation*

*Definition of*
*eGovernment*

By the term electronic government, or eGovernment, we understand the simplification and execution of information, communication, and interchange processes within and between governmental institutions, and also between the governmental institutions and citizens or organizations. The focus is put on electronic governmental services and all public transactions directed at citizens (taxation, social facilities, employment service, social security, official ID cards, health services, etc.) and at companies (taxes, company start-ups, statistical offices, customs declaration, environmental performance, public procurement, etc.).

Figure 1.1 shows options of information, communication, and interchange between the three most important claim groups, governmental institution (A for administration), citizens (C) and companies (B for business). Accordingly, the eGovernment concept comprises the following three options:

*Service exchange*
*on different*
*institutional*
*levels*

- **A2A—Administration to Administration:** The governmental institution itself uses the Internet technologies to unify and improve the processes within their organization. This means that the information and exchange relations on a certain communal level (e.g., on a national level) or between different levels of governmental institutions (e.g., between European level and member state level) are being cultivated. Particular institutional levels can be skipped (e.g., municipality contacts directly an authority on a national level, if the chain of command allows it). The complexity of interaction relations in governmental services is viewed in more detail in the section on technical, organizational, and semantic interoperability (see Sect. 4.1).

*Exchange and*
*relations with*
*the citizens*

- **A2C—Administration to Citizen:** With the option A2C, the governmental institution offers its services to the citizens electronically. This does not only include the twelve governmental services of the European Union (see Fig. 4.2 in Chap. 4 on eService), but rather all relations of information, communication, exchange, and participation between governmental authorities or offices and the public. Beside electronic votes and elections (Sects. 8.3 and 8.4, there are further options of participation like eCollaboration (Chap. 7) and eCommunity (Chap. 9). For example, it is important to facilitate an opinion-forming process before and after votes

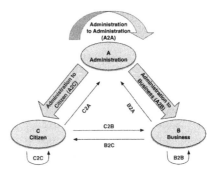

**Fig. 1.1:** How public entities can inform and interact with citizens and companies.

and elections, with discussion forums about ratings and evaluations, subscription services for citizens, documents, and basis of decision making (e.g., spider Web profiles of a congressman to visualize his political goals and actions, see Fig. 8.7 and case study Smartvote in Chap. 8, respectively) up to political controlling.

- **A2B—Administration to Business:** The third option of eGovernment concerns the governmental services directed at companies and organizations. For that purpose, the European Union determined eight service areas (see Fig. 4.3), which range from tax processes over start-ups to open tendering. Also for this kind of services, it results possible and sensible that public offices and government boards recognize the potential of Web-based communication and participation alternatives. For example, a government unit can consider using blogs (see Fig. 9.6 on possible applications of corporate blogs) to interest companies and the public in important topics or causes. Apart from that, the governmental institution can intensify the project works and collaboration with selected companies and organizations by use of software (collaborative working environment, see Sect. 7.5).

*Service exchange between governmental institution and companies*

In order to get a better overview of the variety of exchange relations for eDemocracy and eGovernment, the following section introduces a well-proven eGovernment framework. This framework also establishes the structure of this book (see chapter overview in Sect. 1.5) and can be used for a validation of the quality and depth of participation in governmental services.

## 1.3 Components of the eGovernment Framework

The European Union has realized at an early stage that the eGovernment strategy can only be pushed with clear and measurable action plans. As a consequence, twelve areas for governmental services for citizens, and eight areas for services for companies were defined (Chap. 4 on eService). In order to monitor the performance and quality of the governmental services in a benchmarking of all EU countries and Iceland, Norway, Switzerland, and Turkey (EU28+, see Sect. 4.6), a Capability Maturity Model was developed. The Capability Maturity Model determines whether the governmental service in question is to be categorized as belonging to the information level, the one-way or two-way interaction level, the process level or the personalization level (see Fig. 4.7).

*Governmental services defined by EU*

According to the research of the University of Fribourg, the Capability Maturity Model seems to be qualified to evaluate in certain detail the quality and maturity level of single exchange options. On the other hand, the suggested twenty services for citizens and companies do not go far enough. In particular, the possibilities of eDemocracy are not, or not fully, taken advantage of, that is to say, the options of participation are only exhausted to a small degree (see Level III in Fig. 1.2). Figure 1.2 shows the eGovernment Framework of the University of Fribourg. It constitutes a process model with the following three levels:

*About the Capability Maturity Model of the EU*

- **Process Level I—Information and Communication:** The lowest level provides information and communication facilities in the eGovernment. It focuses on the

*Lowest process level*

design of communal Web portals, and more extensive eGovernment portals, respectively, as well as the use of Web 2.0 technologies. A barrier-free Web access, in compliance with the Web Content Accessibility Guidelines (WCAG) proposed by the World Wide Web Consortium (WCAG (2007)), is imperative (see Sect. 2.5).

*Process level of production*

- **Process Level II—Production**: The second process level contains the actual governmental services required for the options A2A (Administration to Administration), A2C (Administration to Citizen), and A2B (Administration to Business). These services are primarily administration services for electronic procurement (eProcurement), traditional services such as taxation, education, residents' registration, ID card acquisition, etc. (eService), contracts based on digitally signed electronic documents (eContracting) and processing such as electronic shipment, electronic payment, and the guarantee of data security and safety (eSettlement).

*Process level of participation of citizens*

- **Process Level III—Participation:** The participation possibilities on the third process level are of particular importance and are understood as an indicator for a progressive and responsible knowledge society. In addition to electronic voting (eVoting) and electronic elections (eElection), communication concepts must be analyzed, processes for the community formation must be established and a development model for the online citizens must be implemented. Virtual forms of organization and collaboration, including the use of Web 2.0 technologies and social software, respectively, enable the further development of the knowledge society.

*Step-by-step approach to eDemocracy and eGovernment*

Many municipalities or small communities usually start by putting up a Web site, on which they communicate their concerns and projects; within the eGovernment Framework, they stand on the first process level of information and communication. The limited financial means and resources suggest that they link themselves with higher-ranking public institutions and participate in an eGovernment portal. On the second process level, the governmental services for eProcurement, eService, eContracting and secure settlement and performance (eSettlement) can be provided. The highest process level of participation requires a rethinking in administration, e.g., as suggested in the New Public Management (see Sect. 10.1). At the same time, the potential of innovative Web

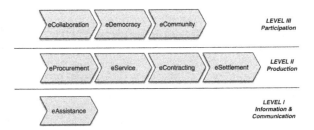

**Fig. 1.2:** Stage model (eGovernment framework) of the University of Fribourg.

| SERVICE DEMAND | | | |
|---|---|---|---|
| | **Administration** | **Citizen** | **Business** |
| **Administration** (SERVICE OFFER) | Administration to Administration (A2A)<br><br>e.g. Types of collaboration of virtual communities | Administration to Citizen (A2C)<br><br>e.g. Opportunity for electronic voting | Administration to Business (A2B)<br><br>e.g. Open tendering of project schemas |
| **Citizen** | Citizen to Administration (C2A)<br><br>e.g. Citizens evaluate public environmental projects | Citizen to Citizen (C2C)<br><br>e.g. Small advertisement on personal homepage | Citizen to Business (C2B)<br><br>e.g. Web site with personal qualification profile |
| **Business** | Business to Administration (B2A)<br><br>e.g. Electronic services for public administrations | Business to Citizen or Consumer (B2C)<br><br>e.g. Products offer in a eShop | Business to Business (B2B)<br><br>e.g. Order from suppliers (supply chain) |

**Fig. 1.3:** Exchange possibilities of eGovernment in comparison with eBusiness and eCommerce.

technologies can be used for different types of collaboration and community formation processes. In the matter of electronic votes and elections, there must be provided secure and transparent software solutions in order to establish trust in the electronic services offered for citizens.

# 1.4 Differentiation from eBusiness and eCommerce

Electronic business, or eBusiness, is defined as initiation, agreement, and handling of electronic business transactions, i.e., a service exchange with the help of public or private communication networks (Internet), with the goal of adding value. Companies (business) can appear as service provider and consumer, as well as public institutions (administration) and citizens or private consumers. It is important that the electronic business transaction creates an added value, be it in monetary form or as an immaterial contribution. *How is eBusiness defined?*

Figure 1.3 shows the three groups of market participants (administration, citizens, and business) with their possible exchange relations. Each of these participants can appear as a provider or as a consumer of services. This gives us a total of nine basic exchange relations.

As illustrated earlier in Sect. 1.2, the exchange relations A2A, A2C, and A2B belong to the eGovernment: Government and administration offices are on the side of the provider and they maintain exchange relations internally (A2A), with the citizens (A2C) or with companies (A2B). Laws and ordinances set the corresponding service mandate. Apart from that, the governmental institution can delegate services to a third party by outsourcing contracts (service level agreements), e.g., to NPOs, NGOs, or private com- *Exchange possibilities of the eGovernment* panies. The exchange options of the eGovernment can be understood as a subset of all eBusiness and electronic exchange relations, respectively, according to the chart in Fig. 1.3.

*Subarea of eCommerce*      Another subset of eBusiness is the actual eCommerce. By the two exchange options Business-to-Consumer (B2C) and Business-to-Business (B2B), companies offer products and services to clients or companies. They are called the two options of electronic commerce (eCommerce). A concrete example for a B2C option would be the operation of an electronic shop by a company. The exchange option B2B constitutes the supply relations between companies (supply chain management, see Sect. 6.1).

While speaking of eGovernment and most of the exchange options of eBusiness, the abbreviation C stands for citizen, when speaking of eCommerce, it stands for consumer. An important feature of the matrix of exchange options is the fact that people can assume the role of a provider as well. For example, the option C2C means that there is an electronic exchange relation between individuals. Also, citizens can provide services for companies (C2B) or administrative institutions (C2A).

*Different roles in eBusiness*      In the numerous collaboration and exchange options of eBusiness and eGovernment, the market participant assumes different roles. At one time, he acts as a service provider, another time, as a service consumer. A citizen can, for example, act as a service consumer and provider at the same time, if he offers his skills on a Web site to the administration or to private companies as a volunteer or as an entrepreneur. This promotes the market and exchange relations of the so-called multi-option society, which will be explained more deeply in Chap. 10 on eSociety.

## 1.5   Chapter Overview

This book focuses on the process areas of eGovernment and dedicates a chapter to each content area (Fig. 1.4). The introductory chapter defines the concepts and introduces to both European Strategy and the eGovernment Framework of the University of Fribourg.

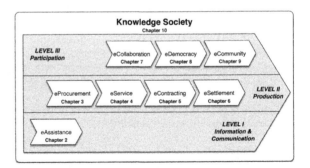

**Fig. 1.4:** eGovernment framework and chapter overview.

Chapter 2 on eAssistance is located on the lowest process level of information and communication. Here, the groundwork for all Web-based information exchange is set. In addition to the discussion of Internet services, a classification of social software and Web 2.0 technologies is given. One of the main focal points is the catalog for communal Web sites, that can be expanded step by step to an eGovernment portal. A barrier-free Web access and a quality assurance in the Internet are important for eAssistance. The case study of the Web site of the Technical Secretariat for Inclusive Management in Disability of Ecuador (SETEDIS) is presented.

*eAssistance (Chap. 2)*

Chapter 3 on eProcurement describes, as a part of the process level production, the Web-based options for procurement and purchase, including the potential benefits for administration. To this end, basic procurement models are discussed, namely sell side (catalog and procurement software are located on the vendors' side), buy side and Marketplace (third party providers with multi-supplier catalog and software platform). The Public Offering via Internet requires a gradual process chain, optionally including auctions. Apart from that, desktop purchasing systems are discussed in order to unburden the purchasers and governmental institution members in the process of procuring MRO goods (maintenance, repair, and operations). The case study of Swiss Federal Railways shows forms of reverse auctions for the procurement.

*eProcurement (Chap. 3)*

Chapter 4 addresses the topic of service management in the eGovernment. First, proceedings of technical, organizational, and semantic interoperability are presented, in order to facilitate heterogeneous system and application environments within and outside of the administrative unit. Afterwards, the governmental services for citizens and companies, as proposed by the European Union, are discussed. A sample catalog for a communal product plan allows for standardizing electronic services and harmonizing them beyond the communities. As an example serves a service oriented eHealth architecture for mobile health services, that is deepened in a case study for the electronic health record of the University of Vienna. To complete the chapter, a Capability Maturity Model for governmental services and a benchmarking, regularly carried out by the European Union, are presented.

*eService (Chap. 4)*

The electronic negotiation process with legally binding agreements is dealt with in Chap. 5 on eContracting. Generic services support the Web-based negotiation process with services for archiving, validation, and settlement. The emphasis lies on the identity management for identification, authentication, and authorization of Web users. The Role-Based Access Control (RBAC) model of the US National Institute of Standards and Technology furthers the separation of access and processing rights (separation of duties). Another focus is the asymmetric encoding with public and private keys that serve to generate digital signatures. The discussion of the public key infrastructure and further basic legal requirements complete the chapter. As a case study serves the face recognition in the biometric passport (ePass), demonstrated by the Fraunhofer Institute for Computer Graphics Research in Darmstadt.

*eContracting (Chap. 5)*

Chapter 6 on eSettlement deals with the handling and completion of electronic transactions. To begin with, the SCOR model is presented, which explains the partial steps of a supply chain. Then, electronic payment procedures are classified and illustrated. It is possible to organize the distribution of digital products and services either online or offline, whereas hybrid forms are also thinkable. While using the exchange options,

*eSettlement (Chap. 6)*

it is imperative that privacy policies and data security maintain guaranteed. In order to protect author rights for digital products or services, digital watermarks can be applied. Two case studies are presented at the end of this chapter, the first one explains the European regulations and puts protection mechanisms and procedure recommendations at discussion. The second case is about consent management system implemented for the BitsaboutMe platform.

*eCollaboration*
*(Chap. 7)*

Chapter 7 on eCollaboration belongs to the third process level, which considers different possibilities of participation for citizens. First, the specific characteristics of document management systems and content management are discussed. There are many applications for wiki tools in the administration, as there are possible advantages for project management, product development, employee suggestion systems, and community formation. The governmental institutions should consider the use of blogs and adoption of software solutions for collaborative working environments and facilitate them, if needed. Virtual types of organization and collaboration improve different strategies for the development of organizations. The case study about virtual campus is brought in by the distance teaching University of Hagen, in which over 50,000 students of the areas culture and social studies, computer science, business administration, and law are registered. Additionally, a second case study about the implementation of accessibility in Massive Open Online Courses, is presented.

*eDemocracy*
*(Chap. 8)*

The process area eDemocracy is outlined in Chap. 8. A participation pyramid is explained by means of the involvement of the citizens and the complexity of public tasks. Afterwards, the variety of electronic votes and elections is displayed, putting a special emphasis on those options via Internet, which are independent of time and place. The sub-processes eDiscussion and ePosting accompany projects for electronic votes and elections. They improve the basis of decision making and voting and advance the personal responsibility of the citizens. In order to ease the complexity, multi-dimensional calculation and illustration methods are used. The step-by-step construction of a Semantic Memory allows the knowledge society to both exercise political controlling and a historiography with multimedia-based facts (audio, video) and documents. The case studies of a VAA for the 2013 Ecuador National Elections and the technical and procedural mechanisms to enhance transparency and trust in Internet voting for the Swiss elections and votes, are presented.

*eCommunity*
*(Chap. 9)*

In Chap. 9, we present communicative strategies (push, pull, customized push) and Web-based tools for community formation. A multi-channel management allows synchronizing the different contact channels (counter, call or communication center, Web portal, amongst others) and media (telephone, e-mail, blog, amongst others). A development model for online citizens includes the user categories online surfer, online communicator, online community member and online citizen. With the help of this model, the governmental institution can estimate the degree of popularity, the capability to communicate and the personal involvement of the citizens. The according key figures allow the institutions to adjust their Web sites better to the needs of the claim groups. Further applications are tools for community formation, like civic network systems, buddy or recommender systems, as well as corporate blogs. The case studies *Participa Inteligente* and the Swiss center for telemedicine are presented at the end of this chapter.

The Chap. 10, about knowledge society, discusses the efforts for decentralization in the New Public Management, efforts that can be realized by means of information and communication systems. Certain processes in the knowledge management, the use of expert systems and knowledge-based data banks, as well as adequate data mining and Web mining methods endorse the transition from an information society to a knowledge society. During this process, the associated dangers and risks must not be neglected. An ethical maxim for the knowledge society with different dimensions is therefore essential. At the end of this chapter, a case study on the so-called cognitive cities is presented.

*Knowledge Society (Chap. 10)*

## 1.6 Bibliographical Notes

Some works on the topic of eGovernment, mostly edited volumes, are available on the market. Asghari (2005) describes in his editor's compilation the digital evolution in the state and points out solutions in the areas of process management, eProcurement, and governmental services. In Bieler and Schwarting's compilation (Bieler & Franz, 2007), some experts in the area of eGovernment have their say on the matter. Apart from communication concepts and forms of collaboration, the legal requirements for the eGovernment are covered.

*Edited volumes and first scientific works on eGovernment*

The edited volume of Gisler & Spahni (2001) gives the basics on service quality in the administration and illustrates applications. Priddat & Jansen (2001) address in their work the changed potentials and the modernization of the state by means of eGovernment. The reference book by Mehlich (2013) introduces to the topic of eGovernment, explains the current development status and gives a prognosis. Basic concepts and current applications of the area eGovernment are compiled by Meier (2002) and Hofmann & Reich (2008). Scheer et al. (2013) illustrate processes of the eGovernment using a process model.

The European Union has launched the eGovernment initiative with the Lisbon Strategy (Lisbon Strategy (2008)). Nowadasys, the European eGovernment Action Plan 2016-2020 was published (European Comission (2016)) in which concrete measures for the implementation are listed. The latest survey and a benchmarking for the countries EU28+ are to be found under European Comission (2017).

There is a remarkable variety of reference books on electronic business, that deal with different aspects of electronic transactions. Bullinger & Berres (2013) published a manual for medium-sized businesses, which assorts basic concepts and practical experience reports for electronic business transactions. Kollmann (2010) Kollmann's reference book gives basic concepts for electronic purchasing and selling as well as electronic trading. Web-based business models are compiled by Hofmann & Meier (2008). Meier (2001) edited volume is addressed to managers and features several articles on initiation, negotiation and handling of electronic business transactions.

*Extensive literature on eBusiness and eCommerce*

Hofmann & Meier (2008) deal with all the elements of a digital value creation chain for eBusiness and eCommerce, illustrating them by the example of an electronic shop. Merz's (Merz, 2002) reference book provides the basic economical requirements of electronic business transactions, but focuses on technological proceedings. Wirtz (2001) textbook describes, after a groundwork part, the strategic and operative management of electronic transactions. The edited volume of Schögel et al. (2002) illuminates different aspects of eBusiness. The work of Schinzer et al. (2005) shows sales structures for electronic shops, organizational principles of Web-based marketplaces and basic forms of procurement in the eProcurement.

*Trends in the information society*     Various books and articles illustrate aspects of and trends for the information society. Gross (1994) has compiled the development and consequences of the multi-option society from a sociological point of view. Ethical principles for the information management are explained in the work of Johnson (2004). In his article, Ruh (1995) postulates, in addition to working and leisure time, additional periods for social work, Me-time, and regeneration.

# Chapter 2

# eAssistance

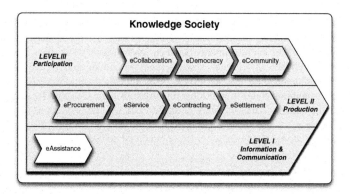

*Chapter 2 procures the basic principles for Web-based information and experience exchange. To this end, Sect. 2.1 outlines the most important Internet services. Trends in the Internet, known by the name Web X.Y, are displayed in Sect. 2.2; in addition to that, a classification of social software is given. In Sect. 2.3, a list of criteria for municipality Web sites allows to make an estimate of the content. A gross architecture for more ample eGovernment portals is presented in Sect. 2.4. The guidelines for barrier-free Web access were created by the W3C and constitute the basis for all public Web sites (Sect. 2.5), with the goal that people with mental or physical handicaps can profit from Web-based information and services as well. In order to assure quality in the Internet, there are criteria for usability, content and ethics to be taken into account, as displayed in Sect. 2.6. Section 2.7 contains bibliographical notes. Finally, the case study of the Web site of the Technical Secretariat for Inclusive Management in Disability of Ecuador (SETEDIS) is presented, in which different forms of access to the Web without barriers are considered.*

© Springer Nature Switzerland AG 2019
A. Meier, L. Terán, *eDemocracy & eGovernment*, Progress in IS,
https://doi.org/10.1007/978-3-030-17585-6_2

# 2.1   Search and Web Services in the Internet

*The network of networks*

The Internet, or network of networks, connects a variety of computers worldwide by use of a protocol (TCP/IP or Transmission Control Protocol/Internet Protocol). It consists of a multitude of computer networks and facilitates the worldwide interchange of data and information. Over the past years, the Internet has established itself as the most important communication platform. Furthermore, it is the basis for electronic exchange relations (eCommerce, eBusiness, eGovernment etc.) and with its multimedia services, it is changing bit by bit even telephony, radio, and television.

As Internet services are considered the following:

*Hypertext documents and navigational aid*

- **World Wide Web or WWW**: The WWW is one of the most important Internet services and makes it possible to interconnect multimedia documents (hypertext documents) from all over the world by links. With the help of HTML (Hyper Text Markup Language), documents are developed, and text, graphics and pictures are arranged on a WWW page. Every hypertext document can link on other web sites that are located on any computer (server) around the world and that are accessible.

*Setup of e-mail addresses*

- **Electronic mail or e-mail**: The e-mail allows the correspondence and the exchange of electronic documents between Internet users. The users deploy electronic mailboxes on computer systems (mail servers) of an Internet provider. Every e-mail address has the fixed form "username@serveraddress." The server address is composed of different domain names that are separated by dots and end with the name of a main domain or top-level domain (abbreviations like, e.g., .eu for Europe, .ch for Switzerland, .de for Germany, .au for Austria, .org for noncommercial organizations, .com for commercial companies, or .edu for research facilities and universities).

*Push principle in the Internet*

- **Discussion lists or mailing lists**: Discussion lists are electronic newsletters. These are regular, often daily released electronic bulletins on an appointed topic or technical subject. The subscribers of the mailing list send their messages via e-mail to the operator of this list (list server), which forwards all incoming messages via e-mail to all the participants. Discussion lists work according to the push principle (see communication strategies in Sect. 9.1), that is, each participant receives the bulletins automatically, without needing to tend to it. The condition for this to work is a subscription, that is, the user has to file his own e-mail address.

*Pull principle for a variety of topics*

- **Newsgroups:** In the Internet, a discussion forum on a given topic is called newsgroup. Unlike mailing lists, the newsgroups work according to the pull principle (Sect. 9.1). Each participant of a newsgroup has to pull the desired discussion entries actively from the designated server (newsgroup server). Some newsgroups have developed into extremely fast news media, because they cover an up-to-date event.

*Exchange of files*

- **File Transfer Protocol, or FTP**: This service makes it possible to copy files from a remote computer onto your own computer or vice versa to load your own files to a remote computer.

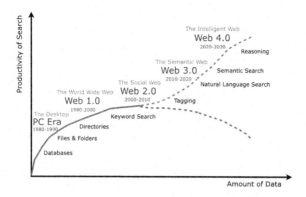

**Fig. 2.1:** Web Evolution, adapted from Spivack (2009).

Apart from these Internet services, comprehensive catalogs, and elaborate searching   *Catalog services*
services that make working in the WWW easier developed. Topical catalogs organize
an area of knowledge in an hierarchical index. These catalogs can be searched for topics
and subtopics in a well laid-out manner. Virtual libraries are topical catalogs that are
provided by libraries or public institutions. Search engines                              *Search engines*
   or search services help the user to find information in the WWW. With the help of    *and search*
a few search criteria, search engines or search robots are capable of compiling the most   *services*
interesting WWW sites in very short time. Search terms can be connected with each
other by logical operators AND, OR, and NOT, in order to narrow down the quantity
of relevant hyper-documents. The operator NOT permits excluding WWW sites that
contain a certain term. In addition to that there are search terms like NEAR that permit
finding documents in the vicinity of a term. Beside textual information, pictures, videos,
or audio elements can also be found with adequate search engines.

Location-based search services provide, in dependence of the location, the necessary   *Location-based*
information about near facilities, services, or partners. This search function is mainly   *search services*
needed for mobile applications.

## 2.2   Web Development

In this section, a description of Web evolution is presented using the descriptor Web X.Y
from the so-called static Web (Web 1.0) to the Intelligent Web (Web 4.0). The amount of
data available in the Web is growing exponentially, for that reason, new mechanisms to
provide relevant information to users are discussed and implemented in both, business
practice as well as for public services. Figure 2.1 shows the evolution of Web in terms
of amount of data available vs the productivity of search. It shows that after the development of so-called Web 2.0, the amount of data increases given that all users of the Web
can be also content generators. The different types of Web development are described
as follows.

### 2.2.1   Web 1.0 – Static Web

*Web 1.0*     The Internet before 1999 is considered by different authors as the "Read-Only" Web or
Web 1.0. This was given since the main role of Internet users was limited to browsing
and consuming (reading) the information published in Web servers in different formats
(i.e., audio, video, and text).

The descriptor Web 1.0 is used to identify first stage in the World Wide Web, which
consisted mainly of web pages connected by hyperlinks. The definition of Web 1.0 is
generally refered to the web when it was a set of static websites with no interactive
content and applications were also in most cases proprietary.

### 2.2.2   Web 2.0 – The Writing and Participating Web

*Web 2.0*     One of the main issues of the first evolution of the Web was the lack of interaction
and contributions of common users. Any advances in software development are often
marked by a version number. The term Web 2.0 originally was used as a key word in a
conference on computer science, to describe the coaction of different Web technologies
and the possibilities of social collaboration in the Internet (social software). The term is
associated with the following concrete developments:

*Subscription*     • **Democratization of the Internet**: The Internet is seen as a platform for com-
*services are*        munication and exchange, in which the contents are contributed dynamically by
*possible*            independent persons and are changed and extended continually by the users. The
                      operators of such platforms do not put up any access restrictions, anyone inter-
                      ested can contribute. The users can arrange a subscription service (e.g., RSS feed,
                      see Sect. 7.4), in order to get continuous updates.

*Mashups are*      • **Combination of existing contents**: Text, pictures, audio and video are newly ar-
*spreading*           ranged in collages and put at the disposal. This is referred to as mashup. Mashups
                      use open interfaces, so that different Web applications can be embedded. For ex-
                      ample, it is possible to design electronic invitation cards with text elements, per-
                      sonal photos geographical maps (e.g., extracted from Google Maps), and music
                      sequences.

*Maintaining and*  • **Formation of social networks**: With the help of Web-based applications, com-
*strengthening*       munities are built in the Internet and relationships are cultivated. After entering the
*relations*           profile information, the user can get to know the other participants of the network
                      and, if desired, utter a request for new relationships and cultivate the exchange.

Social software takes the individual and its wishes into account and at the same time
makes it possible that interested individuals connect with each other and the community
grows into becoming a social network. While other collaborative applications, like e.g.,
groupware (see Sect. 7.5), support the users in their project work, the main concern of
social software is the social context. Figure 2.2 gives a classification of social software.
The three basic goals of such solutions are publication and distribution of information,
communication among Internet users, and nurture of social contacts.

**Fig. 2.2:** Classification of social software, adapted from Hippner (2006).

The subscription service RSS (Really Simple Syndication, see Sect. 7.4) is a distribution service for Web content, which can be drawn on by any participant in an easy way.
With it, the user can request news, findings or recent discussion entries on a particular
topic or knowledge domain, which are delivered automatically in case of a change.

*The subscription service RSS*

Personal or group-related diaries or journals (Weblogs or blogs, see Sects. 7.4 and
9.6), that administer content chronologically, belong to the focal topic information. The
readers of such blogs can comment on content or add to it, in order that the participants
of social networks can profit of new findings. Blogs are often run by private individuals (bloggers) without commercial background, they are subjective and reveal personal
opinions and assessments. Also, blogs are often interconnected, by embedding other
sources of information via RSS.

*Weblogs and corporate blogs*

Podcasts have a purpose similar to blogs, transmitting spoken words instead of information. The term podcasting denotes the production and distribution of audio files
(often as MP3 format), whereby RSS is used, once again, as a distribution service for
spreading spoken news, reviews, audio dramas, readings, music, etc. When podcasts are
complemented with video sequences, the result are multimedia podcasts.

*Emerge of multimedia podcasts*

Social bookmarks are personal link collections that are published and indexed by
other participants. Hereby, taxonomies and ontologies are generated by the participants
of social networks, this means, there is no central authority that determines the key words
(descriptors) and classification hierarchies. The users of social bookmarks manage their
personal bookmarks to their liking, but at the same time they can search collections of
bookmarks. The frequency with which a particular Web site is recommended by the
users serves as an indicator for the quality of that Web site (social choice theory).

*Creating a personal link collection*

Wiki tools (see Sect. 7.3) make it possible to post entries on a topic or a document
quickly. Such tools also facilitate search functions, editing possibilities and protocol
functions, so that various authors can work on the same document. The most popular
wiki probably is the knowledge library Wikipedia, which grants free access for every-
body.

*Functioning of wiki tools*

A representative of the focal topic of communication is instant messaging. This
transmission of messages in the Internet works in real-time and the recipients are able

*Instant messaging*

to respond immediately. Applications of Internet telephony (Voice over IP, IP standing for Internet protocol) widen the set of communication possibilities[1].

*Social networking*      Software solutions for special interest community or social networking belong to the focus Maintenance of Relations. They include building social networks that occupy an area of interest or discuss socially relevant topics. While sometimes it is possible to register in social networks yourself, in other occasions, an invitation is necessary for participation. Tools like discussion forums, chats, or swap sites further the community formation (see Chap. 9). The users' contributions are evaluated by the community or by the software system itself, in order to close the feedback loop.

*No hierarchy in social networks*      Social networks are self-organized communities, they are not subject to any hierarchical order or a set purpose. They live on the variety and intensity of relations: the denser a social network is, the more familiar are the participants with each other. The looser the network is joined together, the less interactions take place. In case of lacking network relations it is possible that the Web-based social network will wither and show little or no interactions any more.

### 2.2.3   Web 3.0 – The Semantic Web

*Web 3.0*      Web 3.0 , also know as Semantic Web, It has been thought of as the basis for web interaction, which generates a significant change in how developers create different websites. However, one of the most important characteristics of this level of Web development is the way people interact with those websites. The research groups and experts in this field consider that this new method for interacural with the web, which seeks to facilitate and make the interaction of people more intuitive. Smart applications, which include more and better functions, are developed with the aim of giving users what they need.

Web 3.0 is considered as a reinvention of the web. Web 2.0 allowed user interaction with dynamic websites that act as applications instead of simply pages of information. In Web 2.0, users can interact with websites depending on the different privileges granted by administrators to their users. To search for information, it is necessary to use several search engines that provide results depending on the quantity and quality of information included with respect to the search. However, the search uses only keywords and provides the information closest to the search criteria used, which does not correspond to the understanding of the context of the search. Web 3.0 is expected to have the ability to understand the context of the user's search and peril; In this way, the system is able to provide the user with the most useful information. Web 3.0 can be compared to an artificial intelligence assistant that understands its user and personalizes everything.

### 2.2.4   Web 4.0 – Open, Linked, and Intelligent Web

*Web 4.0*      There is still no consensus on the name and main characteristics of the fourth generation of the Web, or Web 4.0. However, there are several perspectives on how this could be presented. Web 4.0 has also been called the "active web". In the version of Web 3.0, the use of search engines continues to have a fundamental role in finding relevant information from web pages, which could be used according to the needs of users.

---

[1] Skype: www.skype.com

To understand the concepts that would handle the call Web 4.0 we will use the following example. Currently if a user wants to find accommodation in Paris, for this the user must include in the search engine something like "room + hotel + Paris", in this way the search engine will show an ordered set of web pages, generally hosting search engines. It is expected that the Web 4.0 is quite different from the current one, facilitating the interaction with the user, eliminating several of the necessary steps when using the web 3.0, in this way its use is more direct.

Search engines may not disappear, but they are expected to include different types of virtual assistants who can understand natural language, both spoken and written. It is expected that these assistants have the ability to answer questions as if they were a human assistant. In this way the interaction with the search engine could be of the auditory type with a message such as "get me a room in Paris for next week", and the user will get a reservation in a hotel according to the user's taste (profile) which is something that the Virtual assistant has been able to determine it. The final step will be only the conformation of the reservation. Some examples of how the Web 4.0 is moving forward on this direction are the assistants: *Siri*[2] of Apple, Cortana[3] of Microsoft, and Google Now[4]. These assistants are achieving a greater understanding of natural language processing thanks to machine learning and artificial intelligent systems. Additionally, the so-called "Big Data" is processed more effectively, linking all the information obtained through multiple sources.

The evolution of Web can not be seeing from a business perspective only. Public administration must follow the new trends in the development of technology to provide better and faster services to citizens including also new developments of *eGovernment* towards the so-called *Smart Government*. It extends concepts of *eGovernment*, cloud computing, big data and mobile apps to enhance the way to connect with citizens and better understand their reasoning and requirements. A digital government must improve how authorities deliver public services, strengthening communities and participation. *Smart Government*

## 2.3 Catalog for Municipality Web Sites

Many municipalities have their own Internet presence and maintain an according Web site. These Web sites often differ immensely regarding presentation and contents. The information offers are structured differently and complicate the collaboration between municipalities. The possibilities of communicating are very different as well, more recent forms like blogging, podcasting, or instant messaging are rarely found. When having a closer look on the services that these Web sites offer (for service offers see Chapters 3 to 6), it shows that some electronic services are already available. Nevertheless, there are mainly mere pilot tests for eDemocracy (see Chap. 8) available, because the identity management and the application of digital signatures are still in a developing stage. *Internet presence of municipalities*

---

[2]Siri: https://www.apple.com/ios/siri/
[3]Cortana: https://www.microsoft.com/en-us/cortana
[4]Google Now: https://en.wikipedia.org/wiki/Google_Now

| Public Services | • Organizational structure of the Municipality<br>• Contacts and responsibilities<br>• Services offers and Download of Forms<br>• Communication range |
|---|---|
| Location Promotion | • City Map<br>• Traffic Information<br>• Maps of Districts<br>• Commercial Structure |
| Education and Social Services | • Public Schools<br>• Libraries<br>• Social Institutions<br>• Youth programs |
| Politics | • Council Members<br>• Protocols<br>• Budget<br>• Parties |
| Leisure Time, Culture and Sport | • Events calendar<br>• Cultural Institutions<br>• Associations<br>• Sporting Events |
| Tourism | • Tourism Bureau<br>• Virtual Tours<br>• Restaurants<br>• Hotels |

**Fig. 2.3:** Catalog for municipality Web sites, adapted from Griese et al. (1999).

Figure 2.3 gives us a topical catalog for municipality Web sites. The information and communication offers are mostly wide-ranging and include administrative information, educational offers, cultural, and sporting events up to touristic offers.

*Objectives and target audience for public Web sites*

In order to build a Web site or to evaluate an existing one, some basic questions have to be discussed: What goal does the municipality pursue with the Internet presence? What is the target audience for a municipality Web site (citizens, companies, and/or administrative institutions)? What kind of information and services should be offered? How should the offers be structured, what languages have to be supported, which navigation possibilities should be planned?

*Bundling offers and services*

As discussed in Chap. 1, the Capability Maturity Model for Web-based services in the eGovernment comprises the four steps information and communication, production, and participation. If small and middle-sized municipalities want to serve all process levels in their Web site project, they reach their limits not only for financial reasons. Also from the point of view of citizens and companies, it is time-consuming and difficult to consult different Web sites on different communal levels and to find out where to place their request. For this reason, more and more eGovernment portals are becoming popular, concentrating all municipality offers and services for a region.

## 2.4   Design of eGovernment Portals

*What does the eGovernment portal comprise?*

A portal is a Web site that concentrates information services on certain topics and to that end offers searching, communicating, catalog, and mediation services. eGovernment portals serve the citizens as a gate or entrance to the following services:

- Communication platform of the governmental institution (see Fig. 2.3)

- Use of governmental services (see Sect. 4.2)

- Drawing on services offered by companies (see Sect. 4.3)

- Electronic votes and elections (see eDemocracy in Chap. 8) and

- Processes of community formation (see Chap. 9).

When an eGovernment portal is to be designed, there are several possible functional areas to consider:

- **Provision of information**: The eGovernment portal provides information about administrative activities and offers possibilities to communicate. Topics and contact information for different administrative activities are listed; plans, documents, forms, event calendars, among other things, can be found.

- **Discussion forums**: An administration can run discussion lists, newsgroups, or chat-rooms for specific problems of its own activity and thereby interest the citizens in the concerns of public authorities.

- **Catalog services**: A catalog service makes it possible to build, maintain, and use information and services in a structured way. With the help of a dialog control and adequate searching services, citizens gain efficient access to all areas of interest and required services.

- **Profile maintenance:** The municipality or administration can use its Internet portal to call for profile information of those citizens who regularly draw on services (see Online Community Member and Online Citizen, respectively, in Sect. 9.4). The citizens can submit their preferences and contact information. They subscribe to get information on selected administrative projects or particular factual issues. Together with members of the administrative institution and other citizens, they can continually exchange experiences. In case the citizens have expert knowledge, they may be poised to offer it to the administrative institution when needed.

- **Exchange relations:** The eGovernment portal can be used for the exchange of experiences and services. This means that the portal becomes an electronic trading place, in which prices (see Public Offering in Chap. 3.5) may be negotiated openly or are set by auctions. An administrative unit can consider providing the citizens with particular services for less or even without charge, and bill the remaining claim groups (companies, institutions) normally by the market price. *Public Offering via portal*

- **Project management and groupware:** Many administrative units develop their activities in form of projects, sometimes with the support of citizens. In order to run those projects with the aid of computers, the administrative unit can purchase suitable software for project management or groupware and put it at the disposal of the project members (see Chap. 7). Such services make it possible to carry out Web-based planning, project documentation, and publication. This is especially efficient if the members of the administrative unit and voluntary citizens are geographically widely distributed and want to contribute their know-how at different times of the day. *Promoting forms of collaboration*

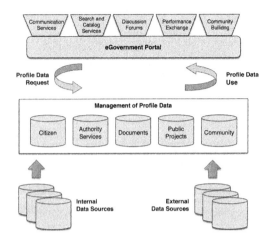

**Fig. 2.4:** Use of personalized services in the eGovernment portal.

eGovernment portals can offer the same structure, contents, and design for all users, or differentiate between claim groups (citizens, companies) or even individuals. Such individualized services pay off in case that the portal offers ample information and additional services, yet the citizens need customized offers.

*Using concepts for personalization*
By personalization we understand the possibility to adapt the content of Web sites, communication channels, products, and services to the citizens' preferences and make them available to them. A personalized service uses personal characteristics and behavioral patterns in order to direct the service to the individual needs of the user.

Figure 2.4 illustrates how personalization works in an eGovernment portal. Visitors and members of the portal use different services such as e-mail, discussion forums, search functions, and service exchange. In doing so, they either enter actively a profile containing their preferences, or a profile is gathered bit by bit by the behavior of the user and the employment of services. The profile data regard the citizen, services, Web site content, project contents and records, work reports, behavioral patterns and behavioral norms in communities, respectively.

## 2.5   Barrier-Free Web Access

*Definition of accessibility*
Accessibility, or barrier-free Web access, is the ability of a Web site to be readable and usable to all users. Web sites and eGovernment portals especially have to be accessible to handicapped people, e.g., to the visually impaired, colorblind, or hearing impaired. Moreover, people with difficulties to move or people who can neither operate a keyboard nor a mouse also have the right to be able to consult Web content of public institutions. People with language difficulties or language disorders, or people with learning difficulties also must be granted the access to the eGovernment portal.

In the legislation of many countries there exist laws for the equality of treatment that protect people from discrimination due to, e.g., a physical or mental handicap. Apart from that, there is legal equality between all citizens, independent of their origin, sex, age, language, or social rank. In 2006, European ministers signed a declaration during the ministerial conference in Riga (Ministerial Declaration of Riga, June 11, 2006) see Riga Ministerial Declaration in bibliographical notes Riga (2006), in order to ensure a barrier-free Web access to all public Web sites until the year 2010. The groundwork for the declaration is provided by the recommendations of the World Wide Web Consortium (W3C), that are published under the name Web Content Accessibility Guidelines (WCAG (2007)). *The EU declaration for barrier-free Web access*

In the ministerial gathering in Riga it was recognized that the information and communication technologies are a strong driving force for growth and employment. What is more, applications and Internet technologies further the exchange even beyond social and cultural boundaries. The most important claims of the ministerial conference can be summarized bellow. *Main claims of the EU*

- Programs are to be developed in order to promote the Internet access and Internet use for elderly people. In particular, the employment ability, working conditions, and the compatibility of family and career are to be improved by innovative Internet solutions.

- Geographical discrepancies have to be diminished by forms of exchange and collaboration between the public and the private sector. In rural and underdeveloped areas, the Internet infrastructure has to be improved by use of broadband technologies, in order to heighten the connectivity and Internet use rate in schools, health centers, and public administration.

- For people with handicaps, access to the Internet must be facilitated and the use of Web-based services promoted. In particular, electronic content and documents for the blind or visually impaired have to be developed according to the WCAG.

- Digital skills and alphabetization have to be improved by specific initiatives. In this enterprise, measures must be directed at the needs of those groups that are threatened of marginalization because of their social situation.

- Cultural and linguistic diversity are to be expanded in the digital space, in order to further the European integration processes.

Using information and communication technologies is hoped to enable an integrative eGovernment, in order to promote public services and further democratic decision making processes on all levels (see Chap. 8).

The WCAG demonstrate, how Web content can be made accessible to handicapped people (see Fig. 2.5). Providers and developers of content are invited to take those Internet users into account who have disabilities or difficulties to see, hear, or move. Perhaps Internet users have difficulties to read or understand a text. With regard to the infrastructural environment, it must be considered that users do not have a keyboard or a mouse, or that they are not able to use them. Furthermore, they might have a display that shows only text, or a small display and a slow Internet connection. *WCAG*

```
┌─────────────────────────────────────────────────────────────┐
│ Web Content Accessibility Guidelines                          │
│                                                               │
│ • Provide equivalent alternatives to auditory and visual content │
│ • Don't rely on color alone                                   │
│ • Use markup and style sheets and do so properly              │
│ • Clarify natural language usage                              │
│ • Create tables that transform gracefully                     │
│ • Ensure direct accessibility of embedded user interfaces     │
│ • Design for device independence                              │
│ • Provide context and orientation information                 │
│ • Provide clear navigation mechanisms                         │
│ • Ensure that documents are clear and simple                  │
└─────────────────────────────────────────────────────────────┘
```

**Fig. 2.5:** Excerpt from the W3C guidelines for Web content access.

*Priority levels*     The WCAG contain an overall of fourteen guidelines, ten of which are given in
*for Web access*  Fig. 2.5. Each guideline contains precise recommendations, together with priority indications (priority 1 = must, priority 2 = should, priority 3 = may). The first guideline
postulates to create text equivalents for pictures, symbols, maps, drawings, video, and
audio. Such text content could be presented to the user in form of synthesized speech,
braille, or visually displayed text. Furthermore, text and pictures should be understandable if seen without colors.

*Repairing*     The incorrect use of markup commands compromises the users' access. When tables
*defects*  are misused for layouting purposes or for titles, in order to, for example, change the
font size, the structure of the site may be difficult to understand and the navigation
complicated. Apart from that, it is recommended to use style sheets to control layout
and presentation.

Other important postulations are: device independence, information on orientation
and navigation, and clearly written documents.

## 2.6   Quality Assurance in the Internet

*How is quality*  Apart from security concerns, quality assurance in the Internet constitutes an important
*defined?*  challenge. The quality of Web sites or Web portals is difficult to define. In most cases,
evaluations take into account usability, content, and ethics. Among the usability criteria
are the following:

- **Accessibility:** It has to be checked whether the Web access has been implemented
  without barriers: Do people with handicaps have access to the Web site or portal?
  Can the contents be retrieved via voice output for the blind or visually impaired?
  Are there text equivalents for pictures or charts? Can the content be retrieved even
  without a keyboard or a mouse? etc.

- **User-friendliness:** This is about evaluating structure, navigation and comprehen-
  sibility. Is the information clearly structured? Is the build-up comprehensible? Are
  there navigational aids? Is the language simple and understandable? Are complex
  terms explained? Are there search options? Is help provided (e.g., FAQ)? etc.

- **Communication:** There must be possibilities to interact and communicate. Is
  there an e-mail address for contact? Do they provide a discussion forum for the

topic? Is it evident who is the contact person for each concern? Are the citizens encouraged to voice their opinion or comment? etc.

It is a particular challenge to screen the content of Web sites. In Web sites or portals dealing with health problems, it is mandatory that the facts be correct and reflect up-to-date medicine. To give an example, the foundation Health on the Net certifies Web sites containing medical information with the quality label HONCode, so that the Internet user can gain trust in the quality of the information provided by the Web site. The HONCode is based on the following eight evaluation criteria:

*The quality certificate HONCode*

- **Authority:** Any medical advice will only be given by medically trained and qualified professionals unless clearly stated otherwise.

- **Complementarity:** The information provided on the site is designed to support, not replace, the relationship that exists between a patient and his or her physician.

- **Confidentiality:** The Web site designers and owners commit themselves to the confidentiality of data relating to individual Internet users, including their identity.

- **Attribution:** There must be clear references to source data. On Web sites with clinical information, the date of its last modification must be displayed.

- **Justifiability:** Any claims relating to the performance of a specific therapy, treatment or medical product will be supported by scientific, balanced evidence.

- **Transparency:** It is mandatory to state contact data of the authors and owners of health Web sites; further help is offered.

- **Financial disclosure:** Funding organizations and sponsors of the Web site are displayed.

- **Advertising:** If advertising is a source of funding it will be clearly stated. There has to be a clear distinction between advertising and medical contents.

Apart from the HONCode, there are further certificates for medical and health related Web sites or other information services. Among the ethical criteria for evaluating a Web site or eGovernment portal are the following:

*Ethical criteria*

- **Authenticity:** The name and address of the institutions and the authors of the Web site are displayed.

- **Protection of privacy:** Privacy policies and data security is guaranteed. The citizens' e-mail addresses may not be divulged.

Due to a drastically growing number of Web sites (information overload), it is necessary to automatize the quality assurance and to use the computer to do it. There are Internet technologies which can analyze the presentation and content of Web sites, and give indications to quality improvements. For example, it is possible to have the above mentioned guidelines checked regularly in an automated or partly automated way.

*Automatic*
*quality check*
The key element of automatic quality checks are methods of Web Mining (see Sect. 10.3) and Web Measurement. For example, there are different models of information retrieval that are able to evaluate the quality of electronic documents. One approach is to rate the quality of certain Web content as good if that content is referenced by links by as many Internet users as possible. In this, scoring models are used, which rank Web contents according to how often they are cited (ranking). According to the hypothesis, higher evaluated Web content comes with higher quality.

## 2.7 Bibliographical Notes

*Basic concepts*
*for Internet and*
*search engines*
An introduction to Web technologies is given in the book by Wöhr (2004); apart from client and server technologies, it deals with aspects of architecture and Web services. Under the headline of Web analytics, the analysis of the behavior of Internet users is understood. Kaushik (2007) reference book gives important basics on this topic, and addresses the issue of Internet technologies and search engines. A handbook on Web mining and related methods of information retrieval was written by Liu (2007).

Gisler & Spahni (2001) compilations, as well as Picot & Quadt (2001), show concrete application examples of eGovernment projects. A survey of Internet portals of municipalities is provided by Griese et al. (1999). Riesch & Zugang (2007) took an inventory of barrier-free Web access of public Web sites in Switzerland.

*WCAG and*
*quality standards*
The declaration of the European ministerial conference in Riga (2006) postulates a barrier-free Web access to all public Web sites until the year 2010. The access criteria are set by the W3C in their Web Content Accessibility Guidelines (WCAG 1.0 and 2.0). The HONCode (1995) is considered as a specific quality standard for medical and health relevant Web sites and is awarded by the Health on Net Foundation. For the automatic evaluation of Web site quality, the habilitation of Mandl (2006) gives different techniques.

*Literature on*
*Web 2.0 and*
*Social Software*
There are some first books and compilations on the topic of Web 2.0 and social software on the market. Alby (2007) and Beck (2007) describe Web 2.0 technologies and applications, Hildebrand & Hofmann (2006) deal in more detail with the possibilities of application of social software. An approach to classify social software is taken form Hippner (2006) article.

*Web 3.0 and*
*Smart*
*Government*
Jain & Kumar (2018) review the various methods and tools to implement the ontologies for eGovernment and how to test them using various reasoners. In the work of Jiménez et al. (2015) they describe a new model of public organization that they call "Intelligent," characterized by the "Smart Government," and they propose a matrix with the elements of this model.

## 2.8   Case Study—Web Accessibility From a Systems Approach

### 2.8.1   Background

The inclusion of persons with disabilities in societies has, among others, a key element: accessibility to information and communication, which can be achieved, at least in a big portion, through Web Accessibility, as we are continually embracing it to better facilitate our businesses, jobs, and social lives. The Ecuadorian experience in this area shows that the social and economic reality of this group of the population, create certain requirements that have to be fulfilled in order to successfully implement web accessibility projects. This issue was somehow addressed by The Ecuadorian Technical Secretariat for the Inclusive Management on Disabilities (SETEDIS), through the implementation of certain features that respond to the users specific needs on its website, combined with the promotion of some projects that respond to the users social realities. From the analysis of the website in the context of the social realities, some proposals for future work are outlined, like a systematic approach with several dimensions for governments to work on web accessibility with efficacy.

Andrea Pacheco,
*Universidad Internacional del Ecuador (UIDE)*

Sergio Luján-Mora,
*Universidad de Alicante*

### 2.8.2   About Social Dimensions and Ongoing Programs for Inclusion

One difficulty for writing this case study was either the lack or the poor official available data about persons with disabilities. Some facts presented are a result of the authors experience in the field and their participation on the projects presented.

**Social Dimensions.**   According to the World Wide Web Consortium (W3C), "The Web is fundamentally designed to work for all people, whatever their hardware, software, language, culture, location, physical or mental ability. When the Web meets this goal, it is accessible to people with a diverse range of hearing, movement, sight, and cognitive ability" (W3C, 2012). However, providing this "designed to work for all" web represents a huge challenge, not only for web designers and developers, but also and especially for governments from developing countries, due to the social and economic reality that persons with disabilities face. In fact, some authors say the barriers to access knowledge do not always have a technological nature, but rather social and economical ones (Varian, 2005), as described next from five different social dimensions:

1. **Empowerment and Demand:** In the case of Ecuador, the data collected by the bio psychosocial study of the "Misión Solidaria Manuela Espejo" showed that the big majority of people with disabilities are in condition of vulnerability due to the lack of resources to fulfill their basic needs, such as access to health, housing, and education (Vicepresidencia de la República del Ecuador, 2012). This situation has led to placing other needs, like technological devices and Internet infrastructure in

a second place, needs that most of the times are not even known by persons with disabilities.

2. **Economical:** The evidence shows that the cost of acquiring a computer with corresponding software and assistive technology, such as adapted keyboards, headphones, large displays, is really high in Ecuador. After making a fast market study, we could conclude that the budget needed with this purpose was around USD 2,500. This budget is prohibitively expensive for most persons with disabilities, as their average income is around 0-30 dollars per month (Consejo Nacional para la Igualdad de Discapacidades, 2005). The reasons for this situation are the lack of national production of assistive technologies and the taxes that their import implies, 42.5% (Servicio Nacional de Aduana del Ecuador, 2014). To address this problem, the government donated computers with screen reading software to students with visual impairments. To the date, there are no official studies of the impact that the donations had. Besides, other kinds of disabilities have not yet been addressed.

3. **Technological Infrastructure:** A study run by SETEDIS on universal accessibility in touristic, governmental and public buildings shows that practically 0% of these entities have either accessible websites, assistive technologies or software as part of their infrastructure for delivering their services, and most of their managers had never considered their need (SETEDIS, 2015).

4. **Social Awareness:** The same study run by SETEDIS included a qualitative research with students and professionals in different fields, in regards to their awareness on universal accessibility. The results showed that only 51% of the respondents knew these terms, and those who knew it, mainly corresponded to persons with studies of fourth level.

5. **Education:** Even if there is no official data about this, it is well known that in Ecuador most people with hearing impairments do not read or write in Spanish, the official language of the country. The majority of this group of the population only finish basic school where they learn sign language; other problem of this situation is that the signs are not standardized at national level, these present variances in all parts of the country.

   In general, persons with disabilities do not have access to the use of technologies for their studies, and those persons who have access to their use in schools, do it a maximum of two hours per week. The digital content is based only in Web and games of frequent usage (UNESCO, 2012).

**Ongoing Programs for Inclusion.** Nowadays, different programs for inclusion are being carried out in Ecuador:

- The national legal framework to warranty universal access to services, education, health, transport, job, and the use of all forms of communication and information is quite solid (Constitución de la República del Ecuador, 2008), (Gobierno de la República del Ecuador, 2012), (United Nations, 2006). In 2014, this legal framework landed its operability in matters of Web, on the Ecuadorian standard NTE INEN-ISO/IEC 40500 (Instituto Ecuatoriano de Normalización, 2014). This standard is based on the internationally recognized standard ISO/IEC 40500 (International Organization for Standardization, 2012), which is based in turn, on the Web Content Accessibility Guidelines WCAG 2.0 (World Wide Web Consortium, 2008) from the W3C. There still remains the need for more standards and technical foundations, but we must know that this is a very good start.

- At the moment of writing this book chapter, NTE INEN-ISO/IEC 40500 is still not mandatory in Ecuador. However, a technical regulation will enter into force soon (Servicio Ecuatoriano de Normalización, 2016). This regulation aims to force the websites of public administration to fulfil the level of accessibility WCAG 2.0 AA until 2017. However, this standard does not consider the features that we will later analyse from the website of SETEDIS.

- SETEDIS is strongly promoting a program of "Participative Inclusion" which is not exclusive to the area of technology and access to information and communication. The program reaches all communities in the country, and is based on periodical "assemblies" where all the persons who live within the community start working together on projects that they find necessary for their development, as it could be the case of digital inclusion.

- Since 2013, SETEDIS has tried to start a project for equipping public places where all the population can have access to the use of technologies and Internet. This project focuses on equipping "Infocentros"[5] mainly in rural areas. Unluckily, this project has not been implemented yet mainly due to administrative reasons. In any case, the project has not been discarded.

### 2.8.3   Case Study: Website of the Technical Secretariat for the Inclusive Management on Disabilities

SETEDIS was created on May 2013. Around three months later of its creation, its official website[6] was launched, which was designed to provide users with a seamless view and user experience. The layout and the interface respect the governmental standards set by the competent authority. During the launch event of the website, the authorities of SETEDIS stated that this was the first "Ecuadorian accessible website", arguing that the site was not only based on the WCAG 2.0 guidelines, but especially because for its creation, the inputs and the social realities of its main users, Ecuadorian persons with disabilities, were considered. With this objective, two focus groups were carried out with the participation of around 20 users with different disabilities. As a result of the analysis of the social dimensions and the main inputs given by the users, several accessibility features were implemented in order to improve the usability and accessibility of the website of SETEDIS, even when the technical norm NTE INEN-ISO/IEC 40500

---

[5]See: http://www.telecomunicaciones.gob.ec/infocentros-comunitarios/
[6]See: http://www.setedis.gob.ec/ (the link no longer exists)

**Table 2.1:** Accessibility features of the website of SETEDIS.

| | |
|---|---|
| | Screen reading tool embedded in the webpage to mitigate dependence on additional software for navigation. This tool aims to combat in the short term the problems identified in the "Economical", "Technological Infrastructure", and "Social Awareness" dimensions, given the fact that most Ecuadorian people with visual impairment cannot afford assistive technologies and access to Internet. Also, the common places where they could access this service do not have the infrastructure with this purpose. |
| | Colour tool to allow users to choose the combination of colours of their preference. This tool lets them choose more comfortable interfaces according to their perception or specific needs. |
| | Menu and videos were also published with subtitles and sign language videos to mitigate the problem of the dimensions "Education" and "Technological Infrastructure" as this feature is complicated to maintain due to the vast quantity of information in the website. Having this in mind, SETEDIS has already started a collaboration program with a private Ecuadorian enterprise for creating an avatar which could automatically interpret the information of the website in sign language. The creation of this avatar could also help on the standardization of sign language at national level and will drastically reduce the cost of providing information in sign language. |
| A + − | Options for increasing or decreasing text size without modifying the structure and distribution of the interface on the webpage so the content is still readable and clearly structured if it is browsed with a device that does not support style sheets. The tool mitigates in part the problem of the "Technological Infrastructure" dimension. |
| F2 | Shortcut to navigate to the beginning of the webpage as users mentioned to get lost while searching information and this function takes them back to the beginning. |
| TAB | Shortcut to navigate through focusable elements (typically links and form controls) within a webpage. |
|  | All images throughout the website have been assigned an alternative text (alt attribute), which describes the contents or function of the image. |

does not mention anything about them. The main accessibility features implemented are shown in Table 2.1.

Of course, the website of SETEDIS itself does not solve all of the problems that we have brought to attention in our analysis. That is why the functioning of the webpage must be supported on other projects and plans as we propose next.

## 2.8.4   Future Work and Conclusions

The problem of exclusion and the digital gap of persons with disabilities shown in this document, imply that this problem must be counteracted at governmental level. If governments do not act in this way, persons with disabilities will keep facing poor education

**Table 2.2:** Systems approach and Proposals for Ecuador.

| Dimensions of Analysis | Short Term | Medium Term | Long Term |
|---|---|---|---|
| Empowerment and Demand | *Through the "Participative Inclusion" program teach to persons with disabilities, their rights and the role of technology in their lives. This will start empowering them and increasing the social demand for ICTs. | Start projects of digital inclusion with "basics" training, free access to technologies and Internet in public places such as Infocentros and libraries. | Boost a program with a multiplier effect in which socially empowered persons with disabilities, help others in the use of ICTs. |
| Economical | Eliminate taxes for the import of assistive technologies and software. | *Start a program of promotion for the local production of assistive technologies and software. | Eliminate subsidies and ICTs donation programs (Further discussion). |
| Technological Infrastructure | *Equip public places with Internet service with assistive technologies, at least infocentros and schools. *Implement the features of the website of SETEDIS in all governmental sites. | Start the adaptation of the norm "NTE INEN-ISO/IEC 40500" including the extra features from the website of SETEDIS. Include representatives of civil society during the process. | Equip all public schools, universities, libraries, with assistive technologies and software. Make the adapted norm "NTE INEN-ISO/IEC 40500" mandatory |
| Social awareness | *Start awareness programs of inclusion in the curricula from basic school. *Collect data and run continuous studies in all dimensions about persons with disabilities. | Start massive awareness programs through TV, radio, and campaigns. | Create mechanisms of management, control and especially incentives for compliance with the technical standards on Web accessibility. |
| Education | *Go deeper on teaching Spanish in special schools. *Gradually make it more intensive the use of ICTs. | Provide professional development training on universal accessibility and make it mandatory at least for public workers. | Start the standardization of sign language at national level. Include "Universal Accessibility" in the curricula of universities in all relevant faculties. |

levels, minimal job opportunities and economical dependence. The question remains on how should governments address the problem warranting effectiveness and efficacy of their actions. To tackle this problem, we think the systems approach applied in Ecuador can be a good point to start. This systems approach based on the same dimensions of our analysis and the specific proposals for the case of Ecuador is outlined in Table 2.2 .

In Table 2.2, the proposals that initiate with and asterisk and highlighted are the priority ones represent those in the authors' opinion. We call it systems approach because all elements have a relation among them, working on isolated projects would probably end up on failure. Furthermore, working from a systems approach will probably reveal other concerns that have not been considered in this document and could also trigger some other problems, especially from an administrative point of view, due to the diverse public institutions that should work together to start the actions proposed. Other need or proposal, non-specific to the case of Ecuador, is the improvement of the methodology of analysis of accessibility of governmental websites with a combined method based on three components:

- Automated testing, where a suite of web accessibility evaluation tools (AChecker, Examinator, TAW, WAVE) help determine if web content meets accessibility guidelines.

- Manual inspection, where experts use different methods to evaluate the accessibility of a website without involving users.

- User testing and system analysis, where users with disabilities have to perform a set of tasks in order to detect accessibility barriers.

Finally, it would be appropriate that governments from other developing countries study this systems perspective and some of the actions proposed for Ecuador, as these countries usually face similar realities.

## 2.8.5   References

- Consejo Nacional para la Igualdad de Discapacidades (2005). *Ecuador: la discapacidad en cifras. Análisis de los resultados de la Encuesta Nacional de Discapacidades.* Accessed 14-07-2015, from `http://www.inclusion.gob.ec/wp-content/uploads/downloads/2013/11/Pol%C3%ADtica-P%C3%BAblica_Subsecretar%C3%ADa-de-Discapacidades.pdf`.

- Constitución de la República de Ecuador (2008). *Registro Oficial No 449.* Ecuador, Octubre de 2008.

- Hayashi, E. C., & Baranauskas, M. C. C. (2008). *Facing the digital divide in a participatory way–an exploratory study.* In Human-Computer Interaction Symposium, pp. 143-154, September 7-10, Milano, Italy.

- Instituto Ecuatoriano de Normalización (2014). *NTE INEN-ISO/IEC 40500 "Tecnología de la información - Directrices de accesibilidad para el contenido Web del W3C (WCAG) 2.0 (ISO/IEC 40500:2012, IDT)".*

- International Organization for Standardization (2012). ISO/IEC 40500:2012 (W3C) Information technology – W3C Web Content Accessibility Guidelines (WCAG) 2.0.

- Gobierno de la República del Ecuador (2012). *Ley Orgánica de Discapacidades.* Registro Oficial N° 796. Ecuador. Instituto Ecuatoriano de Normalización (2015).

Reglamento Técnico Ecuatoriano INEN 288 "Accesibilidad para el contenido Web".

- Servicio Ecuatoriano de Normalización (2016). *Reglamento Técnico Ecuatoriano RTE INEN 288 "Accesibilidad para el contenido web"*.

- Servicio Nacional de Aduana del Ecuador (2014). *Tráfico Postal Internacional y Mensajería Acelerado o Courier*. Accessed 13-07-2015 from `https://www.aduana.gob.ec/envios-courier-o-postal/`

- SETEDIS (2015). *Accesibilidad Universal en el Ecuador: Diagnóstico en las Provincias de Imbabura, Pastaza y Santa Elena*. Quito: Edicuatorial.

- UNESCO (2012). *Informe sobre el Uso de las Tecnologías de Información y Comunicación (TIC) en la Educación para Personas con Discapacidad*. Accessed 14-07-2015 from `http://unesdoc.unesco.org/images/0021/002163/216382s.pdf`.

- United Nations (2006). *Convention on the Rights of Persons with Disabilities and Optional Protocol*.

- Varian, H.R. (2005). *Universal Access to Information*. In: Communications of the ACM, 48(10), p. 65-66.

- Vicepresidencia de la República del Ecuador (2012). *Estudio Biopsicosocial Clínico Genético de las Personas con Discapacidad en Ecuador. Misión Manuela Espejo*.

- World Wide Web Consortium (W3C) (1997). *WAI early days*. Accessed 05-07-2015 from `http://www.w3.org/WAI/history`.

- World Wide Web Consortium (W3C) (2008). Web Content Accessibility Guidelines (WCAG) 2.0. Accessed 13-07-2018 from `https://www.w3.org/TR/WCAG20/`

- World Wide Web Consortium (W3C) (2012). *Accessibility*. Accessed 05-07-2015 from `http://www.w3.org/standards/webdesign/accessibility`.

## Acknowledgment

Special thanks to the Technical Secretary of Disabilities, Dr. Alex Camacho, for boosting and supporting all projects. Also, greetings to architects Fernanda Páez and Katherine Chacón for their support while writing this case study.

## Contact Address

**Universidad Internacional del Ecuador (UIDE)**
Av. Simón Bolívar y Av. Jorge Fernández, Quito, Ecuador
Tel. +593-2 2985-600
Internet: http://uide.edu.ec
eMail: anpachecoba@uide.edu.ec ∣ a.pachecob@alumnos.upm.es

**Universidad de Alicante**
Carretera San Vicente del Raspeig s/n
E-03690 San Vicente del Raspeig (Alicante), Spain
Tel. +34 965 90 34 00 ext. 2962
Internet: http://accesibilidadweb.dlsi.ua.es/
eMail: sergio.lujan@ua.es

## Profile of Authors

### Andrea Pacheco Barzallo

Andrea earned her architectural degree from the Pontifical Catholic University of Ecuador (PUCE) and her master degree in Management of Technology and Entrepreneurship from the Swiss Federal Institute of Technology Lausanne (EPFL). She worked at Nestlé International Headquarters in the development of high hygiene standards for food factories and laboratories. She has lectured "Technological Innovation Potential in the Construction Industry" and "Constructive Systems" at the Faculty of Architecture and Urbanism of the Central University of Ecuador. Nowadays she is the National Coordinator of Universal Accessibility at the Technical Secretariat for the Inclusive Management on Disabilities in Ecuador (SETEDIS), where she has promoted the adoption of national accessibility standards, directed and published several research projects of accessibility in more than thirteen cities of the country, and directed the creation of the "Ecuadorian Methodology for the Elaboration of Accessibility Plans" which received the "Best Practice" award from the European foundation "Design For All". She has represented SETEDIS at several international conferences and projects of international cooperation with Uruguay, Brazil, Germany and Dominican Republic.

### Sergio Luján-Mora

Sergio is an associate professor of the Department of Software and Computing Systems at the University of Alicante, Spain. He has developed and executed several MOOCs in computer science. He has implemented web applications since 1997. He has also published several books related to programming and web development. His main research topics include MOOCs, OERs, e-learning, web applications, web development, web accessibility and usability and e-learning. His current research work can be found at http://gplsi.dlsi.ua.es/slujan/english.

# Chapter 3

# eProcurement

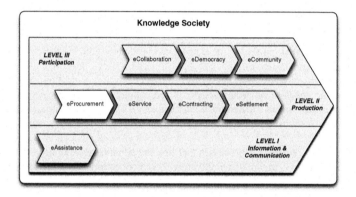

*Chapter 3 describes Web-based processes of procurement and purchasing for the administration. In Sect. 3.1, partial steps of the eProcurement process are explained and new potential benefits for the administrative institution are shown. Section 3.2 deals with the procurement model Seller-Side, while Sect. 3.3 focuses on the Buyer-Side and Sect. 3.4 on the market solution. To this end, we will discuss the software services for both the administrative institution and the suppliers' side, including intermediaries. The Public Offering via Internet is a process that starts, as displayed in Sect. 3.5, with publishing a public order and requesting the submission of offers, then it evaluates these offers and awards the contract. In order to determine prices in a dynamic way, Sect. 3.6 presents some current auction possibilities. The purchase of indirect goods with the help of desktop purchasing systems is presented in Sect. 3.7. Section 3.8 gives a summary of the literature. The case study discusses the procurement of Maintenance, Repair, Operations (MRO) goods (indirect goods for maintenance, repair, and operations) for the Swiss Federal Railways. In this, inverse auctions are used to obtain purchasing advantages.*

© Springer Nature Switzerland AG 2019
A. Meier, L. Terán, *eDemocracy & eGovernment*, Progress in IS,
https://doi.org/10.1007/978-3-030-17585-6_3

## 3.1   Internet-Based Procurement Process

*Difference between eProcurement and ePurchasing*

By eProcurement, we understand the Internet based procurement process. This includes not only the purchasing, which is limited to the operational partial steps of the procurement, but also includes strategic and tactical tasks such as selecting suppliers and negotiating framework contracts.

The procurement process is divided into the following six partial steps:

- Standardizing and specifying the procurement

- Selecting suppliers for products and services

- Negotiating contracts

- Ordering products and services

- Checking the delivery

- After sales services.

*Strategic, tactical and operational sub-processes*

For administrative purposes, these tasks can be divided into strategic, tactical and operational sub-processes, as shown in Fig. 3.1. The strategic level includes the standardization of the procurement, questions of make or buy and controlling. The analysis of the specific needs or ordering patterns of the institution, as well as negotiations of framework contracts, are situated on the tactical level. The operational purchase, on the other hand, is responsible for tendering, selection between offers and control and purchase of services.

*Cultivating connections to suppliers*

In the eProcurement, the processes that link the administrative unit to its suppliers are not the only concern, but also cultivating these connections. That is why the partial steps specification and selection are put onto the strategic level, in order to facilitate long-term, promising ties with the suppliers.

*Direct goods*

From the point of view of the administration, the products and services that are to be procured can be classified differently. Direct goods are trading goods or advances that enter directly the in-house effort. Counted among these are raw and auxiliary materials that go directly into the product as basic material.

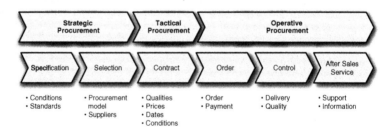

**Fig. 3.1:** Process steps for eProcurement.

Indirect goods are products and services that are needed for running the administra- *MRO goods*
tion. They do not enter the final product and are usually called MRO goods. They are
operating supplies, like energy that is consumed during the work process, etc. Commodi-
ties and investment goods that are needed to produce the final product are also counted
among them.

Under Public Offering (see Sect. 3.5) we understand the entirety of relations and *Public Offering*
processes of public procurement orders. This includes publishing a public order and
requesting the submission of offers, evaluating these offers, awarding the contract, and
carrying out the procurement process. This brings along high potential in the following
aspects:

- **Shortening the processing time:** The use of information and communication
  technology evades manual, time-consuming, and repeating process steps including mailing. Apart from reducing the number of process steps, it also downsizes
  the supervision effort. Corresponding surveys have shown that the throughput
  time of a conventional ordering process is cut in half when using electronic procurement.

- **Reduction of procurement costs:** The process costs in eProcurement can be reduced. Furthermore, it is possible to obtain lower acquisition prices by using dynamic pricing mechanisms (see inverse auctions in Sect. 3.6 and the case study).
  MRO goods like office supplies or articles for office automation are needed on a
  regular basis and are usually cheap, but high costs may be produced by manual
  or uncoordinated procurement transactions. The ratio between merchandise value
  and procurement effort can be measured in the eProcurement.

- **Quality improvement in the decentralized procurement:** With the help of desktop purchasing systems (see Sect. 3.7), the purchase runs decentralized as a part of
  the eProcurement. Thanks to electronic support (catalog management), it is possible to keep the administrative effort and error-proneness down and at the same
  time profit from already negotiated prices and conditions.

- **Increasing the transparency:** The possibility to access the electronic procurement process independently of time and place increases the transparency for the
  administrative units and the suppliers. In addition to that, controlling functions
  give an up-to-date status on the procurement and possible consequences for the
  budget.

Apart from these potential benefits of eProcurement, it must be laid sufficient stress *Protection*
on privacy policies and data security. It is particularly necessary to apply digital sig- *through public*
natures in contracts and to maintain corresponding infrastructures (public key infras- *key*
tructure, see Chap. 5 on eContracting). Diverse models for eProcurement have been *infrastructure*
developed, depending on the characteristics of the software solution and on where the
procurement catalog is maintained. In the following sections, the procurement models
Seller-Side, Buyer-Side, and Marketplace are presented.

## 3.2   Procurement Model Seller-Side

*Purchasing
software and
catalog on the
sellers' side*

In the procurement model Seller-Side, the supplier provides the purchasing software and an electronic catalog. In this scenario, the purchaser has to apply for each supplier and has to familiarize himself with different software solution and navigational aids. Some suppliers with Seller-Side solutions offer further functions for personalization, product configuration and compatibility checking. For example, the purchaser can determine administration specific rules in the procurement process.

*User profile
setup*

The eProcurement according to the Seller-Side approach requires the supplier to provide the whole business logic for the procurement procedure in an information system (purchasing software, eShop), including the product catalog. In Fig. 3.2, the most important software elements and functions on the suppliers' side are listed. The purchaser's user profile, as well as his rights and obligations (login, authorization, acquisition limits, attribution of cost centers, among other things) have to be covered by the supplier's software and maintained. In case the purchaser has to handle several suppliers with Seller-Side systems, this means an extensive work and maintenance effort.

*Supplier uses
content
management*

The supplier employs a content management system (see Sect. 7.2) for the electronic catalog entries. He creates the product description and the product classification and determines the actualization procedures. The process of ordering and handling are also done with the help of software. Search services for articles and services and a shopping cart are provided, orders can be received. ePayment solutions are employed for billing. Depending on the maturity of the supplier's software, different kinds of reports on the buying behavior and the purchase of goods and services can be generated.

*Use of electronic
shops*

An eShop is a typical option for procurement after the Seller-Side principle. It supports the phases of information-getting, agreement, and fulfillment in online orders. As examples serve Amazon as a supplier of books and other information articles, and Dell for ordering computers and peripheral devices.

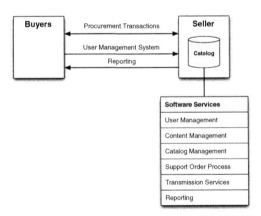

**Fig. 3.2:** Software services in the electronic procurement (Seller-Side) according to Schubert & Ecademy (2002).

Depending on the degree of maturity of the eShop, the purchaser can specify com-   *Configuration of*
plex products with the help of a configurator. For the supplier, this means an automati-   *products*
zation of consulting services, a reduced effort in capturing data, and the possibility to
delegate responsibilities to the purchasing institution.

An eProcurement system according to the Seller-Side model facilitates, depending   *Interface to ERP*
on the degree of development, integration into the Enterprise Resource Planning (ERP)   *systems*
system of the supplier. In this case, the system gives further information like stock on
hand, availability or customized prices. It is not necessary to register the orders a second
time in the ERP system of the supplier.

It is obvious that a relationship between the procuring institution (purchaser) and   *Reveal structure*
the supplier has to be established in order to run the Seller-Side version successfully.   *of setup and*
In particular, the shop system also requires information on the organizational structure   *procedures*
of the administrative unit that is procuring. The record of change orders has to be designed appropriately. The administrative unit finds itself confronted with a multitude
of information systems when procuring products from several suppliers. This requires
significantly more information and training.

Another problem is the integration of the procurement process into the purchaser's
information systems. A possible approach to solve this problem is the cXML standard
(XML specification on catalog formats), offered by Dell to its mayor clients. Using
cXML, orders can be sent via Internet.

## 3.3   Procurement Model Buyer-Side

In the procurement model Buyer-Side, the purchaser must host and maintain the corre-   *Procurement*
sponding software, including an extract of the product catalog. It is possible to define   *software and*
customized catalogs in which articles of different suppliers are combined to a multi   *catalog on the*
supplier catalog. This is convenient for the administrative institution, because the pro-   *buyer's side*
curement can be done with a consistent product display. Apart from that, the regulations
for the procurement process, like compliance with contracts, responsibilities in the ordering process or authorization procedures, can be customized, though with an increased
effort. At any rate, the procurement process remains independent of the supplier and the
arising process data can be collected and analyzed.

As Fig. 3.3 shows, most eProcurement services are situated on the side of the admin-   *User*
istration. In particular, the user administration including the administration of authoriza-   *administration*
tions and access rights is executed by the governmental institution. They also determine   *and*
the steps of the ordering process with the specific organizational properties like approval   *authorizations*
procedures and workflow control. The product catalog can be enriched and expanded to
a purchase catalog for all MRO goods. Though this requires an increased maintenance
effort from the administrative unit, the result is a customized eProcurement solution for
the governmental institution. It is easier to integrate it into the existing software environment and to link it to the ERP systems.

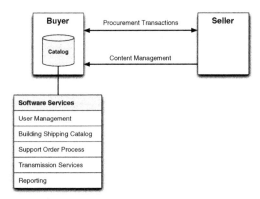

**Fig. 3.3:** Software services in electronic procurement (Buyer-Side) according to Schubert & Ecademy (2002).

*Desktop purchasing for the administrative unit*

Applications for procurement that are run by employees are called desktop purchasing systems (see Sect. 3.7). They are located at the workplace of the consuming or requesting person and are adapted to the process of the procuring administrative unit. They offer a consistent user interface, can factor in organizational specific standards and are usually well integrated into the operative information systems. The precondition for its successful operation is a catalog of all products that are available and priory negotiated with the supplier. This catalog often is referred to as multi sourcing product catalog because it contains the product data of different suppliers.

*Advantages of Web-based procurements*

Desktop purchasing systems are most commonly executed as Web applications on the user's side. They back up the procurement process of all involved posts within the institution. Consequently, the requesting person can apply for the order over the intranet, the head of the cost center can authorize it, the purchaser can order the product, the goods recipient can affirm the delivery and accounting can pay the bill. The depth of the integration on the supplier's side determines whether the products can be procured without further interaction and whether the bill is sent from the supplier to the buyer electronically.

## 3.4   Marketplace Procurement

*Intermediary runs Marketplace solution*

In the eProcurement Marketplace option, a platform is run by an intermediary. An intermediary (in digital products often referred to as infomediary or information broker) has the task to bundle information or products and put them at disposal on his platform. He consolidates the providers' offers and makes comparable product offers to the consumers. He establishes contacts between providers and consumers and, if required, carries out procurement transactions in the name of the administration (purchaser's side).

If providers and consumers meet directly on Web-based marketplaces, the intermediary trade is eliminated (disintermediation). But why do intermediaries and infomediaries occur and offer their services?

The Internet is based on an open standard, the density of regulation is maintained as deep as possible. The result is a multitude of solutions, which are though all based on Internet technology, different from each other. For the procuring organization, this creates a problematic lack of comparability of products (price, quality, availability, etc.). The intermediary assumes this service and charges for it. *Comparison of products and prices*

Another argument is that he brings together supply and demand. Empirical studies show that a lot of time goes into searching a suitable provider or demander. An intermediary can unite a multitude of providers and a multitude of procuring companies on his platform and thereby reduce significantly the search effort for the market participants. *Search and Navigation*

Another pro argument for an eProcurement solution of the type Marketplace is its independence regarding the place. The anonymization that comes along with this bears the risk of electronic transactions for the procuring organization. The intermediary guarantees a successful transaction and consequently receives remuneration for this job. If desired, the intermediary himself carries out the procurement procedures, while keeping the anonymity. *Anonymity is advantage in procurement*

The actual design of the intermediary's procurement platform may have different forms. It ranges from Yellow Pages, tendering platforms and auctions to trade-specific platforms. Also, the operators employ a multitude of different price models.

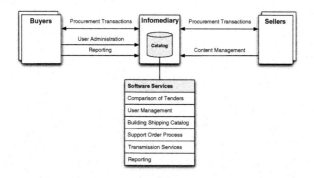

**Fig. 3.4:** Software services offered by an intermediary for eProcurement.

Figure 3.4 shows the intermediary's software services for procurement processes (purchaser's side) and presentation of supply (provider's side). The operator of the platform intends to create advantages to the procuring institution by offering his own software services that is representing offers and comparing them. The suppliers submit their product catalogs on a regular basis and remain responsible for the content management of their offerings.

In general, it can be said that the intermediary's activities consist in providing information of high quality to both sellers and buyers and to guarantee smooth procurement transactions. Previous experiences have shown that only intermediaries with a sufficient level of specialization reach the required quality and liquidity. This explains why vertically organized intermediaries have quite more success in comparison to horizontally established platform owners.

In contrast to the procurement models Seller-Side and Buyer-Side, with intermediaries it is possible to compare different providers. Bringing together several providers increases the liquidity of markets and results, in the best case, in efficient markets, for example, regarding price fixing. Depending on the needs of the providers and demanders, it is possible to ensure anonymous procurement of products and services for the market participants.

## 3.5   Public Offering via Internet

*What is Public
Offering?*
By Public Offering, we understand the awarding of public contracts by administrative entities. This regards constructions, restorations, repairs and procurements of any kind that the administrative institution itself is not able to do or does not want to do. The act of awarding a public contract must not be arbitrary, but has to follow fixed and comprehensible rules. The purpose of taking various providers into account is to increase competition and diminish discrimination of tenderers. That's why it is mandatory to establish a transparent process for the awarding of public orders via Internet.

*Process steps for
the awarding of
public contracts*
The awarding process consists of standardized process steps, they are presented in Fig. 3.5 and described bellow.

- **Announcement:** The administrative institution or entity publishes the public order in a Public Offering portal. The tendering text outlines the order, specifies the work, fixes the deadlines and announces the registration modalities.

- **Registration:** Before entering a public tendering process, all interested parties have to register themselves. Apart from that, an electronic certificate confirming the applicant's authenticity has to be filed (see Chap. 5 on eContracting).

- **Awarding:** After checking the registration, the applicants receive the detailed awarding documents. This interchange of documents is carried out in an encoded way and secured with digital signatures (see Chap. 5). The interchange and deposit of document parts can be prepared with software help (offering assistant).

- **Submission:** When a provider decides to submit an offer, the required work contracts are described and prices are put together. The encoded and signed offer is submitted within the time limit.

- **Evaluation:** The administrative institutions analyze the received offers. The evaluation of the offers is based on criteria that were set up in the tendering text. After a pre-selection, it is possible to discuss open topics with the authors of the best offers.

- **Processing:** The preselected providers are informed of the preliminary decision and invited to clarify topics that are still open. The negotiation results contribute to the decision making.

- **Awarding:** The contract is awarded to the best provider. The other providers are informed. The handling of the order can begin.

**Fig. 3.5:** Process steps for the awarding of public contracts.

The access to national and international procurement markets for governments and administrative entities has both advantages and disadvantages. In case that economical aspects are decisive for winning the contract, local providers may find themselves confronted with stronger competition. On the other hand, if ecological aspects play a decisive role for certain procurement objects, the local industry can be strengthened. These and more aspects can be taken into account in the tendering text by employing respective evaluation criteria.

*Advantages and disadvantages for local providers*

## 3.6   Conducting Auctions

Auctions or public sales are particular ways of finding and fixing prices that are utilized more and more by administrative institutions. Offers can be called for in a regulated tendering process. The auctioning process, which may be outsourced, determines who wins the contract.

The purpose of an auction is to lead the price negotiation in a dynamic way. Different providers will calculate the willingness to pay of the institution differently. This asymmetry of information can be exploited by the administrative institutions in their eProcurement process. If a provider sets his prices too high, he will not win the contract and will not be able to sell his products or services to the administrative institution. If he sets the price too low, he will not exhaust the profit margin optimally.

*Dynamic pricing via auctioning*

Auctions are an important instrument of dynamic pricing. They are a part of a standardized course of action as shown in Fig. 3.6, regarding buying and selling products and services. The auctioning process, as part of the tendering and procurement process, can be carried out by the administrative institution itself or a third party provider. There are different types of auctions, namely English, Japanese, Dutch, highest-price auctions, and Vickrey auctions:

*Standardized auctioning process*

- **English auctions:** In the English auction, the bidding process begins with a starting price. Every participant bids several times and may beat his former bid. As in electronic auctions the bidders do not physically meet at the trading place and

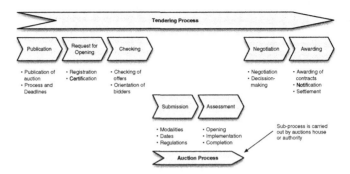

**Fig. 3.6:** Tendering process with auction.

they do not know how many bidders participate in the auction, electronic auctions are ended at a previously determined time. The winner of the auction is the bidder who has given the highest bid at this time. In other words, in electronic auctions, the bidding does not go on until there is only one bidder left who gets the tender.

- **Japanese auction:** This type of auction is equivalent to the English auction, but here the bidders do not announce the price by themselves. The price rises continually until there is only one bidder left.

- **Dutch auction:** This type of auction is designed the other way around. At the beginning of the Dutch auction, a high price is announced and then gradually lowered until there is a bidder who accepts that price. In this mechanism of continually lowering the price, the first bidder gets the tender.

- **Highest-price auction:** In the highest-price auction, the participants give secret bids that are revealed simultaneously at the end of the auction. The bidder with the highest bid gets the tender. The bidders are not allowed to change their bid or submit more than one bid. On the Internet, highest price auctions are not very common, they are mostly employed for trading industrial products or real estate.

- **Vickrey auction:** This auction is equivalent to the highest-price auction. The winner is the bidder with the highest bid. But here, the winner does not pay the price of the highest bid, but the price of the second-highest bid. For that reason, the Vickrey auction is often referred to as second-price auction.

Auctions are meant to reveal the bidders' willingness to pay. In the English and Dutch auction, this happens during the bidding process and in the highest-price auction, it happens at the end of the previously secret auction.

*Addition to conventional distribution channels*    The hosts of these auctions have the intention to open up new marketing channels and they hope for publicity effects. Primarily, auctions serve to increase the number of potential consumers. Auctions in the Internet often focus on certain products and consumer segments and complement the traditional distribution channels.

The operators of auctions or auction portals are intermediaries who increase the transaction volume by innovative services (advertising, catalog services, expert reports, encouragement during the auction, payment processing, etc.). As a precondition, the operator has to win the providers' and bidders' trust and guarantee a high quality auction processing.

Due to the high popularity of auctions, some providers of electronic shops give their consumers the opportunity to choose between buying the article in the electronic shop or in an auction. To give an example, newly published books can be offered in the electronic shop, while out-of-date books or such that are officially sold out can be traded in auctions. This prevents the cannibalization for one and the same book. Hence, auctions provide alternative distribution channels for some business models.

*Avoiding cannibalization*

An idea that is currently used by administrative institutions is to have inverse auctions. This type of auction is similar to tendering, as the administration announces its preferences and the providers of products and services have to enter a competition. On Internet platforms like www.travelbids.com, the user registers a desired travel destination and travel agencies submit their offers within 2–3 days. In the case study in this chapter, the Swiss federal railways use the inverse auction type in order to obtain a centralized procurement process and better prices.

*Benefits of inverse auctions for administrative institutions*

## 3.7   Desktop Purchasing

The purchase of indirect goods or MRO services can be done with the help of information systems (desktop purchasing). These systems consolidate the product and service offers of different suppliers in a multi sourcing product catalog. The browser-based user interface of these systems facilitates the non-regular access by members of the administrative institution, who check for offers of MRO goods when needed and order them individually. Progressive desktop purchasing systems feature interfaces to the operative information systems and ERP systems, respectively, and make it possible to integrate the procurement of indirect goods into the administrative processes.

*Procurement of MRO goods*

Today, there are different providers of software systems for desktop purchasing. An overview of the functionality is given in Fig. 3.7: Even the search for potential suppliers is supported by the desktop purchasing system. With the help of the so-called reversed marketing, the search for providers and the selection is made easier. Reversed

*Functionality of desktop purchasing systems*

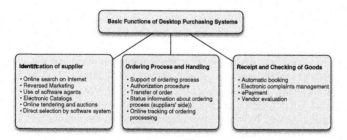

**Fig. 3.7:** Software support for desktop purchasing systems.

marketing aims at publishing specific information for potential suppliers (ground rules for procurement, quality features, topics to negotiate, etc.), be it on the Web site of the procuring company or with help of a desktop purchasing system, or to announce the need for goods, shipping conditions and payment modalities. Here, the administrative unit is inclined to buy, takes the initiative and runs the marketing.

The ordering process, including handling and shipping, is also done within the desktop purchasing system, the authorization process is initialized and carried out step by step. Of special interest is the tracking function, which displays the up-to-date status of the order at the supplier's and during transportation in the desktop purchasing system. This way, the person who activated the order is always kept informed.

*Checking target dates and goods*  The receipt and booking of goods are noted in the desktop purchasing system and synchronized directly with the ERP system, depending on how deep the two systems are integrated. After checking the incoming goods and target dates, statistics are compiled and complaints are released, if needed. This way, the procuring institution is always up-to-date regarding the quality of the suppliers.

Desktop purchasing systems can decisively unburden the logistics and purchasing departments of the administrative institution. A variety of services can be procured efficiently, ranging from workplace design and office installations, to traveling services or events.

*Providers of desktop purchasing systems*  Ariba Technologies Inc. offers a desktop purchasing system with a user-friendly front end. The system includes a powerful search engine with which wanted product groups can be specified by selectable criteria. The partial work steps in the procurement process are supported by a workflow component. Providers of product catalogs must submit their specifications in catalog interchange format (CIF) format, so that the information can be added to a multi supplier catalog.

The company CommerceOne sells an eProcurement solution under the name BuySite. This platform supports the procurement of MRO goods, the handling, billing, and process controlling.

Apart from standalone desktop purchasing systems, the producers of ERP systems have started to widen their product range toward functions for procuring direct and indirect goods (see, e.g., SAP Enterprise Buyer Professional).

## 3.8   Bibliographical Notes

*Literature on eProcurement*  Appenfeller's and Buchholz's work (Appelfeller & Buchholz, 2005), as well as the one of Dolmetsch et al. (1999); Dolmetsch (2000) and Nekolar's book (Nekolar (2013)) give an overview of the topic of eProcurement and the management of supplier relations. They set themselves apart from other investigations by concrete applications, functionalities, and architectural aspects. Brenner and Wilding's research work is dedicated to the procurement over the Internet, as well (Brenner & Wilking, 1999). In the work of Schubert & Ecademy (2002), several case studies are dealt with, illustrating the different market models for eProcurement (Seller-Side, Buyer-Side, Marketplace, etc.).

*Public procurement*  The peculiarities of Web-based procurement in public institutions are explained in the work of Friedhelm et al. (2002). This work describes legal issues, apart from econonomical and technical aspects.

# 3.9   Case Study—Inverse Auctions at the Procurement Agency of Swiss Federal Railways

### 3.9.1   Background

The strategic purchasing department of the infrastructure division of the Swiss Federal Railways (SBB for its initials in German) procures goods and services for the infrastructure, and goods for the company. Negotiations in form of inverse auctions have been defined as strategic devices in the procurement process. Taking into account the existing procurement volume and the number and type of procurement cases, scenarios for application were developed. As a policy, the purchasers were instructed to lead a certain amount of auctions, but acceptance was low. There were all kinds of concerns. Apart from that, the need for handicap auctions (auction bids are weighted differently depending on a previous detailed evaluation of the offers) and package auctions (different articles are auctioned at the same time) were analyzed. Furthermore, the SBB extended its vision and sought the collaboration with the federal government and its companies.

Heidi Rubi,
*Swiss Federal Railways SBB*
and

Joachim Weiss,
*Swiss Federal Railways SBB*

It became obvious that in everyday business, auctions cannot always be realized as planned. For example, there were too few procurement cases for handicap auctions. What was more, the general tendency toward framework contracts, outsourcing of complete product lines or strategic partnerships made it impossible to keep the target number of auctions. As well from the financial point of view, inverse auctions reached their limit, because in some cases, the generated costs for platform maintenance and support threatened to exceed the expected cost saving effect by far. The need for an easy-to-use and low-cost platform became stronger every time.

The strategic purchasing department of SBB first ran an electronic price negotiation over the Internet in 2001. Taking into account the existing procurement volume and the number and type of procurement cases, scenarios for application are now developed on a regular basis. Public-law customers must comply with the federal law on public procurement and the according ordinances. Under certain circumstances they may lead negotiations in the form of inverse auctions, where it is especially important to keep confidentiality.

### 3.9.2   Case Studies of Inverse Auctions in the SBB

The procurement cases of the strategic purchasing at SBB are meant to show how inverse auctions facilitate transparent price negotiations. The case examples were led according to the same ground rules:

- The providers' submitted offers must pass a quality check in order to be approved for the inverse auction.

- The bidders do not know how many competing parties participate in the auction.

- The bidders are informed about their own rank, but not about the highest offer in the auction. This means that the bidders cannot orientate themselves at the currently highest offer when giving their own bids. Based on their own calculations, they may bid in order to improve their position in the auction.

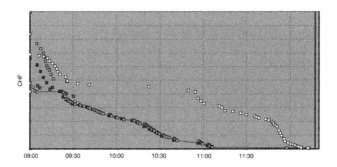

**Fig. 3.8:** Procurement of a service (case A).

- The base period for the auction is 30 min. If someone bids in the last 5 min of the period, the auction is prolonged for another 5 min. The maximum prolongation possible is 180 min.

- The bidders have to underbid their own bid, but not necessarily the best bid. A minimum step size of a 0.5% of the last bid is determined.

Each auction was preceded by a test auction 2 days earlier. This allowed the bidders to get to know the platform and the settings and solve rising questions before the actual date. This training auction was carried out with fictional prices, so that no conclusions could be drawn regarding the real auction.

For privacy policy reasons, no names or values can be published here. Furthermore, no specific description of the procured article is given in order to prevent possible conclusions regarding the auctions.

### 3.9.3   Case Example A—Procurement of a Service

The horizontal time axis shows the duration of the conducted auction, the $y$-axis depicts the bids in Swiss francs. The span of the $y$-axis is proportional and represents the span between the highest starting bid and the last or best bid. Starting from the opening bid, the individual bids given by the individual bidders in the course of the auction are shown. The currently best bid is linked with a line on the time axis.

Figure 3.8 shows the procurement of a service for which the providers need special equipment and know-how. The international providers' calculation was in some cases influenced by the laws in their respective countries and indirectly as well by the prices for raw material and their development on the world market. Partial contributions of third parties also played a role in the calculations.

The contract that was to be awarded had 1 year's volume. The value of this procurement order has been approximately 1.5 million Swiss Francs in the past years. Some surrounding conditions had changed and the purchaser had reason to assume that he would be able to award the contract for a lower price.

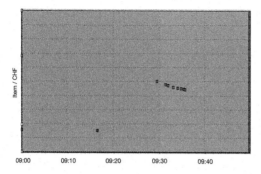

**Fig. 3.9:** Procurement of a piece of clothing (case B).

All written submitted offers of the providers undercut the previous procurement price. In the further course of events it became obvious to the purchaser that the previously successful tenderer and at least one other competitor were interested in the contract, as both companies had just invested in the development of the technical preconditions. The bidder Black, depicted in Fig. 3.8 (with the fourth best starting bid), is the current contractor. The gap between the best and the worst starting bid is approximately 65%.

The auction ended with an improvement of about 40% toward the best starting bid and about 100% toward the highest starting bid. There had been seven bidders from Europe admitted to the auction, which took almost three and a half hours total. During this span, the bidders gave 184 bids. The result surpassed the purchaser's expectations.

### 3.9.4   Case Example B—Procurement of Clothing

In this procurement example, the concern is the yearly requirement of a clothing item of the SBB with a contract value of a little over half a million Swiss Francs. The amount to be delivered is ordered from the provider during the year according to a delivery plan. In this package auction, several related pieces of clothing (e.g., the same cut but another color of fabric) were negotiated to a standard price per piece, independent of the size.

The SBB had been procuring these articles for some time now and their prices have been determined by a inverse auction. In Fig. 3.9, the course of the auction is shown, exemplarily for one article. In order to give the bidders enough time to redo their calculations during the auction, the prolongation time was set to 10 minutes instead of the usual 5 min.

There were five providers admitted to the auction after a qualitative suitability test including a test for washing performance, etc. The starting bids were almost 50% apart. The purchaser expected a reduction of costs of 5–10% compared to the best bid. This auction, however, closed after only two prolongation periods, without reaching a new best bid. The auction did not improve the prices of any of the negotiated articles. The contract had to be awarded for the starting bid price, to the bidder with the best starting

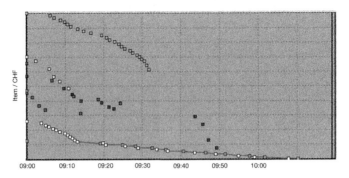

**Fig. 3.10:** Procurement of a piece of work-wear (case C).

bid. The auction serves as an example for the fact that not every inverse auction that is carried out guarantees a better price.

The possibility of the bidders having had an agreement can be discarded. The reasons for the failure must be sought in the current market situation. It is one possible cause that one provider could have more favorable production circumstances than the others and therefore entered the auction virtually without competition. Furthermore, the previous auctioning of the same good probably had an influence on the pricing as well.

### 3.9.5   Case Example C—Procurement of Working Clothes

In this procurement example, the concern is the yearly requirement of SBB working clothes with a contract value of 300,000 Swiss Francs. The amount to be delivered is ordered from the provider during the year according to a delivery plan.

Figure 3.10 shows one article exemplarily for all articles negotiated in the package auction, for which a standard price per piece was negotiated, independent of the size to be produced. In contrast to the previously shown article, in this case different articles were produced with one and the same fabric. Further articles from this product line segment were practically negotiated at the same time. The order for each article was placed with that provider who had the best price for the particular article. The prices of the articles of this product line segment had never been negotiated in an auction before.

There were eight bidders from Switzerland and neighboring countries admitted to the auction, after qualitative suitability tests and sampling inspections with wearing tests and other every-day tests. In order to give the bidders enough time to redo their calculations during the auction, the prolongation time was set to 10 min instead of the usual 5 min. The starting bids were almost 50% apart and the purchaser expected a reduction of costs of 5–10% compared to the best bid. The expectations were met in this case, the auction results were a little over 10% compared to the best starting bid. This auction was quite successful, because all bidders with the exception of one participated actively and gave 89 bids during the auction.

### 3.9.6   Case Example D—Procurement of a Service

This procurement case deals with a service in the pure sense of the word. The order is not linked at all to raw materials or fabrication. The particularity of this auction was that only two bidders were admitted to it, as they were the only ones who had matched the quality requirements. The purchaser was sure that both providers had active interest in getting the contract. Both starting bids were a 50% apart.

It was then up to the bidder on second place to improve his bid enough to gain the lead (see Fig. 3.11). The success of the auction depended on his engagement and interest in the auction. Already after nine bids and merely 20 min, he had taken the lead in the auction. The auction lasted a total of 70 min and closed after eight prolongations of 5 min. Fifty-three bids were given by only two bidders, leaving the bidder with the worse starting bid as the winner. He had improved himself by 100% and in the end had undercut the better starting bid by over 25%.

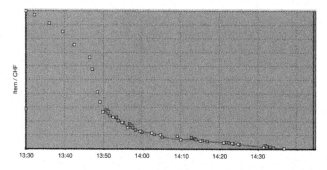

**Fig. 3.11:** Procurement of a service (case D).

### 3.9.7   Opportunities and Risks

The auctions comply with the federal law on public procurement and the implementation rules, because they guarantee transparency, equal treatment, competition, and cost-effective use of public resources. In the auctions at SBB, the bidders do not know how many fellow bidders participate in the auction. They neither know who participates in the auction nor which bidder gave what bid. Confidentiality, which is strictly mandatory, is provided and each bidder starts with the same preconditions.

All auctions are carried out with prolongation time. In case someone bids shortly before the end of the auction, every bidder has the chance to react and adapt his own price to the new situation. All auctions were being hosted on a platform that featured multiple functions and that could be configured for each auction individually. For the purchaser who has only a couple of auctions a year, this may not result easy. That's why the help of the provider and the competence center at SBB are necessary. Such auctions are comparatively expensive and in a lot of cases, the achieved savings are neutralized by the involved costs.

For the reasons above mentioned, a platform was needed which would lead quickly and easily to the goal. In collaboration with the Federal Institute of Technology in Lausanne, an auction platform was developed over which the purchaser can handle even his smaller everyday procurements in a time-saving way and with a reduced effort. The purchaser enters his procurement plans into the platform, sets the publishing date and the date of the starting bid and determines the deadline. He can manage his providers and provider groups in the system, relating them to an auction. The platform notifies the bidders of the current course of the auction via e-mails. The platform only allows a couple of individually different settings, it is based on a simple defined standard.

Inverse auctions are a particular type of price negotiations and present advantages to both purchasers and providers. The auction platform is transparent and serves for fair pricing. It supports the purchasers in their purchasing process; if used well, it results in reduced processing costs. It is wrong to think that the benefit of a inverse auction always must be a lower procurement price.

When planning a inverse auction and agreeing on objectives, alternatives like outsourcing of product lines or strategic partnerships can be considered. However, in everyday business it is quite common that apart from these efforts, one has to deal with smaller procurement amounts. Even in these cases, a low-cost and user-friendly auction platform has a chance for the future.

## Contact Details

Swiss Federal Railways SBB
Strategic Purchasing
Mittelstrasse 43
CH-3000 Bern 65
Internet: www.sbb.ch/einkauf
eMail: eauction@sbb.ch

## Profile of Authors

### Heidi Rubi

Heidi Rubi is head of the contract management and projects area of strategic purchasing in the infrastructure division of the Swiss Federal Railways in Bern. She is an attorney specialized in procurement issues. The competence center for auctions is located in her department.

### Joachim Weiss

Joachim Weiss is a specialized expert in strategic purchasing in the infrastructure division of the Swiss Federal Railways in Basel. Since 2001, he has been working with inverse auctions at SBB, and in this capacity has organized and led purchasing auctions on the Internet for SBB and other governmental corporations.

# Chapter 4

# eService

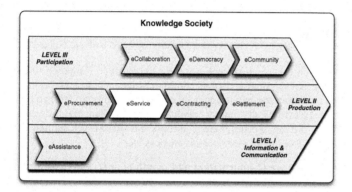

Chapter 4 deals with the service management for eGovernment. Section 4.1 makes an argument for the interoperability of systems in order to facilitate exchange relations between heterogeneous system landscapes. The 12 process areas for public services to citizens, as proposed by the European Union, are presented in Sect. 4.2, whereas the eight areas for companies are shown in Sect. 4.3. In the line of an effect-oriented administration, municipality product catalogs were created and then digitized step by step (Sect. 4.4). A service-oriented application architecture for mobile eHealth services is presented in Sect. 4.5. The European Union runs a regular benchmarking to evaluate and compare administrative services (Sect. Sect. 4.6). Section 4.7 gives bibliographical notes. The case study presented at the end of this chapter is related to the service management dealing with electronic health records from scientists of the Medical University of Vienna that introduce to the project "electronic health record," coordinated by the Austrian Ministry of Health.

© Springer Nature Switzerland AG 2019
A. Meier, L. Terán, *eDemocracy & eGovernment*, Progress in IS,
https://doi.org/10.1007/978-3-030-17585-6_4

# 4.1   Technical, Organizational, and Semantic Interoperability

*What is*
*interoperability?* Interoperability denominates the ability of heterogeneous information and communication systems to exchange information efficiently and in a way so that no data gets lost, both within organizations and between different ones. At this, three levels have to be considered:

- **Technical interoperability**: Computer systems and communication networks are linked to each other with the help of exchange formats and protocols. Open and standardized interfaces help to make heterogeneous information systems compatible.

- **Organizational interoperability**: The processes within the administration and the ones between the administration and the citizens or between the administration and companies have to be adjusted with the help of appropriate models.

- **Semantic interoperability**: The meaning of the exchanged information is interpreted correctly by the involved application systems and handled accordingly.

*Advantages of*
*interoperability* Interoperability makes it possible for the administrative institution to utilize their often heterogeneous system and application landscapes within and outside of the institution. In particular, the public administration services are available to both citizens and companies electronically. Interoperability may be challenging, if diverse information systems in different countries are required. Figure 4.1 gives a fictitious application scenario. The following interrelationships are possible:

- **Direct exchange of information and handling of services inside a state**: Citizens and companies, respectively, draw on governmental services in situ, i.e., within the state borders.

- **Exchange between administrative institutions of different countries**: Emigrated citizens or branch offices of companies in foreign countries contact the local

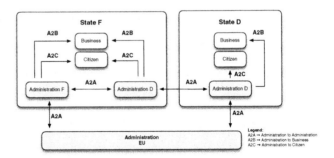

**Fig. 4.1:** Complex interrelationships for governmental services.

administrative institutions in substitution of their own, or embassies of their home country, in order to handle services with their country of origin.

- **Exchange of information and services with a European institution**: Individual administrative bodies, companies or citizens interact through European institutions in order to handle particular governmental services.

Considered as an example for complex application scenarios, job placement offices act in all Europe. In doing so, they may have to offer some services in different languages. Additionally, country-specific regulations have to be taken into account when making job arrangements and the processing has to be done with electronic agreements that are in accordance with the law (see Chap. 5 on eContracting and Public Key Infrastructure). *Exemplary application scenario: Europe-wide job placement*

The coordination and counseling department (KBSt) of the German federal government has published standards for the interoperability in the eGovernment under the abbreviation Standards and Architectures for eGovernment Applications (SAGA). Apart from interoperability, the purpose of this is to promote openness, scalability and reusability of the architectures and information systems, while at the same time reducing or limiting costs and safety risks. The SAGA proposition specifically deals with the following models and procedures: *The SAGA standard*

- **General concept and legal framework**: In the first topic area (enterprise viewpoint), the general conditions of eGovernment applications are listed and differentiated from the concept of service. Next to the general concept of eGovernment, the organizational and legal preconditions are discussed and the interrelationships in eGovernment applications demonstrated.

- **Data models and data exchange**: The second topic area of the architecture model of SAGA deals with data modeling and standardization of data models (Information Viewpoint). In this, one aims for an XML repository with UML diagrams and XML schemas that offers the different data models in a standardized form for reuse.

- **Service oriented software architecture**: An exemplary software architecture (reference architecture) is described in the third topic area under the headline of computational viewpoint. As a possible realization, a component-based procedure for the multi-layer architecture is proposed, in which the rules of Service Oriented Architecture (SOA) are applied.

- **Infrastructure, protection and safety**: The setup of an eGovernment infrastructure is comprised in the forth topic area called Engineering Viewpoint. It puts systems and system components into separate security zones, according to a classification of protection and security requirements.

- **Standardization**: In the fifth topic area of SAGA, the standards for IT architecture and data security are listed in detail.

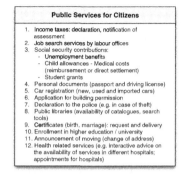

**Fig. 4.2:** Public services for citizens according to EU program.

Diverse appendices contain reference projects for ePayment (see Chap. 6), virtual post offices, forms (see Chap. 4), content management (see Sect. 7.2), eGovernment portals (see Sect. 2.4) or Public Key Infrastructure (see Chap. 5).

## 4.2   Electronic Governmental Services for Citizens

*Process areas*
*for citizens*
In 2007, the European Union has analyzed the governmental services for citizens and determined 12 basic process areas (see Fig. 4.2); further eight governmental services for companies are presented in Sect. 4.3.

*Handling of*
*income tax*
The governmental services for citizens comprise declaration, fixing and handling of income taxes (process area no. 1 in Fig. 4.2). The basic idea is that an eGovernment portal puts the necessary information and electronic tax forms (see Sect. 4.4) at disposal. The highest level of declaration and handling of income taxes is reached, when all incurring steps can be followed electronically. In other words, in the future there will be no paper printouts, manual signatures, or conventional mailing necessary. Rather, this stage of development requires a functioning Public Key Infrastructure (see Chap. 5 on eContracting) that includes digital signatures and thereby verifies electronic documents as legally binding.

*Job search*
*services*
Governmental job search services (process area no. 2) put databases with job offers and requirement profiles at disposal. Electronic job portals assist during the search for a job by comparing profiles and special requirements of providers and demanders and submitting job arrangements in an efficient way. By these governmental services, mobility and attractiveness in European countries are to be increased and the costs and efforts for the placement procedure are to be lowered.

*Social security*
In the area of social security (process area no. 3), mayor concerns are those governmental services regarding unemployment benefits, child allowances, reimbursement or direct settlement of medical costs according to state regulated health insurance plans and application and granting of student scholarships.

Another governmental service (process area no. 4) for citizens concerns ordering    *Issue of personal*
and issuing official documents (ID card, passport, driver's license, social security card,    *documents*
etc.) Primarily, the goal is to simplify the ordering procedure for official ID documents
by making it possible to order the required documents on the eGovernment portal. Later
on, the main concern will be to facilitate all necessary process steps electronically in the
same medium. For example, the administrative institution is to take action and notify
citizens in case the validity of official documents ends and they have to be renewed.

Process area no. 5 deals with the registration of cars, be they new, used or imported    *Car registration*
from abroad. Applications for building permissions and renovations are dealt with in
process area no. 6. Area no. 7 is about filing charges with the police, for example, after
a theft or breaking and entering.

Process area no. 8 deals with public libraries and their services. One particular goal    *Public libraries*
is to make catalogs and search services for books, magazines, and DVDs electronically
available. The services for ordering, making reservations, delivering and the administration of rented items are to be digitalized.

In the future, requests and deliveries of birth or marriage certificates will be facil-    *Enrollment and*
itated electronically, as well, according to process area no. 9. Apart from that, regis-    *registration of*
trations for public schools or enrollment in a higher education institute can be done    *residence*
electronically (process area no. 10). Registrations of residence and changes of address,
especially within the state borders, are to be carried out electronically (process area no.
11).

Electronic health services like registering in a hospital or calling on medical services    *Services for*
are facilitated via eHealth (process area no. 12). In Sect. 4.5, the corresponding service    *eHealth*
oriented architecture for mobile health services is presented. The case study at the end
of this chapter is dedicated to the electronic health record, as publicized by the European
Union in their priority program eHealth. Research programs investigate the interoperability of mobile health services in order to facilitate counseling and tele-medical care.

## 4.3  eGovernment Services for Businesses

The European Union has determined eight governmental services for businesses (see    *Mandatory*
Fig. 4.3), which add to the above mentioned for citizens. Process area no. 13 deals    *social insurance*
with the contributions the company pays for the mandatory social insurance of their
employees. The whole course of business regarding the social insurance is to be facilitated electronically over an eGovernment portal or a service provider. This concerns the
declaration and charges for retirement arrangements, public health insurance services,
invalidity, etc.

The declaration, fixing and handling of corporate income taxes are covered in pro-    *Handling of*
cess area no. 14. Application, decision making and handling regarding value-added tax    *taxes*
are the topics in area no. 15.

| **Public Services for Business** |
| --- |
| 13. Social contribution for employees |
| 14. Corporation tax: declaration, notification |
| 15. VAT: declaration, notification |
| 16. Registration of a new company |
| 17. Submission of data to statistical offices |
| 18. Customs declarations |
| 19. Environment-related permits (incl. reporting) |
| 20. Public procurement |

**Fig. 4.3:** Public services for businesses by EU program.

*Founding companies*  The registration of start-ups and the handling of decision making procedure within the administrative institutions are made possible by the processes of area no. 16. In the future, all process steps needed for a registration are to be taken online.

*Privacy policies of statistical offices*  The exchange of data among the statistical offices and between the statistical offices and the companies happens electronically (process area no. 17), as well as the declaration and handling of customs formalities (area no. 18) and the processes required complying with environmental law (area no. 19).

*eProcurement in administrations*  The process steps for Internet based procurement are determined in area no. 20, ranging from the specification and selection of suppliers to negotiations, delivery and final checking. Here, the models and procedures proposed for eProcurement in Chap. 3 come into operation.

## 4.4   Municipality Product Plan

*Effect-oriented administration*  Municipal administrations make more and more use of concepts of business management and instruments for improving and controlling their administrative tasks (effect-oriented administration, New Public Management, see Sect. 10.1). To this end, the municipality's performance and outcome goals have to be defined, including corresponding instruments for measurement, usually with the help of a municipal product catalog or product plan.

*Product plan of Baden-Württemberg*  Figure 4.4 shows the municipal product plan of Baden-Württemberg (1996) as an example. The purpose of this is to obtain uniform and continuous municipality services and to facilitate the desired comparability of public budgets. According to the New Public Management, something is called a product, if the following preconditions are given:

- The creation of a product requires several tasks.
- The units of quantity and performance that are needed to create a product can be defined and gathered.
- There is a demand or a service mandate for the products within and outside the administration.

| Group Products | Value Ranges |
|---|---|
| Centralized Management | • Internal administration<br>• Safety and order |
| Education and Culture | • School boards<br>• Culture and science |
| Social Affairs and Youth | • Social assistance<br>• Children, adolescent and family support |
| Health and Sports | • Health care services<br>• Sports promotion |
| Environmental Formation | • Spatial planning and development<br>• Constriction and housing<br>• Supply and waste disposal<br>• Traffic and equipment<br>• Nature and landscape<br>• Environment protection<br>• Economic development and tourism<br>• Control |
| Public Finance | • Finances |

**Fig. 4.4:** Exemplary catalog, adopted from the product plan of Baden-Württemberg (1996).

In the eGovernment, the municipality product plan is of great importance, as the individual products are realized as electronic governmental services (eService). Before having an extensive restructuring of an eGovernment portal, the following clarifications have to be done:

*Necessary clarifications in the institutional process management*

- Analysis of the activities for supply and maintenance of individual products (process analysis).

- Redo of the processes, taking the administration into account (change management) and using progressive information and communication infrastructure.

- Standardization of the electronic governmental services, in accordance and collaboration with other municipalities, in order to guarantee benefits and reusability.

Whenever governmental services are restructured to be digital, there are changes in the administrative organization, in the process handling and in the user groups. Whether such a digitalization of the municipality product catalog is worth the trouble or not, depends strongly on how open the administrative institution is to cooperation projects and to standardization of their services.

Figure 4.5 sketches how municipality products are implemented in electronic governmental services. An important factor is that the individual process steps from the point of view of the administration and from the point of view of the claim groups (citizens, companies) are attuned to each other. The best way to achieve that are regular surveys, for example quality measurements and benchmarking, respectively (see Sect. 4.6) on the provider's side, and consumer satisfaction measurements on the other side (see the development model for online citizens in Sect. 9.4 and the corresponding key figures for the success measurement in Sect. 9.5). Figure 4.5 is explained with more detail during the discussion of the multi-channel management in Sect. 9.2.

*Quality measurements in service management*

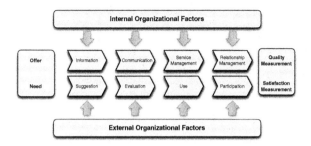

**Fig. 4.5:** Implementation of municipality products in electronic governmental services.

## 4.5   eHealth Architecture for Mobile Services

*What does eHealth mean?* By eHealth or electronic health, we understand the use of information and communication technology for quality improvement, clearer basis of decision making, increase in efficiency and guarantee of regional and worldwide health care. Its use, e.g. in telemedicine or in disease management, requires a rethinking from all participants, that is care providers (physicians, therapists, pharmacies, laboratories, hospitals), insurance providers, care recipients (patients), and public entities.

The following areas of application are considered a challenge to eHealth:

- **Web based provision of information and prevention**: Web sites and eHealth portals offer information, support and counseling in health concerns for patients, physicians, therapists, and other experts. Physicians and other health specialists have the chance to educate themselves further and follow up on developments (tumor data banks, AIDS, gene diagnostics, and others). Prevention programs help to prevent diseases and to cut down health care costs.

- **Computer aided process optimization**: Studies in hospitals show that for reasons of quality and security, some of the processes should be redone and supervised with more help of technical devices (workflow management systems). The processes have to be analyzed and adapted to changing demands, in order to improve the cost effectiveness.

- **Electronic patient dossiers**: The electronic health record is a collection of all medical data of a person (see case study in this chapter). It provides time- and place-independent medical data in form of text, images and sound files, in order to support the decision-making process. The electronic health record contains, apart from medical facts, administrative and organizational data and information relevant for coverage and billing.

- **Tele-consultation and tele-medicine**: In tele-medicine, information and communication technologies are used for medical diagnostics, health care, and further education. In tele-surgery, a non-present surgeon carries out a complete or parts of an operation with an endoscope that is controlled via Internet.

- **Disease management**: This comprises systematic and evidence-based forms of treatment of chronically ill patients. The patient receives mobile devices or personal emergency call systems, which transfer information or collected bio data to a medical communication center (see case study in Chap. 9) or to the treating doctor (home care).

- **Data protection and data security**: The identification, authentication and authorization of the users of electronic health services are carried out with the help of digital signatures (see Chap. 5 on Public Key Infrastructure). Patients can give clearance on their electronic health data with their personal patient health card. Doctors, therapists and pharmacists own access cards (health professional cards), with which they can consult the health record after previous authorization.

- **Community formation**: As a result of qualified health portals (see quality assurance in the Internet and HONcode in Sect. 2.6), prevention programs or possibilities of community formation in the Internet (see Chap. 9 on eCommunity), the patient develops into a well-informed patient.

In order to open up the application fields of eHealth, suitable platforms have to be created and linked to each other. Figure 4.6 presents the eSana architecture that facilitates the mobile access to medical information systems or communication centers. A layer model (in this case with three parts) and the communication between client and server have to be defined and implemented according to the basic principles of SOA. *Setup of eHealth platforms*

The topmost level controls the emission of physiological parameters from the eSana-Client to the eSanaServer. It serves as a basis for evaluation (see middle layer) and counseling (lowermost level). The physiological parameters can either be sent automatically from the medical device to the mobile device of the insured person, or manually entered into the eSanaClient. *The eSana architecture*

The middle layer provides tools to evaluate the received parameters. Statistics (graphic or text based) can be retrieved from the eSanaServer. Also, reports can be generated automatically. The lowermost layer makes counseling available for the insured person. In this layer, not only the patient but also authorized specialists (doctors,

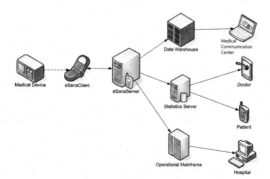

**Fig. 4.6:** eSana architecture for mobile health services, according to Savini et al. (2007).

physiotherapists, etc.) gain access to parts or all collected physiological parameters. The eSana architecture can be used for counseling services, health care, or prevention programs. As an example for a mobile application, we will consider the specific patient group of diabetics.

*Application example for diabetes patients*

One approach to improve the medical care of diabetics is the health passport that is carried by many diabetic patients. It contains a record of the time and type of examination that have been done. The health passport can be led electronically, for example, by a medical communication center (see case study in Chap. 9). As a result, the data can be evaluated directly and compared to historical values, if required. The doctors in charge and the patients can follow the development of the diabetes values independently of time and place. Statistical evaluations can be retrieved directly on their mobile device.

Diabetic patients are requested to stick to a certain diet and exercise schedule. The patients themselves with a mobile device can measure parameters like weight, blood pressure, or blood sugar. Doctors or digital agents supervise the parameters (HbA1c, total cholesterol, systolic and diastolic blood pressure, triglycerides or HDL). They detect changes in the course of the health care and can intervene in critical situations.

*Options of evaluation*

Apart from observing the individual values, it is possible for the physician to make aggregated evaluations for the whole patient collective: What is the status of blood sugar and blood pressure self-monitoring, diabetes education, diet counseling, data entry, etc.? Aggregated evaluations show, whether new or changed treatments bring the desired progress, whether special examination methods improve diagnostics or whether certain criteria are suitable to predict the risk for a disease.

## 4.6  Capability Maturity Model for the eGovernment Benchmarking

*Capability Maturity Model for governmental services*

The eGovernment services undergo a regular benchmarking in 34 countries – the European Union Member States, as well as Iceland, Norway, Montenegro, Republic of Serbia, Switzerland, and Turkey – referred to as EU28+. The eGovernment Action Plan assesses these services and covers four priority areas measured by one or more indicators, included in the so-called top level benchmarks:

- **User-centric Government**: it assesses the availability and usability of public eServices and examines ease and speed of using those eServices.

- **Transparent Government**: it evaluates the transparency of government authorities' operations, service delivery procedures and the level of control users have over their personal data.

- **Cross-border Mobility**: it measures the availability and usability of services for foreign citizens and businesses.

- **Key Enablers**: it assesses the availability of 5 functionalities, such as Authentic Sources and eID.

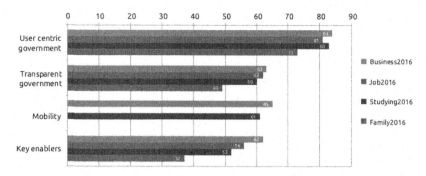

**Fig. 4.7:** Results for top-level benchmarks per life event (EU28+, 2016).

The benchmark measurement of 2017 selected four life events that cover the most common domains of public services for both businesses and citizens: starting a business and early trading operations, losing and finding a job, studying, and family life. Life events are associated with businesses or citizens experience. They provide the starting point for the assessment providing a score for each benchmark element: user-centric government, transparent government, cross-border mobility, and key enablers. Figure 4.7 presents the scores for the benchmarks for each of the life events measured in 2016. Cross-border mobility is not measured for life events "losing and finding a job" and "family life".

The results per country of the latest benchmarking (eGovernment Benchmark 2017. Taking stock of user-centric design and delivery of digital public services in Europe, see bibliographic notes) presents the average scores for the four top-level benchmarks, per 2016 life event. They are shown in Fig. 4.8. To summarize the results of the European developments in eGovernment results on how the indicators developed over time.

*Results of the benchmarking*

- **User Centricity**: Europe records a twelve percentage increase (from 73% in 2012 to 85% in 2016). Mobile friendliness of public websites is rapidly increasing –

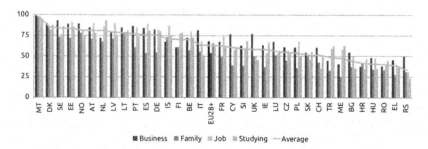

**Fig. 4.8:** Country ranking – average results for top-level benchmarks per 2016 life event (EU28+, %).

though still only 1 in 2 public websites allow to properly read information and navigate public websites on a mobile device.

- **Transparency**: The results on transparency in public services show that in several services, the level of transparency is still very low. This is a barrier for citizens to continue browsing online for information. On the other hand, the results of the indicators improved in countries such as Germany, Finland and Iceland. On the other hand, Slovakia and Switzerland also made substantial progress but there are still problems to be attacked in order to reach acceptable levels with absolute scores that are behind the EU average.

- **Cross-border service delivery**]: The results presented by this online availability indicator show that the countries with the best performance are Sweden and Finland (100%). In addition, other countries that have improved notably in recent years are Latvia, Poland and France, offering online channels to other European countries. Online availability of cross-border services in 2016 approximates the level of maturity of services at the national level in 2012. It is important to identify that the provision of cross-border services have the capacity to continue improving in the following years. As an example, indicators on eID and cross-border electronic documents are in the process of being developed, however, these will allow other cross-border online services to be developed.

- **The deployment of key technological enablers**: Fig. 4.8 shows that services in the family life event are not moving forward. This progress is not as fast as other indicators with only a 3% growth since 2012. The benefits for users and public authorities are evident (e.g. efficient, effective, time-saving) but they do not have satisfactory growth and maturity.

Year after year, Europe makes progress in the implementation of eGovernment plans. Nevertheless, as it is shown in Fig. 4.8, there are still weak points that require action to move forward the goals proposed in the EU Action Plan 2016-2020.

## 4.7   Bibliographical Notes

*Literature on interoperability*
Definitions of technical, organizational, and semantic interoperability for the eGovernment are given in the SAGA publication (SAGA, 2011) of the German Federal Ministry of the Interior. The basic concepts of service-oriented architectures can be found in the focal issue by Fröschle & Reinheimer (2007).

*Governmental services in the EU*
The European Commission determined the governmental services for citizens and companies in the eGovernment initiative, see European Comission (2007). For some years, the electronic governmental services in the EU area and in selected countries have been undergoing a benchmarking. The latest survey and a benchmarking for the countries EU28+ are to published by European Comission (2017).

*New Public Management*
The New Public Management (Schedler & Proeller (2000); Norbert & Adrian (2006)) demands of the administration to act and plan in an effect-oriented way. In many places, product catalogs have been designed with the help of suitable programs. These

programs structure and put together the range of tasks with performance plans and measuring instruments. A popular example is the municipal product plan of the federal state of Baden–Württemberg in Germany, which is published by the Ministry of the Interior (Baden-Württemberg, 1996). In Switzerland, similar catalogs were created; mentionable are the examples of the canton of Zurich (GAZ, 2003) and Solothurn (AGS, 2002).

In the works of Haas (2006) and Jähn & Nagel (2003), basic principles in the area of eHealth are imparted. Medical information systems and electronic patient dossiers are dealt with in Haas' book (Haas, 2005). The example of eSana architecture for mobile eHealth services is based on the research work of Savini et al. (2007).

*Works on eHealth*

# 4.8   Case Study—The Austrian Electronic Health Record System ELGA

## 4.8.1   Background

Univ.-Prof.
Dipl.-Ing. Dr.
Georg
Duftschmid,
*Medical
University of
Vienna*

The ongoing specialization of modern medicine accelerates medical progress on the one hand, but requires a high level of interdisciplinary collaboration on the other hand. At the same time and due to new techniques of data collection and evaluation, the quantity of health-related data accumulated per patient, continually increases. The exchange of these data is a crucial condition for efficient collaboration of cooperating health care institutions.

The integration of all medical data belonging to a patient in a trans-institutional electronic health record (EHR) has thus become a key topic of medical information technology. Such records enable authorized health service providers and patients to retrieve full edited medical records at anytime and anyplace. Decisive improvements to modern health care are particularly expected if the EHR system covers a wide geographic area, as is reflected by the growing number of national EHR systems[1].

The following case study depicts the nation-wide Austrian EHR system ELGA (short for Elektronische Gesundheitsakte, "Electronic Health Record") that has been operational since 2015.

Univ.-Prof.
Dipl.-Ing. Dr.
Wolfgang Dorda,
*Medical
University of
Vienna*

## 4.8.2   Case Study

First, we outline the health telematics context in Austria, on which ELGA builds upon. The most essential components of the Austrian health telematics landscape are:

Health information network (GIN) and eCard system: At the end of 2005, the eCard system was launched in Austria and replaced the previous paper based system of health insurance certificates. The system is based on smartcards for identification of patients and medical practices, and reading devices in the medical practices. The GIN is an intranet that connects the medical practices with the data processing center of the main association of social security providers. In ELGA, the cards for doctors and patients serve as a key to access patient data. In combination with other information networks, the GIN is used as a medium for the exchange of ELGA-specific data.

Ao.Univ.-Prof.
Mag. Dr. Walter
Gall,
*Medical
University of
Vienna*

ELGA Law (ELGA-G): This law[2], passed as a part of the Austrian Health Telematics Law, defines the legal framework for the usage of ELGA. Amongst others, it specifies the initial set of document types that are stored in ELGA, who may access patient data in ELGA and for which purposes, the rights of ELGA participants, how long ELGA data have to be stored, and the details of the logging component to ensure reproducibility of any activity within the ELGA system. Further, the ELGA-G defines penal provisions for violations of its regulations.

---

[1]https://gateway.euro.who.int/en/indicators/ehealth_survey_84-has-a-national-ehr-system/
[2]http://www.bmgf.gv.at/cms/home/attachments/5/6/5/CH1045/CMS1338460371868/elga_nrbeschluss_bgbla_2012_i_111.pdf

Additional legal regulations that are relevant in the context of ELGA are specified in the Austrian Law for Data Privacy[3] and the European General Data Protection Regulation[4] as well as in the Austrian Law for eGovernment (E-GovG)[5]. The E-GovG includes provisions for the implementation of the ELGA patient portal and for the generation of the unique identifiers of ELGA patients.

The core technical components of the ELGA infrastructure are:

- Index of patients and health service providers: One of the main functions of the central patient index is to link the different patient identifiers of local health information systems with a central patient identifier to enable the integration of distributed data of a patient. The index of health service providers is a complete registry of all individual and institutional care providers who are authorized by the ELGA-G to access ELGA data.

- ELGA patient portal: This portal[6] enables patients to access their personal ELGA data as well as the access protocol for their data. It also serves patients to adapt the default access rights of care providers to their data and allows them to completely opt out of ELGA. Further, the portal offers citizen access to general, quality assured medical knowledge, for example, with references to professional societies, support groups, and welfare institutions.

- Authorization component: This component comprises clear rules on who, when and under what conditions can retrieve what ELGA contents as defined in the ELGA-G. The patient may also override the default access rights, e.g., to grant his or her family physician extended rights.

- Log component: This component stores all activities, such as access to patient data or modifications of access rights, to ensure full reproducibility.

- ELGA domains: ELGA is organized in a set of domains that are implemented according to the IHE XDS[7] specification. Each domain contains a document registry, where not the source data itself are stored, but references to the source data and descriptive meta data. The source data remain at the place of origin, which means they are stored in distributed document repositories.

ELGA data are formatted according to the HL7 CDA[8] standard. For the initial set of document types as defined in the ELGA-G, corresponding implementation guides[9] and computable HL7 template[10] specifications have been published. Additional document

---

[3]https://www.ris.bka.gv.at/GeltendeFassung.wxe?Abfrage=bundesnormen&Gesetzesnummer=10001597

[4]https://eur-lex.europa.eu/eli/reg/2016/679/oj

[5]https://www.elga.gv.at/fileadmin/user_upload/Dokumente_PDF_MP4/Recht/e-Government_Gesetz.pdf

[6]https://www.gesundheit.gv.at/

[7]https://wiki.ihe.net/index.php/Cross-Enterprise_Document_Sharing

[8]http://www.hl7.org/implement/standards/product_brief.cfm?product_id=7

[9]https://www.elga.gv.at/technischer-hintergrund/technische-elga-leitfaeden/index.html

[10]http://elga.art-decor.org/index.php?prefix=elga-

types will be added to ELGA as needed. Currently the following document types are covered by ELGA:

- Discharge letter, i.e. the closing medical report written after an in-patient hospitalization.

- Medication prescriptions by physicians and drug dispensings at pharmacies.

- Radiology reports, i.e. the results of radiological exams with the diagnostic findings.

- Laboratory reports, i.e. the results of lab analyses.

ELGA applies the following international standards within its document exchange framework:

- Integrating the Healthcare Enterprise (IHE) technical framework as communication architecture

- HL7 Reference Information Model (RIM) as basic data model

- HL7 Clinical Document Architecture (CDA) as document standard

- Logical Observation Identifiers Names and Codes (LOINC) for designating document types and laboratory parameters

- Digital Imaging and Communication in Medicine (DICOM) 3.0 and Web Access to DICOM (WADO) for radiology images.

The implementation process and the current status of the ELGA system can be summarized as follows: A first pilot project that focused on the exchange of medication data in a limited geographic region was conducted in 2011. Considering the insights gained during the pilot project, the ELGA system was set up and first became operational in fall 2015. The first phase of the ELGA rollout focused on connecting all Austrian hospitals to the system. This phase was completed in summer 2018. In parallel the second phase of the ELGA rollout started in early 2018 and focused on outpatient physicians and pharmacies. This second rollout phase is currently still in progress.

### 4.8.3  Opportunities and Risks

As described earlier in the section on the initial situation, the implementation of the ELGA system is expected to bring along a number of potential advantages: With ELGA, the physician knows all prior diagnostic findings and risk factors, a shift is made from institution-centered to patient-centered data availability, the juncture between hospitals and office based physicians is improved and the efficiency of the health care system can be increased by using savings potential. All in all, ELGA contributes to an improved quality of patient care.

Despite the positive opinions about ELGA the implementation of an EHR system does not automatically lead to the desired improvements in the health care system. For this reason, the following ELGA key factors had to be considered in the implementation process:

**Patients' rights—data protection:**   The respective patient's right to grant access to his or her sensitive health data and the practical enforcement of privacy policies are of great importance for public acceptance. On the other hand, the concerned person's right to get optimum treatment has to be considered as well. The compromise found for ELGA was the possibility for the patients to adapt the default access rights of care providers to their data – even at the level of each single document.

**Involvement of health care professionals:**   According to international experience, the users' acceptance of an EHR system is a key factor. The project to implement an EHR system can only be successful, if it involves the users actively. After years of controversial discussions the roll out of ELGA was quite smooth, maybe due to a financial incentive payed for the implementation of ELGA.

**Risk of information overload:**   The possibility to have insight into the full spectrum of a patient's health data can lead to overlooking the most essential points. Only by careful and needs-based topical preparation of the information ELGA can contribute to the expected improvements in patient care —instead of leading to information overload and liability issues.

To this end, the following activities take place in the ELGA context:

- The specification of a 'patient summary' will be finalized in the near future.

- To reduce the amount of data ELGA stores medication data only for one year and other data for ten years

- To alleviate automated searching it is planned to gradually increase the amount of structured data. At the moment only the laboratory reports and medication data are fully structured.

Worldwide, eHealth and the implementation of national EHR systems are still at a developing stage; they have to be evaluated with corresponding objectivity, in order to recognize risks on time and obtain optimum benefit. Therefore, the medical computer science research must be integrated into the national ELGA development. Research can also play an important role in developing ELGA's content goals and detail specifications, and for knowledge management and the health care system: Finding and setting the supported workflows, the standardized architecture of ELGA and the obligatory medical terms should be done in cooperation with the medical universities.

## Further Reading

- Ammenwerth, E., Duftschmid, G., Gall, W., Hackl, W., Hoerbst, A., Janzek-Hawlat, S., Jeske, M., Jung, M., Woertz, K., Dorda, W.: A nationwide computerized patient medication history: Evaluation of the Austrian pilot project "e-Medikation". Int J Med Inform. Sep; 83(9):655-69 (2014)

- Hackl, W., Hoerbst, A., Duftschmid, G., Gall, W., Janzek-Hawlat, S., Jung, M., Woertz, K., Dorda, W., Ammenwerth, E.: Crucial Factors for the Acceptance of a Computerized National Medication List: Insights into Findings from the Evaluation of the Austrian e-Medikation Pilot. Appl Clin Inform. Jun 4;5(2):527-37 (2014)

- Janzek-Hawlat, S., Ammenwerth, E., Dorda, W., Duftschmid, G., Hackl, W., Hörbst, A., Jung, M., Woertz, K., Gall, W.: The Austrian e-Medikation pilot evaluation: Lessons learnt from a national medication list. Stud Health Technol Inform. 192:347-51 (2013)

- Duftschmid, G., Rinner, C., Kohler, M., Hübner-Bloder, G., Saboor, S., Ammenwerth, E.: The EHR-ARCHE project: Satisfying clinical information needs in a Shared Electronic Health Record System based on IHE XDS and Archetypes. Int J of Med Inform. Dec;82(12):1195-207 (2013)

- Deutsch, E., Duftschmid, G., Dorda, W.: Critical Areas Of National Electronic Health Record Programs - Is Our Focus Correct?, Int J of Med Inform. 79(3):211-222 (2010)

- Dorda, W., Duftschmid, D., Gerhold, L., Gall, W., Gambal, J.: Austria's Path toward nationwide electronic health records. Meth Inf Med. 47(2), 117–123 (2008)

- Dorda, W.: Informationsmanagement im Gesundheitswesen - Der Elektronische Gesundheitsakt ELGA: Chancen und Risken. Klinik. 6-07:21–22 (2008)

- Dorda, W., Duftschmid, G., Gerhold, L., Gall, W., Gambal, J.: Introducing the electronic health record in Austria. Stud Health Technol Inform. 116:119-24(2005)

- Duftschmid, G., Wrba, T., Gall, W., Dorda, W.: The strategic approach of managing healthcare data exchange in Austria. Methods Inf Med. 43(2):124–132 (2004)

## Contact Details

Section for Medical Information Management
Medical University of Vienna
Spitalgasse 23, A-1090 Wien
Internet: https://cemsiis.meduniwien.ac.at/en/mim/
eMail: georg.duftschmid@meduniwien.ac.at
wolfgang.dorda@meduniwien.ac.at
walter.gall@meduniwien.ac.at

## Profile of Authors

### Univ.-Prof. Dipl.-Ing. Dr. Georg Duftschmid

Georg Duftschmid is a professor for medical computer science at the Medical University of Vienna/Austria. His primary research area is eHealth, in particular information models of the health care system and the electronic health record. He wrote both his diploma and Ph.D. theses in computer science at the Vienna University of Technology and habilitated in medical computer science at the Medical University of Vienna. He is the head of the Section for Medical Information Management and Associate Editor at BMC Medical Informatics & Decision Making.

### Univ.-Prof. Dipl.-Ing. Dr. Wolfgang Dorda

Wolfgang Dorda is a retired university professor for applied medical computer science. He was the head of the Center for Medical Statistics, Informatics and Intelligent Systems at the Medical University of Vienna. He was head of extensive computer science projects at the university hospitals of Vienna and counselor to the minister of health in the Commission for Standards and Guidelines for the Employment of Informatics in Austrian Health Care, and in the telemedicine platform of the federal Austrian government. He finished studies as physician (Medical doctor), mathematician (Master) and computer scientist (PhD).

### Ao.Univ.-Prof. Mag. Dr. Walter Gall

Walter Gall is a professor for medical computer science at Medical University of Vienna. He works at the Section for Medical Information Management, with a primary research focus on hospital information systems, electronic health record, modeling, and information retrieval. He is an engineer in high frequency and communication technology, got his Ph.D. at the Faculty of Social Sciences of the University of Vienna and habilitated in medical computer science at the Medical University of Vienna.

# Chapter 5

# eContracting

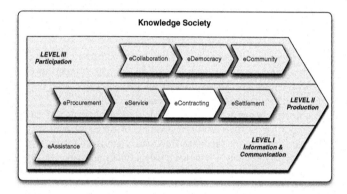

Chapter 5 analyzes the electronic negotiation process and shows how electronic agreements can be designed to be legally binding. First, Sect. 5.1 discusses the elements of electronic contracts, and later on, Sect. 5.2 introduces to generic services for the negotiation process. The identity management, as presented in Sect. 5.3, deals with user identification and user administration. Asymmetric encoding procedures (Sect. 5.4) make it possible not only to encode and decode documents, but also to generate digital signatures (Sect. 5.5). With these, the Law can declare electronic contracts legally binding on Electronic Signatures. In Sect. 5.6, the Public Key Infrastructure is explained, which is needed to issue digital signatures and certificates. Then, Sect. 5.7 presents the basic concepts of blockchain technology and its applications, including eGoverment. An overview of laws and ordinances on data protection and data security is given in Sect. 5.8. Section 5.9 provides bibliographical notes. A case study by the Fraunhofer Institute for Computer Graphics Research demonstrates how the face recognition in the biometric passport (ePass) works.

© Springer Nature Switzerland AG 2019
A. Meier, L. Terán, *eDemocracy & eGovernment*, Progress in IS,
https://doi.org/10.1007/978-3-030-17585-6_5

## 5.1   Electronic Contracts

*Unmistakable proof of origin for electronic contracts*
Speaking in legal terms, a contract is a legally binding arrangement between two or more people (contract partners), whose basic characteristic is a statement of intention. Since a couple of years ago, contracts can be closed on the Internet with the help of electronic information and communication technologies. In this matter, electronic agreements require unmistakable proofs of origin or digital signatures in order to be recognized in front of a court (see law on electronic signatures in Sect. 5.8).

An electronic contract is nothing else than a legally binding digital document that answers the following questions:

- Who are the contract partners?

- What is the content of the agreement?

- How are the electronically determined obligations put into practice?

- When are the determined goods or services due?

- What legal framework conditions apply?

*Advantages of electronic contracts*
In contrast to paper-based contracts, the contents of electronic agreements have the advantage that program systems of software agents can check them for completeness and further process them. This means that additional services can be implemented as well, like a notification service in case of delayed or no delivery.

*What does eContracting comprise?*
There are software systems for the reception and maintenance of electronic contracts, which keep a log of the individual contents of the agreement for the contract partners, allow version control, facilitate electronic signing and support the handling and controlling of the agreement. Under the concept of eContracting, we understand the complete process of negotiation and handling of an electronic contract, consisting of the following partial steps:

- Valid log of the negotiating positions

- Electronic storage and administration of the contract parts, including a version control

- Agreement on rights and obligations

- Legally binding conclusion of the contract with digital signatures

- Controlling of the fulfillment of the subject matter of the contract.

*Reducing costs and effort*
In the eGovernment, it is parted from the idea that electronic contracts and negotiation processes reduce the administrative workload and related costs. Apart from that, it is expected to mostly evade sources of errors by the use of software-based control mechanisms, and also to have better control over the fulfillment of agreements (monitoring with notification services). In the following section, we will go a little deeper into the details of the electronic negotiation process with its individual services.

## 5.2   Generic Services for the Negotiation Process

Electronic negotiation processes make it possible to apply generic services for particular steps of agreement and handling (Fig. 5.1). These services comprise identification of contract partners, electronic negotiation including conclusion of contract, contract archiving, contract enforcement, and electronic mediation.

Before entering negotiations, contract partners need to clarify the identity of their opposing party. To that end, certain entities or institutions are needed, which issue certificates stating the identity of natural or legal persons. This certification authority (see Trust Center in Sect. 5.6) must guarantee that the contract partner actually is the person he claims to be (authentification). In order to issue such certificates electronically, the certification authority requests documents of the participant of the negotiation in advance and, in most cases, a physical contact. *Certification of identity necessary*

A certification authority is a trusted third party, which issues temporary certificates on market participants and contributes them to the contract negotiation process. The identification of the contract partners is considered a generic service, as one can always come back to the proper certification entity in different negotiation processes. This way, a correlation of the partners involved in an electronic negotiation process with real-life persons and institutions is guaranteed. *Task of the certification authority*

The generic service for identifying contract partners can be complemented by a validation component. With it, it can be checked whether the framework of the contract, including possible contract templates (that is, drafts for specific development steps), have the correct form. This service can advert risks and propose how to handle them. Depending on the specific needs, the validation service is provided either by software agents or by designated administrative entities. If the validation service is an acknowledged institution, it can be drawn upon to represent one party in front of an arbitrating court. *Application of software agents*

The negotiation service helps the contract parties to negotiate the subject matter of the contract. Special software systems, called electronic negotiation support systems, assist in the negotiation process by multimedia communication components and cooperative negotiation environments. Depending on the degree of maturity of these software *Electronic negotiation*

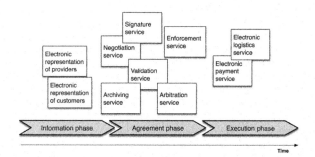

**Fig. 5.1:** Generic services for eContracting according to Runge (2000).

systems, possible solutions can be generated and already existing partial positions can be optimized.

*Logs in catalogs*  On the basis of electronic catalogs, the software system determines the optimum exchange conditions and logs them in the intended contract. An additional archiving service classifies the contract versions and ensures the respective contract outcomes. Both administration and handling of the negotiation process are supported, including the description of the corresponding statuses. The negotiation service can serve to compare supply and demand, or it can be complemented by auctions (see Sect. 3.6) and technically mature software agents for ample electronic negotiations.

*Monitoring of the agreement process*  In case of a technically mature software agent, the negotiation service provides functions for supervision and controlling of the negotiation process. This service, often called monitoring, controls the negotiation process and revises all individual agreement documents and related aspects of security. During the handling phase, this service can cover the supervision of delivery deadlines and methods of payment.

*Tasks of enforcement services*  Naturally, an electronic market is not a priori protected from market participants who do not want or cannot fulfill their agreed negotiation positions. If a contract party does not fulfill its obligations, an enforcement service is needed. This service can include proactive measures, in order to achieve that individual contract parts are fulfilled after all, or to obtain compensation for the non-fulfillment of these parts. Apart from that, reactive measures like rating systems or blacklists aim at preventing belated contract partners from being admitted for future transactions, in extreme cases.

*Use of an online arbitrating court*  If, despite the preventive and security measures, the situation develops into a legal conflict, an online arbitrating court can be consulted for possible arbitration. This arbitrating court only comes into action once it is authorized by the contract partners, the lawsuit is filed via electronic media. The online arbitrating court negotiates with the contract partners and gives them advice, for example, via Internet conference or chat-room. If an amicable settlement is reached, the arbitration procedure is closed after publishing the settlement. It is possible to end the proceeding by an arbitral verdict. This has the effect of adjudication and is enforceable at law (e.g., electronic arbitration with cyber-settle[1]).

## 5.3   Identity Management

*Recognition and administration of users*  During the electronic negotiation process, being able to identify the contract partners anytime is necessary. In general, working with electronic information and communication systems requires sophisticated procedures for user recognition and user administration. The term identity management summarizes these. The identity management comprises all processes and stored data on user administration and supports the following tasks:

- **Identification**: The users, or contract partners, are distinctly identified. The identity can be detected by non-ambiguous names, artificial identification keys, or non-ambiguous multiple combinations.

---

[1]http://cybersettle.com

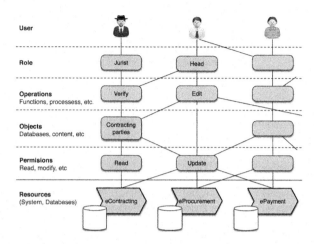

**Fig. 5.2:** Possible applications in the RBAC model.

- **Authentication**: This task comprises checking the authenticity of the users or contract partners. The idea is to determine whether a user actually is who he claims to be. When information and communication systems are applied, it is common to attribute a password. In the electronic negotiation process and for receiving legally valid contracts, these passwords are not sufficient anymore. Rather, a digital signature (see Sect. 5.5), often described as a personal seal or digital fingerprint, must be used.

- **Authorization**: Apart from the identification and authentication, the identity management requires a distribution of rights and obligations that are granted to a user or contract partner. The authorization comprises processing functions (access right and/or modification right) and the right to consult or change certain stored data (resource right).

The identity management is not only important for eContracting, but it is also applied in all process levels (information & communication, production, participation) of the eGovernment framework. Hence, this is the way in which user recognition, certification, and authorization work within governmental services, in the eProcurement, in ePayment and in the eCommunity and eDemocracy processes (see Chap. 8). *Identity management affects all process levels*

Another task of the identity management is it to develop and put into practice a model of different roles for users or contract partners. Figure 5.2 shows the Role-Based Access Control (RBAC) standard of the National Institute of Standards and Technology (NIST), USA. The RBAC model is based on the following five components: users, roles, operations, objects, and permissions. One user can have different roles, and vice versa, one role can be occupied by different users (e.g., representation). A role contains all permissions that a user needs in order to fulfill his or her tasks in the negotiation process or while working with information systems. *Aiming for standardization with the RBAC model*

**Fig. 5.3:** Recognition symbol for biometric passports (ePass).

*Importance of role concepts*    A well-engineered role model must prevent that mutually exclusive tasks are exercised. Therefore, during specification of user roles, conditions have to be set that allow a separation of access and modification rights (separation of duties). This is important for the eGovernment, because it requires the dual control principle for critical electronic administration processes (e.g., budgeting and release in eProcurement, application and approval in ePayment or system controls in eVoting). Therefore, new amplifications of the mentioned RBAC model integrate rule-based approaches to approval and checking of permissions.

*Biometric recognition procedures*    Another challenge is the biometric recognition procedures, which have undergone great progress during the past years. Under biometrics we understand measurement and analysis procedures for persons or, in general, for all living things. In order to recognize people, the biometric procedures use biometric behavior characteristics (lip movements, voice modulation, patterns in body movements, etc.) or body parts (facial geometry, iris characteristics, fingerprints, etc.).

*Passports with biometric data*    The International Civil Aviation Organization (ICAO) of the United Nations requests all member states to store biometric parameters of the passport holder electronically on the machine-readable travel document (MRTD, also called ePass in some countries including Germany). Electronic passports with biometric data carry the recognition symbol shown in Fig. 5.3. Following the requirements of the ICAO, an ePass contains a contactless chip to store the passport photograph and other biometric data like fingerprints or iris patterns of the holder. In the future, there are to be digital signatures on the ePass in order to guarantee integrity and authenticity of the stored data (see case study on face recognition in this chapter).

## 5.4   Asymmetric Encryption

*Service exchange without direct contact*    With the progressing development and utilization of the Internet, the security of electronic processes gains importance. As the service exchange in the electronic market often occurs over big distances and without personal contact, special security measures must be met in order to establish trust. It has to be ensured that electronic documents come from the desired addressor. Also, sensitive data like electronic contracts may not be altered on the way. Additionally, it is requested that the addressee confirms the receipt of electronic documents correctly.

*Electronic contracts must be legally valid*    The digital signature is an electronic signature with which electronic documents and contracts are signed in a legally valid way. The electronic signature can be considered as a seal, which is put onto the electronic document before sending it (see Sect. 5.5). The addressee of the document is able to recognize whether the seal is correct and obtains the guarantee that the document was transmitted without being manipulated or damaged.

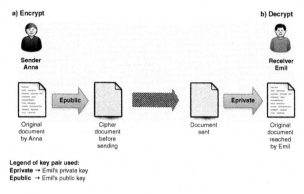

**Fig. 5.4:** Encoding (**a**) and decoding (**b**) in asymmetric encoding procedures.

In order to introduce a digital signature into the electronic market, asymmetric encoding techniques are used. On the contrary to traditional encoding techniques, in which the same key is used for both encoding and decoding, the user in the electronic market is given an asymmetric pair of keys. In other words, encoding and decoding require two different keys, a private and a public one. The public key is openly accessible and can be published on the user's homepage or in public indices. The private key, on the other hand, is provided specifically to the negotiation and contract partners. It guarantees that unwanted third parties cannot see the transmitted documents.

*Importance of digital signatures*

Figure 5.4 shows the asymmetric encoding and the encoding and decoding of an electronic document. In the example, Anna (sender) wants to transmit an electronic document that is encoded, and therefore unreadable for the public, to Emil (recipient). To this end, the asymmetric encoding technique is used, in order to render the document illegible for other market participants (cryptographic procedure). In the following, the same encoding technique will help to create digital signatures and add them to the document. Only with that digital signature can the recipient verify the authenticity of the addressor (see the following Fig. 5.5, in which the encoding of the document and the sealing were done at the same time).

*Functionality of asymmetric encoding*

In the asymmetric cryptographic procedure, Anna encodes her original document or contract according to Fig. 5.4 with Emil's public key $E_{public}$, before transmitting the document to the desired addressee. This document stays illegible for all market participants except for Emil, who owns the necessary private key. Thus, on the receiver's side, the document is decoded with Emil's private key $E_{private}$. Emil, and only Emil, can therefore read and understand the document. The asymmetric encoding is not only used for encoding and decoding documents, but also for sealing documents with digital signatures.

*Use of public and private keys*

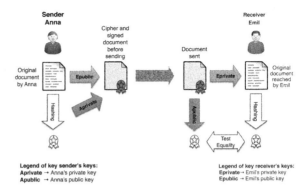

**Fig. 5.5:** Encryption and sealing electronic documents.

## 5.5   Sealing Electronic Documents with Digital Signatures

*What are digital signatures needed for?*

Under a digital or electronic signature, we understand a procedure that guarantees the authenticity of a document and its sender. When the sender is identified and indicated by the name, it is additionally necessary to prove his or her "authenticity." This means, that as the receiver of an electronic document or contract, one desires to know for sure that the sender actually is the person he claims to be.

*How is the digital signature created?*

The digital signature can be carried out with the help of asymmetric encoding techniques, as well. Figure 5.5 illustrated, how the digital signature is generated and added to the electronic document. It is important to note that in normal cases, the asymmetric encoding is applied twice:

- Utilization of the receiver's set of keys: Emil's (receiver) private key $E_{private}$ and public key $E_{public}$ are needed for encoding and decoding of the electronic document or contract.

- Utilization of the sender's set of keys: Anna's (sender) private key $A_{private}$ and public key $A_{public}$ are used for the digital signature and to guarantee the authenticity of the sender of the electronic document.

*Overlap of asymmetric encoding techniques*

In Fig. 5.5 it becomes clear that the concealment of the document (asymmetric encoding for reasons of cryptography) overlaps with its sealing (asymmetric procedure for digital signatures). For this to work, a digital signature must be generated in an adequate way, and attached to the encoded document.

*Application of the hashing algorithm*

How then is a digital signature generated? For that purpose, a so-called hashing algorithm has to be utilized. A hashing algorithm uses the original document to generate a hash value or digital fingerprint, respectively (represented by a sun-like symbol in Fig. 5.5). This hash value has the following characteristics:

- The hash value or digital fingerprint has a fixed length for any document.

- The hash value or fingerprint does not make it possible to conclude the original document.

- Any altering in the original document leads to a different hash value or different fingerprint, respectively.

These important features of the hash algorithm make it possible to utilize the fingerprint or seal as a digital signature. Hence, digital signatures are nothing else than encoded hash values. First, the hash value generated from the original document has to be encoded with Anna's private key ($A_{private}$) and attached to the already encoded document. After transmitting the document, Emil (or the software that is installed on the receiver's side) separates the digital signature from the encoded document. Emil transforms the encoded document into the original document with the help of the private key $E_{private}$. At the same time, a hash value is drawn from the original document, using the same hashing algorithm as the sender.  *Signatures are encoded hash values*

The digital signature separated from the transmitted document (black seal on the receiver's side in Fig. 5.5) is transformed back to the original hash value by Anna's public key ($A_{public}$). Now, a test is run to see whether both seals are the same. In case they coincide, Emil can assume that the original data arrived in sound condition and that the "real" sender sent them, as to say, Anna. So firstly, Emil can check whether the original document hasn't been altered after sending. Secondly, he can verify whether the sender is the market participant he claims to be.  *Testing the sameness of hash values*

There are several methods for encoding, which will not be discussed here in detail. One widespread method is the so-called RSA procedure, which was invented and published by the researchers Rivest, Shamir, and Adleman. The technique lying behind it is a prime factorization, which can be declared secure and indecipherable, depending on the length of the chosen keys.  *RSA algorithm is based on prime factorization*

The Pretty Good Privacy (PGP) procedure is a cryptographic procedure to encode electronic documents or data and mark them as authentic. It, too, is based on the Public Key procedure and is mainly used for e-mails with attachments.  *Pretty Good Privacy*

## 5.6   Public Key Infrastructure

Several Law of electronic signatures countries which request a Public Key Infrastructure have passed national laws on electronic signatures (see Sect. 5.8), in some areas there exist supraregional agreements, for example, in Europe. The concern of these laws and acts is to recognize electronic documents as objects of legal protection and to determine framework conditions for certification authorities. In this matter, it is spoken of PKI or Public Key Infrastructure, which denominates the infrastructure needed to issue digital signatures and certificates.  *Law of electronic signatures*

A certification authority or Trust Center is an institution (natural or legal person), which certifies the correlation of public signatures to natural persons. Thus, the principal task of a certification authority is to reliably identify a person and to confirm for the electronic market the correlation of the requested public key with this person. These  *Tasks of a Trust Center*

**Fig. 5.6:** Tasks of the Certificate Authority (CA).

authorities obtain a license for their task, namely by application at the corresponding regulatory authority.

*Registration authority*      A certification authority has a wide range of tasks, as illustrated in Fig. 5.6. For example, it functions as a receiving office (registration authority), which means that digital signatures can be applied for there. To this end, it has to securely identify the applicant. It requires a personal contact and the presentation of a valid ID card and notarized documents, respectively. This is necessary if the applicant claims an occupational title and a reference as doctor, lawyer, tax consultant, or accountant.

*Certification authority*      Apart from the receiving office, the Trust Center is the central element of the certification infrastructure and serves to issue keys and certificates (certification authority). Here, digital signatures, that is pairs of private and public keys, are generated and issued. Accordingly, security requirements in this procedure are high. Any abuse in the course of the key generation, for example, prohibited copying of the private key, must be excluded. Therefore, the people working in a certification authority must have sufficient technical know-how and abilities.

*Components of a certificate*      A certificate is a digital attestation of the correlation of a public key and the holder of this key, which is a natural person. The certificate contains:

- Name of the signature holder

- Attributed public key

- Identification of the hash algorithm for using the key

- Beginning and ending of the period of validity of the certificate

- Name of the certification authority

- Restrictions during use

The issue of certificates and the generation of keys have been standardized. Widely known is the X.509 standard, issued by the ISO (International Organization for Standardization). This standard gives a consistent scheme to exchange certificates worldwide and to apply them to use digital signatures.

The certification authority has to ensure that the certificates are not falsified under-    *Concealment of*
hand. Particularly, the secrecy of private keys must be guaranteed. This is accomplished    *private keys*
by storing the private key on a smartcard (see, for example, ePass in Sect. 5.3). This
way, not even the holder of the smartcard can make a copy of his or her private key and
pass it along intentionally or unintentionally.

In addition to the above outlined tasks, certification authorities have to maintain a    *Use of time*
time stamp system. For eContracting, for example, it can be important to attribute time    *stamps*
specifications to parts of the negotiation. In such cases, the certification authority must
confirm these time specifications in the role of a trustworthy third party institution. A
time stamp system must guarantee with certainty that a particular document was presented at a particular time in a particular version. With regard to keeping deadlines, a
time stamp system is indispensable.

A certification authority can permit to put a pseudonym into the certificate instead    *Use of*
of the real name, if a corresponding request has been made. With this option, the holder    *pseudonyms*
of a digital signature does not have to reveal his identity in the electronic market. This is
legal, because the applicant is known by name to the certification authority. For bigger
institutions or governmental entities, using pseudonyms can result useful. As natural
persons can only request the digital signature, the pseudonym helps in transaction of
the kind "by delegation to" or "on behalf of." Data protection laws protect holders of a
signature key with a pseudonym. The identity of the key holder may only be revealed, if
it is needed for crime prosecution or if the public safety is in danger.

## 5.7   Blockchain as a Distributed Ledger with Consensus

On October 30, 2008 Satoshi Nakamoto (alias) published an email under the title, "Bit-    *Blockchain, the*
coin P2P e-cash paper" and with the words: "I've been working on a new electronics    *origins*
cash system that's fully peer-to-peer, with no trusted third party" (Nakamoto (2008)).
As most important characteristics, he pointed out:

- Double spending is prevented with a peer-to-peer network.

- No mint or other trusted parties.

- Participants can be anonymous.

- New coins are made from Hashcash style proof-of-work.

Satoshi Nakamoto substantiated its contribution with his research paper 'Bitcoin –
A Peer-to-Peer Electronic Cash System' (Nakamoto 2008b). The following section introduces into the block chain technology, which is based on the use of public and private
(secret) keys (see Public Key Infrastructure in Sect. 5.6). The shortest formulation for
the characterization of the blockchain stands in the title of this section and can be written
as an equation: Blockchain = Distributed Ledger + Consensus. We owe this shortened
definition to Niklaus Wirth, who tended to say in its lectures at the ETH in Zurich: "Programs = Data Structures + Algorithms" (Wirth (1976)). In modified form we define the
blockchain (software) as a Distributed Ledger (data structure for decentralized record
keeping) plus Consensus (consent algorithm for fraud prevention).

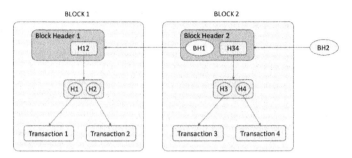

**Fig. 5.7:** Blockchain with two blocks, adopted from Drescher (2017).

### 5.7.1   The Blockchain Data Structure

*Blockchain data structure*   The blockchain is a distributed peer-to-peer network of ledger books, where the individual data blocks are concatenated (Bashir (2017); Berentsen & Schär (2017)). To ensure integrity and security in the blockchain, key pairs consisting of a private key and a public key of the public key infrastructure are used. In the following, the data structure of the blockchain will be presented. In addition, we will show how to solve a cryptographic task and how the proof-of-work will be done. At last, we discuss the collective decision problem (consensus finding) in determining the longest block chain.

Figure 5.7 shows a simplified data structure of the blockchain with two blocks. Block 1 contains a block header 1 and uses a Hash Tree with root H12 via the hash values H1 and H2 to refer to the two transactions 1 and 2 which appear as leaves of the hash tree. Accordingly, the second block is organized, with the block header 2, the hash tree H34 and with the references H3 and H4 to the transactions 3 and 4. Since Block 1 is the first block in the blockchain data structure, it has no predecessor and thus no reference to a preceding block header. Block 2, in contrast, contains block header 1 (BH1) of its predecessor in block header 2 next to the hash tree H34. Accordingly, the block header 2 can be used for further links; BH2 is declared the so-called head of the blockchain.

In a distributed peer-to-peer network containing the simplified data structure of the blockchain of Fig. 5.7, a network node cannot only crawl individual blocks including the block header, hash tree, and transaction data but can scroll backwards in the entire blockchain. By this, all transaction data transferred to the system can be visited. The head of the block chain (see BH2 in Fig. 5.7) should not be mixed with the term block header. The above blockchain in the example consists of the two blocks 1 and 2, each with its block header 1 resp. 2, the hash tree H12 resp. H34, and the transaction data 1, 2, 3 and 4; as well as the head BH2. If a new block 3 is generated, it would be appended to the current header BH2 of the blockchain after a successful check.

Now, we will also shortly discuss the effects of a change in the blockchain. In particular, it is pointed out that a change in one part of the block can trigger a whole cascade of changes in the entire blockchain. The principle of all-or-nothing is a basic principle of every blockchain data structure: If, for example, data is changed in the first block of the blockchain in a particular transaction dataset, then the entire blockchain must

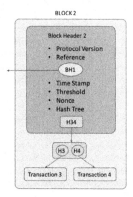

**Fig. 5.8:** Block with extended header for PoW.

be adapted. If, however, the modification of the transaction data in this block is denied because the polluter has no rights to this change, then nothing happens.

### 5.7.2   Solving a Cryptographic Task

In this part, we look at the question of how to make a distributed consensus decision in a peer-to-peer network when expanding the blockchain data structure. The point is to collectively select a transaction history for block extensions. For this purpose, the nodes must deliver their newly created blocks for examination and acceptance to all partner nodes in the network. If there are several concurrent block versions, the so called miner node with the fastest block calculation effort will win and its blockchain extension will be taken (see Sect. 5.7.3).

*Blockchain cryptographic task*

The creation of a new block candidate requires little computational effort. This would mean that block candidates could be created faster than peer-to-peer consensus building. For this reason, creating a block with artificial computational effort helps to find enough time for the consensus finding process. Every node that wants to create a block must provide a so called Proof-of-Work (PoW) by solving a cryptographic task.

In order to find a consensus within the peer-to-peer network, the block header must be extended by a few important elements (see Fig. 5.8):

- The protocol version specifies which policy is used when creating a block.

- The reference is the reference to the previous block; here in the example, BH1 refers to block 1.

- The timestamp indicates when the block was created.

- A level of difficulty (threshold) is needed to set the number of bits equal to 0 at the beginning of the nonce number sequence.

- The nonce (number used once) is a preliminary sequence of numbers that is generated once for a specific purpose (here PoW).

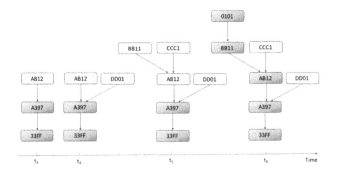

**Fig. 5.9:** Choosing the longest blockchain by consensus, adopted from Drescher (2017).

- The hash tree refers to the transaction data; In our example, H34 (root of the Merkle Tree) points to the hash values H3 and H4 resp. to transaction 3 and 4.

When new transaction data is generated or transaction data is changed, the nodes (often referred to as miners) must solve the cryptographic task in competition. We are looking for the bit sequence (Nonce), which has only zeros in the first forty places. Such a proof of labor is computationally intensive, it must be carried out in the normal case by 240 experiments. If a solution to the cryptographic problem is found, the miner node distributes his result to the peer-to-peer network for verification.

### 5.7.3   The Criterion of the Longest Block Chain

A peer-to-peer network with distributed book entries has no central control authority. For this reason, the nodes in the network have different levels of knowledge about the development of the blockchain. Despite these adversities, they are anxious to build a clear transaction history over time.

If there are new blocks due to user exchange options, these blocks are distributed in the network and verified with PoW. The solution, i.e., a bit string with 40 zeros at the beginning of the number string for the block to be checked, is verified by the nodes. If there are several concurrent blocks at the same time that should be included in the blockchain, then the criterion of the longest chain applies. This states that nodes independently select the path in the tree-like chain structure that is the longest and thus contains the most blocks. This criterion is based on the fact that the longest path in a tree of blocks has made the largest computational effort.

Fig. 5.9 shows the structure of a blockchain at different times. The two already discussed blocks 1 and 2 correspond to block 33FF (Block 1) and A397 (Block 2). They form the current block chain at time $t_3$ when a new block AB12 is to be inserted at the same time. However, block AB12 is still in the queue, since the associated PoW has not yet been fully rendered or verified.

At time $t_4$, another block, block DD01, wants to dock onto the current block chain and points to block A397, by competing block AB12. At time $t_5$, the two blocks BB11 and CCC1 appear, both referring to block AB12, since AB12 now has done its PoW. However, at time $t_5$, the majority of the nodes have not yet agreed whether or not to declare AB12 as the longest chain of blocks. Since there is no unique longest path at time $t_5$, BB11-AB12-A397-33FF and CCC1-AB12-A397-33FF are in competition, one must wait.

Only at time $t_6$, the competitive situation dissolves, since in the meantime, a new block 0101 would like to refer to BB11. The longest block can now be selected, it is 0101-BB11-AB12-A397-33FF. The miners of the blocks AB12, BB11 and 0101 are paid out, the miners of the two blocks DD01 and CCC1 have to reorient themselves and restart their blocks for linking. In our example, all nodes in the peer-to-peer network at time $t_6$ declare block 0101-BB11-AB12-A397-33FF as binding. The head of the block chain, i.e. the block header 0101, is targeted to dock new blocks to the current blockchain.

### 5.7.4  Blockchain Options for eGovernment

An idea for the further use of the blockchain technology is the identity management. While in the real world the identity of persons can be ascertained with official documents such as passports or driver's licenses, so far no such possibility exists in the online world. Today, most Internet users have a variety of accounts managed with different usernames and passwords.

*Blockchain Applications*

The accounts provide access to the deposited resources on the different information systems. With the blockchain, an application can be developed in which only a single digital identity is needed. Systems that require information from the user can query them via the blockchain if the user gives them access. Figure 5.10 shows some examples of blockchain applications in different areas, including eGovernment (Gianpietro-Zago (2018)).

In recent years, a number of blockchain-based identity management systems have been developed. Bitnation[2] attempts to build a 'world identity'. People from all over the world can sign up there and become citizen of bitnation. The bitnation pass is stored in a decentralized blockchain.

*Blockchain for eGovernment*

The United Nations unveiled a first prototype digital signage solution at the ID2020 Summit in June 2017. This prototype is based on a blockchain solution from Accenture and runs on Microsoft's cloud solution Azure. This solution is intended to help people who have no official identification documents. A beta test is planned for 2020.

The company ShoCard[3] from Cupertino, USA offers a blockchain-based solution of the same name, in which people register and then share their personal data with others. ShoCard already offers a variety of services for companies, for example to realize a ShoCard-based user login or an age check.

Electronic voting is another topic in which a blockchain can be used. In contrast to the classic choice of paper, there is no longer a common ballot box in which all ballot papers are selected. Instead, each candidate receives his own digital ballot box. If a voter wishes to vote for a candidate, he will execute a transaction with a token issued

---

[2]Bitnation: `https://tse.bitnation.co/`
[3]ShoCard: `https://shocard.com`

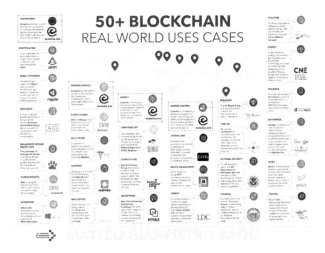

**Fig. 5.10:** Applications of Blockchains, adopted from Gianpietro-Zago (2018).

by the electoral commission. At the end of the election, the number of votes a candidate
has received can be directly determined by the number of transactions. Furthermore,
each voter can verify that his vote has been counted. One problem with this approach
is anonymity. Although outsiders cannot draw conclusions about the election of a person, the election commission can use the token, however, to draw conclusions about the
voting behavior (Noizat (2015)).

In recent months, a number of attempts have been made worldwide to carry out
voting on the basis of blockchain technology. In Switzerland, the city of Zug has set
up a blockchain distributed over three data centers. Citizens can vote with their digital
identity via an app on their smartphones. Experiences of this first public experiment
should be evaluated and analyzed (see media release of the city of Zug from June 8,
2018[4]).

The startup Agora[5] offers a blockchain-based e-voting system, which has already
been used for a presidential election in Sierra Leone (Rubtcova & Pavenkov (2018)).
More details on the architecture used by Agora for blockchain-based eVoting are presented in Sect. 8.5.

## 5.8   Legal Aspects

*Multitude of*        For some time now, there have been legal framework conditions for the use of electronic
*legal ordinances*    information and communication services. The most important laws and ordinances con-
                      cern the following areas:

---

[4]City of Zug: http://www.stadtzug.ch/de/ueberzug/ueberzugrubrik/aktuelles/
aktuellesinformationen/?action=showinfo&info_id=529072

[5]Agora: https://www.agora.vote

- **Digital signature and Public Key Infrastructure**: The laws on electronic signatures regulate how the granting of private and public keys and the issuing of certificates has to be organized. Apart from directives for building a PKI infrastructure, they are mostly concerned with security regulations about the electronic exchange of legally secured documents.

- **Data protection and data security**: Data protection aims at protecting personal data from misuse. In contrast to that, data security is about protecting data from disappearing or manipulation. Laws regulate both data protection and data security. In addition to that, in some countries Data Protection Officers counsel citizens and explain their rights to them (right to information, right to correction).

- **Copyrights and patents**: When dealing with digital goods, corresponding bills have to be adapted and amplified in the area of copyrights and patents. The protection of authors of information objects is difficult to realize, although digital watermarks and other techniques do exist (see Sect. 6.5). On the one hand, such watermarks have to be embedded into the information objects; on the other hand, it has to be proven whether information objects are illegally copied and used for own purposes.

- **Right to domain name and trademark right**: The address in the Internet is primarily determined by the domain name. The addressing is done with the Unified Resource Locator (URL), which is composed of the access code (Internet Protocol), the server and domain name. Both the issue of domain names and the regulation of legal disputes over the claim of individual names is momentarily still in development, although there have been created some legal foundations nationally and internationally.

- **Telecommunication law**: The telecommunication market has been liberalized distinctively over the past years. Former monopoly holders have to accept alternative market providers, respecting fair conditions of competition. Apart from the actual network operators (carriers), Internet access providers and Internet service providers originated, which facilitate access to the Internet or electronic services.

- **International advertising guidelines**: The International Chamber of Commerce, see www.iccwbo.org) in Paris has developed guidelines regarding online advertising. The main idea is to obligate providers to lay open their identity towards Internet users. Sending messages in extreme numbers (spamming) is only permitted within commercial newsgroups, and only if the sending of advertising messages is not strictly forbidden in these newsgroups.

The selection of legal regulations and efforts made in this chapter shall illustrate how deeply the handling of electronic communication channels changes society. As the Internet spans the whole world, single nation laws are not remotely sufficient any more. In fact, individual regions as well as the global community have to impose themselves framework conditions, so that privacy protection be guaranteed in the electronic market and in the eGovernment.

*Supranational agreements are necessary*

## 5.9   Bibliographical Notes

*Literature on*
*eContracting*
The area of eContracting is still young, so accordingly there are only a few publications. The standard works are mainly confined to legal aspects. The edited volumes Handbook Electronic Business by Weiber (2013) and Internet & Electronic Business by Meier (2001) both contain a chapter on electronic contracting in electronic markets. Runge (2000) doctoral thesis illustrates the role of eContracting in electronic trading. Apart from a frame of reference, Runge proposes design elements and shows a case example from the American insurance industry. An introduction to identity management was composed by Mezler-Andelberg (2008). The author describes a process-oriented model with the levels personal data, resources, authorization and authentification. Gipp & Beel (2005) summed up the most important biometric techniques for the ePass in their book on the ePass. Furthermore, the authors address aspects of data protection and data security.

*Works on*
*cryptography*
There are quite a lot of publications on the topic of cryptography and encoding techniques. Especially worth mentioning are the introduction into cryptography by Buchmann (2010), the book on security and encoding in the Internet by Schwenk (2002) and Brands' (2002) book (Brands (2013)) on encoding algorithms. Bitzer's and Brisch's book ((Bitzer & Brisch, 2013)) imparts basic knowledge on digital signatures. The function of signatures, certification authority, smartcard and asymmetric encoding are illustrated by numerous examples. Hochman's work ((Hochmann, 2001)) discusses legal questions in correlation to the PKI infrastructure and illustrates the basic concepts of encoding and certification.

*Publication on*
*Internet law*
The handbook on Internet law by Kröger & Gimmy (2000) and the book on online law by Strömer (1997) are primarily directed at commercial lawyers and attorneys. Both books give an overview on legal requirements of the information society. In particular, legal questions for online providers and participants of electronic commerce are discussed, next to issues of data protection and copyright. The work of Dittmann (2013) is dedicated entirely to digital watermarks. With them, copyright claims in the electronic market can be lodged, clients can be identified and checks for integrity can be carried out.

*Blockchain*
Section 5.7.3 is based on the German research paper 'Blockchain = Distributed Ledger + Consensus' by Andreas Meier and Henrik Stormer (Meier & Stormer (2018)). In the work of Bashir (2017); Drescher (2017), the authors provides the insights and concepts of blockchain technology. Berentsen & Schär (2017) provides details on the development of crypto currencies such as bitcoin. In the chapter (Noizat (2015)), the author describes how to leverage the availability of the Bitcoin blockchain as a secure transaction database, to log votes and audit vote results.

# 5.10   Case Study—Face Recognition in the Biometric Passport

## 5.10.1   Background

Traditional authentication mechanism, such as knowledge-based authentication (PIN and password) or authentication through tokens (keys), have clear disadvantages. Passwords and tokens can be passed on, whereby violating security protocols, or the authentication factor can be lost and forgotten. This problem is even more serious, when a token - such as a passport - is deemed more trustworthy due to the embedded physical security features (such as holograms) or the fact that it's produced by a governmental authority, but on the contrary not used by its rightful owner. Amongst other motivating arguments, this situation has resulted in the decision that biometric data of passport holders are nowadays being stored electronically. Biometric characteristics cannot be forgotten or passed on offhandedly. Biometric recognition can ensure the confirmation of a person's identity the physical border control process.

Prof. Dr. Christoph Busch, *Hochschule Darmstadt (HDA), Germany and Norwegian University of Science and Technology (NTNU), Norway*

The conditions for the transition to biometric passports (ePass) were decided by the International Civil Aviation Organization (ICAO, 2015). Following an EU-resolution (EU, 2004), all EU Member States started issuing passports including electronically-stored facial images since November 2005. Meanwhile, fingerprints are being stored in ePassports as well.

## 5.10.2   Case Study on Biometric Data in Passports

Biometrics can be considered an computer supported method for the recognition of individuals. By international standards, the term biometrics is defined as follows: *"automated recognition of individuals based on their behavioural and biological characteristics"* (ISO, 2012). Biometric methods analyse a person's behaviour and/or the features defining their biological characteristics. Those biological characteristics can either be categorised as anatomical characteristics - which concern the body's structures - or as physiological characteristics - which are the body's functions such as voice or a handwritten signature.

The biometric authentication process confirms an unmistakable link between an individual and their identity. This is regardless of where that identity is being stored, whether it is on a physical token - such as a traceable document or a passport - or in a central database. The process of biometric recognition can be characterised by the following steps:

- Measurement of the biological characteristics with suitable sensors (camera, microphone, etc.), and storage as digital representation

- Pre-processing with the goal of data improvement or data cleansing

- Extracting features to distinguish significant patterns

- Comparing features to a biometric reference

The biometric recognition process requires participants to be enrolled into the system beforehand, in order to create the necessary reference data. In the case of e-passports, a photographic image is taken either with a professional photographer or with a Photo-Booth and then submitted with the application at a registry office.

Biometric systems can be designed as verification systems or identification systems. A verification system confirms a user's identity claim by comparing the probe image to the reference. Provided biometric systems are combined with an authentic document (such as an ePass), a reference image can be stored on said document. A comparison is made to that exact reference image (1:1 comparison) at the time of verification. In the case of an identification system however, the recorded image is compared to a potentially large number of stored images (1:n comparison), to distinguish the most similar candidates. The similarities between both images must reach a certain threshold in order for a reliable match between an identity and its reference image to be confirmed.

Figure 5.11 shows one of the biometric verification system's challenges: the result of a comparison between a current photograph and its reference image is a comparison score. The resemblance is determined when the similarities exceed a certain threshold. If the individual in the photograph has an altered appearance compared to when the reference image was taken, the chances of that threshold not being reached increase. The reference image in illustration 1 is only outdated by five years. In accordance with current EU regulations, however, passports in many countries are valid for up to 10 years.

An RFID-chip was chosen as the storage medium for biometric passports in accordance with ISO 14443. At close range (up to ca. 25 cm), the chip can be read with a contactless interface (913,56 MHz). Passports generally have a capacity of 72 Kbyte, enabling the storage of a facial image (ca. 12 Kbyte) and two fingerprints (ca. 10 Kbyte each). The images are also compressed into standard formats (JPEG, JPEG2000 or WSQ). Apart from the biometric files, further information is saved in a logical data structure.

Figure 5.12 shows the first and most important data groups of logical data structures in electronic Passports according to the ICAO 9303 specification for Machine Readable Travel Documents (MRTD) (ICAO, 2015). Data group DG1 contains information, which is also printed onto the Machine Readable Zone (MRZ) on the data page in analogue form, such as the passport holder's name, nationality, and date of birth. Data group DG2 and DG3 respectively contain the images of the face and fingerprints. DG4, designated for iris scans by the ICAO, is currently not being used in European countries.

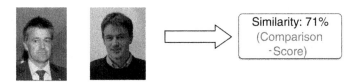

**Fig. 5.11:** Biometric verification.

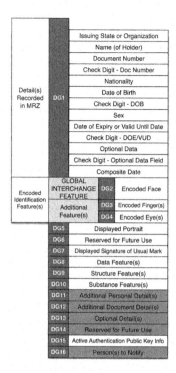

**Fig. 5.12:** Logical data structure in the ePassport.

To safeguard the saved data's authenticity and integrity, the data has been secured with electronic signatures. In addition, two security protocols have been implemented to protect the biometric data. The face image is secured by means of a Basic-Access-Control (BAC) protocol. This mean access to the MRZ's data can only be granted through a scanning device with visual contact to the passport, from which an access key can be derived. Fingerprints are additionally secured through the Supplemented Access Control (SAC) protocol. That is to achieve that fingerprints, which are categorised as sensitive information, can only be accessed by reliable scanning devices from reliable countries.

### 5.10.3   Opportunities

The opportunities provided with biometrics are exemplified by the challenges posed to the acceleration of border control. This topic is becoming increasingly important considering the high growth of traffic at airports and seaports considering for instance a cruise-ship with multiple thousands of travellers that must be boarded and de-boarded in a short time window.

As early as 2003 the Australian government has been pioneer working on the challenge of border control optimisation. This brought forth the SmartGate project, which aims to achieve easier, faster, and more secure processes. Analysis of the research data from the SmartGate system's operational phase has among other things indicated the decreased the duration of border control for travellers: the results show an improvement from 48 seconds in the case of manually operated border control, to 17 seconds in biometrics-supported control. An equivalent optimisation was reached in Germany with the EasyPASS system. A similar implementation based on e-passports, was established with the VBeGATE-system at the Faro airport in Portugal and other European airports starting in 2007. Again process optimisation is the main goal. Since 2D-face recognition cannot prevent circumvention in terms of a presentation attack (ISO, 2016), considering a presented photograph or electronic display (e.g. tablet computer) can result in the same positive comparison score, when compared to the stored passport photo, as it would be expected with a bona fide presentation of a human being, operators must take care of presentation attack detection (PAD) mechanism.

One approach is that border crossing gates are overlooked by border control officers. Their work is supported by an automatic video analysis of the passenger traffic flow in the eGates with the intention to detect the presence of additional individuals in the eGate, or to detect when those individuals leave the gate in the direction contrary to the passenger flow. As an alternative or additional countermeasure dedicated software algorithms analyse the probe and the reference images and provide the PAD functionality. In either case and as a general constraint 2D face recognition it is essential for the reference image in the passport to be of very high quality. Important criteria include a frontal angle, good contrast, sharpness and exposure, a neutral facial expression and no coverage of the face's characteristics (such as eyes and mouth) by hair, glasses or hats. If these quality criteria are not met, this results in a very low recognition accuracy by the biometric system.

To increase the accuracy of biometric face recognition and the robustness against presentation attacks, 3D face recognition methods have been investigated. The approach is based on three-dimensional scanning of the face, for which multi-camera-systems are being used. These have been long-established in photogrammetry: analysing a collection of photos, their respective cameras' angles are included in the calculations and - using a set of 2D photos and the triangulation principle - depth information is compiled. Alternatively, an active acquisition system can be constructed, which consists of an active component - projecting coloured lines or patterns onto the face - and one or more sensors. The resulting three-dimensional facial representation allows for an easier reference image comparison than a frontal photo when the individual has their head tilted or when the camera is at an inconvenient angle. However, before a probe image is compared to the reference model, the face's model has to be rotated to reach a proper alignment. Only then can the similarities, which are deduced from geometric information like the measure of curvature or distance between geometric surfaces, be determined. On top of that, the colour information is graded with texture characteristics (Busch and Nouak, 2008). 3D face recognition consists of significantly more information than the conventional two-dimensional face recognition, meaning that the number of false positive or false negative decisions (e.g. a passport holder not being recognised by the system) taken by the biometric system can be reduced (Busch et al., 2012).

Another goal of the biometric passport is to strengthen the link between a passport holder and the document itself, in order to reduce the risk of that passport being misused by any third parties. That specific risk (misuse of legal documents by unauthorised persons) is also linked to so-called Visa-shopping, the extent of which at the Schengen-area borders and its effects are hard to quantify. The German Federal Criminal Police Office (BKA) detected 655 cases of misuse of legal documents in 2006, during a time period in which there were 3100 other cases of document falsification. With the deployment of ePassports it was expected that misuse to be significantly reduced by biometric verification of photographs and fingerprints (Ziercke, 2007). This expectation is the reasoning behind the integration of two fingerprints in the European e-passport on top of the photographic image required by the ICAO: with a two-finger-verification, a better performance can be achieved compared to the usage of only a photographic image. However, if the biometrics-supported border controls at the outer EU-borders were to be based on two-finger-verification alone, the EU would virtually become a biometric island: the verification of the biometric characteristics of the e-passport would merely be possible for EU citizens, traveller with other origin (i.e. non EU member state citizen) would not have the corresponding references in their passports.

### 5.10.4   Risks

Despite the potential of biometric e-passports, their introduction might be considered as new risks for passport holders. These will be examined and discussed with appropriate countermeasures in the following section.

In some European countries, a central storage of citizen's biometric data was introduced parallel to the introduction of e-passports. This is not only unnecessary, it also doesn't reflect the European culture of data protection that has been growing during the past decades and has now converged to the General Data Protection Regulation (GDPR) (EU, 2016). Whenever possible, biometric systems should be designed without central databases (TeleTrust, 2008).

A frequent point of criticism is the risk of identical reproduction of an e-passport. The possibility of a cloned passport is, however, rather low due to the physical security feature integrated into the page of the ePassport. Even with an exact reproduction of the RFID chip[6] and its logical data structure, the gains for an attacker would be minimal: thanks to the digital signature on the hash values of the individual data groups, replacing biometric data in a Passport would be detected, if the hash values are checked. In case a duplicated document would resemble the image of a look-alike, detection of a misuse would still be possible through fingerprint verification. Furthermore it would be easier to request a passport duplicate by feigning to have lost the original, without having to go through to the technical complications of cloning one.

An additional risk concerns unauthorised access to a passport without the knowledge of the passport holder. This is a concern to the de facto MRZ data's high entropy, which must be considered in the context of deriving the cryptograph strength of the access

---

[6]http://www.heise.de/newsticker/meldung/76379

key for the chipreader to the RFID communication. However, due to constraint of the proximity-cards (max. 25 cm) and the estimated 12 days (Kügler and Naumann, 2007) necessary to even obtain just 220 keys (apporx. 6 numbers), such an attack seems highly unrealistic. Access to the photographic image (DG2) is no real break through for an attack, as a photo of the e-passport holder could be achieved quite easy by other means (e.g. via social networks or remote photography).

## 5.10.5   Conclusion

The advantages of biometric reference data for optimisation of automated border control processes are quite obvious. Most of the risks raised at the time of introducing ePassports have seen appropriate countermeasures. Before the RFID's introduction in passports and ID-cards, simulation studies were done to test those chips' durability. Afterwards, the producers predicted a durability corresponding the legal validity of passports (10 years). After years of experience with can in fact conclude that the majority share of the RFID chips will last 10 years. There is an additional risk related to the biometric characteristics themselves, which are subject to changes caused by ageing (or even beautification surgeries). The comparison of a facial probe image to a ten-year-old reference image is a challenge even for manual inspection by border control officers. In the same line we have to anticipate that automatic biometric face recognition will be challenged with this task. Maintaining face recognition accuracy under the influence of ageing and/or poor image quality remains a task for future research.

## Further Reading

- C. Busch, A. Nouak, 3D-Gesichtserkennung für die unbeaufsichtigte Grenzkontrolle, in Tagungsband Sicherheit 2008, GI-LNI, April 2008

- C. Busch, M. Brauckmann, R. Veldhuis, F. Deravi, T.Kevenaar, A. Nouak, H. Seibert, F. Weber, J.-M. Suchier: Towards a more Secure Border Control with 3D Face Recognition, in Proceedings of the 5th Norsk Informasjons Sikkerhets Konferanse (NISK), November 2012

- EU-Council Regulation No 2252/2004 - of 13 December 2004 on standards for security features and biometrics in passports and travel documents issued by Member States

- EU-Council Regulation No 2016/679 - of 27 April 2016 on the protection of natural persons with regard to the processing of personal data and on the free movement of such data, and repealing Directive 95/46/EC (General Data Protection Regulation)

- ICAO, Doc 9303, Machine Readable Travel Documents, Seventh Edition, 2015

- ISO/IEC JTC1 SC37, ISO/IEC 2382-37: Harmonized Biometric Vocabulary, online: http://www.3dface.org/media/vocabulary.html

- ISO/IEC JTC1 SC37, ISO/IEC30107-1: Biometric presentation attack detection - Part 1: Framework, 2016

- D. Kügler and I. Naumann, Sicherheitsmechanismen für kontaktlose Chips im deutschen Reisepass, in DuD 3/2007, S. 176-180, March 2007

- TeleTrust e.V. Arbeitsgruppe BIometrie, White Paper zum Datenschutz in der BIometrie, March 2008

- J. Ziercke, Stellungnahme zum Passgesetz, Expertenanhörung im Innenausschuss des Deutschen Bundestages, April 2007

## Contact Details

Hochschule Darmstadt, CRISP, Schöfferstr. 10
64295 Darmstadt, Germany
Internet: https://www.christoph-busch.de
eMail: christoph.busch@h-da.de

## Profile of author

### Prof. Dr. Christoph Busch

Christoph Busch is member of the Department of Information Security and Communication Technology (IIK) at the Norwegian University of Science and Technology (NTNU), Norway. He holds a joint appointment with the computer science faculty at Hochschule Darmstadt (HDA), Germany. Further he lectures Biometric Systems at Technical University of Denmark (DTU) since 2007.

He received his PhD in the field of computer graphics in 1997. In the same year he joined the Fraunhofer Institute for Computer Graphics (Fraunhofer IGD) as head of the department Security Technology. Prof. Dr. C. Busch has since been responsible for the acquisition, the management and the control of various applied research and development projects.

# Chapter 6

# eSettlement

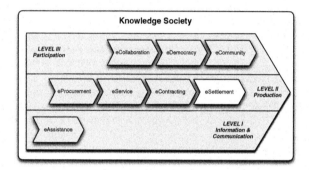

*Chapter 6 deals with processing and settlement of transaction in governmental institutions. Section 6.1 explains the sub-steps of a supply chain and the reference model Supply Chain Operations Reference (SCOR). Section 6.2 classifies electronic payment methods and briefly introduces to some ePayment solutions. Section 6.3 describes online and offline distribution and hybrid forms, respectively, and the advantages and disadvantages that occur when they are used. In the settlement, like in all process steps of the eGovernment, data protection and data security play an important role. Section 6.4 discusses data protection elements and shows measures to protect the privacy of citizens. Section 6.5 argues, how the copyright of digital documents and objects can be protected by digital watermarks. Section 6.6 deals with security measures including risk classes and describes how to secure data and applications with the help of firewalls. Bibliographical notes are provided in Sect. 6.8. In Sect. 6.7, the basic concepts of the General Data Protection Regulation (GDPR) introduced in the European Union, is presented. The Salzburg Research Society works on data protection in electronic data exchanges, among other things. Two case studies are presented at the end of this chapter, the first one explains the European regulations and puts protection mechanisms and procedure recommendations at discussion. The second case is about consent management system implemented for the BitsaboutMe Platform.*

© Springer Nature Switzerland AG 2019
A. Meier, L. Terán, *eDemocracy & eGovernment*, Progress in IS,
https://doi.org/10.1007/978-3-030-17585-6_6

# 6.1    Sub-Steps of a Supply Chain

*The term*
*eSettlement*

By the term eSettlement, we understand the electronic handling and settlement of trans-actions, including confirmation, electronic payment (ePayment, see Sect. 6.2), distribution of material and immaterial components (eDistribution, Sect. 6.3) and further supporting functions. For the governmental institution, the eSettlement means a challenge, because the individual processing steps have to be carried out with guaranteed data protection. As the individual steps in the settlement process of an electronic transaction must harmonize with preceding and following process steps, it is helpful to regard the supply chain as a whole.

*Supply Chain*
*Management*

A supply chain comprises all process steps necessary to fulfill the request or mandate of a citizen. When needed, all involved administrative units, and additionally the respective suppliers and producers of products and services, must be taken into account. Also, merchants and in-betweeners, carriers or other intermediaries are part of a complex supply chain.

*The reference*
*model SCOR*

The development of a reference model for supply chains is based on the idea to get a grip on the complexity and varieties of a supply chain by describing the processes systematically. Next to the description of activities during the individual process steps, the SCOR reference model (SCOR=supply chain operations reference) captures performance key figures, best practices, and software functions (SCOR (2004)).

*Plan, Source,*
*Make and*
*Deliver*

The reference model SCOR associates all tasks of the supply chain with one of the four basic process parts, planning (P=plan), procurement (S=source), production (M=make), and delivery (D=deliver). Figure 6.1 shows the process view in the SCOR model. First of all, the order-related information flow from (1) to (4) takes place, as part of the process part related to execution: The citizen places the order (1), which is received by sub-process D (deliver). This results into the production order (2), in case the citizen places an order (e.g., ordering an ePass, see governmental services and case study in Chap. 5). For the sub-process of production M (make), an order to provide material is placed, which causes the supplier under (4) to order material components. Thereby, the sub-process of procurement S (source) is activated.

*Material flow in*
*the SCOR model*

The material flow in the supply chain of Fig. 6.1 runs opposite to the information flow in steps (5)–(8): The supplier provides the material requested under (5). This procurement step S (source) supports the production by placing orders to provide material (6). During production step M (make), products and services are created (7). Step D (delivery) picks out, packs and ships the ordered products to the citizens under (8).

*Planning the*
*supply chain*

Many sub-processes in the supply chain cannot just be triggered when citizens submit requests. In fact, they have to be initialized and prepared early for reasons of planning procedures, particularly, if it is a question of material procurement and time-consuming production processes (e.g., production of secured carrier documents including embedded chip card for the ePass). To this end, the SCOR model includes a sub-process for planning the supply chain: Following market prognoses (9), procurement scenarios are developed in (10), by analyzing procurement possibilities (11) on the market at an early stage and negotiating them with the respective suppliers. Also, basic production data is taken into account in the planning process (12), supplemented by supplying information of the respective distributor. In summary, the data on planning,

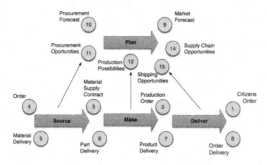

**Fig. 6.1:** Sub-steps within the supply chain according to the SCOR model (SCOR (2004)).

production and supply (11) to (13) constitute the planning horizon (14) of the supply chain.

Every governmental service for citizens (Sect. 4.2), for companies (Sect. 4.3) and for carrying out electronic votes and elections (Sects. 8.3 and 8.4) must be designed and implemented as a process based supply chain. For any of those sub-steps, the question whether to make or buy arises, this is, the governmental institution decides which sub-processes are to be carried out by the institution itself and which are to be carried out by third parties as contract partners.

*Make or Buy for governmental services*

With the help of appropriate measurement categories, services, supply performance, and expenses of production and logistics in the supply chain are continuously registered and provided for reporting. For flawless order deliveries, the corresponding part can be calculated and studied in detail. The productivity of added value, range of inventory or asset turnover are further key factors for evaluating the quality of a supply chain.

*Key figures for measuring quality*

## 6.2   Classification of Web-Based Payment Systems

In governmental services, deliveries, or partial deliveries have to be paid, in case of need, by the citizens or companies. The term ePayment describes the electronic payment process needed to carry out the supply chain without changing media.

*What is ePayment used for?*

Web based payment systems can be classified by different criteria. ePayment solutions can be distinguished by the amount of the money to be transferred, by creating categories like picopayment, micropayment and macropayment. Picopayment denominates trifle amounts (less than 1 cent to maximal 1 Euro), e.g. for visiting pay content Web sites or receiving electronic documents. Micropayment is for services between 1 and several Euros. The macropayment class comprises transfers of bigger amounts of money.

*Pico-, micro- and macro-payment*

In commercial environments, it is important to distinguish electronic payment systems by the criteria anonymous and non-anonymous. Often, individual persons or companies want to pay for the procurement of products and services anonymously, that is, the provider or supplier does not know the identity of the paying person. An important

*Anonymous and non-anonymous payment*

classification alternative for ePayment procedures is the time of the payment. For that purpose, three categories are created, namely pre-paid, pay now, and pay later:

*Money card and paysafecard*

- **Electronic payment alternative pre-paid:** In this category, the money transfer has to be effected before the delivery. Possible solutions can be realized by means of hardware or software. Widely spread in Germany is the "GeldKarte"[1] (money card), which is based on a smartcard previously topped-up with credit. A pre-paid solution based on software is the paysafecard procedure[2] popular in Austria; here, the PIN (personal identification number) is obtained electronically and a previously provided credit can be used.

*PayPal and Pago platform*

- **Electronic payment alternative pay now:** The electronic payment alternative pay now requires for an amount of money to be transferred during the order. A popular example is the credit card based PayPal[3] of eBay, which can be used between governmental institutions and citizens, governmental institution and companies, and also among citizens themselves. PayPal is run in Europe by the PayPal Ltd. in London and regulated by the British financial service authority in accordance to the EU directive on eMoney. The company Pago eTransaction Services GmbH[4] in Cologne provides a platform on which the user can make electronic payments with the internationally established means of payment Visa, MasterCard, Maestro and so on, as well as with regionally positioned direct debit methods.

*Click & buy*

- **Electronic payment alternative pay later:** In the payment alternative pay later, the money is transferred after delivery. This solution is especially interesting for transferring trifle amounts (pico- or micropayment). For it is not worth the trouble to pass through many transaction and booking steps for every picopayment. Rather, all trifle amounts are added and settled with a billing procedure, for example, once a month. One example is the click&buy[5] system by the Firstgate Internet AG, which provides a platform for the handling of trifle amounts. After registering, the citizen can draw on pay content of all providers who accept this currency. The amounts of individual purchase transactions are added and then charged to the buyer monthly, and at the same time credited to the provider or governmental institution.

*Innovative ePayment solutions*

Apart from the here described electronic payment alternatives, there are plenty of innovative solutions that were not able to establish themselves on the market. For example, there were systems proposed which are able to generate and exchange electronic coins (cyber cash) or coupons. In this scenario, correspondent banks and financial institutions, respectively, that are connected to the system would have carried out the conversion from electronic coins or coupons into hard currency and vice versa for the citizens. Such payment systems would be interesting especially for trifle amounts, in order to avoid high transaction costs in the ePayment.

---

[1] www.GeldKarte.de
[2] www.paysafecard.com
[3] www.paypal.com
[4] www.pago.de
[5] www.clickandbuy.de

When making payments independently of time and place with the help of a mobile device, this is called mPayment (mobile payment). In mobile procedures, network carriers and operators have to collaborate with established banks and financial institutions, because, for example, macropayments are often handled over the giro accounts of the citizens.

*mPayment independent of place and time*

In Fig. 6.2, the sub-steps of mPayment are shown, demonstrating the case that citizens draw on services from the governmental institutions. After the initiation step (1) and the authorization of an mPayment transaction (2), the amount charged by the governmental institution is debited with the billing method (3) chosen by the citizen. In the following, the governmental institution receives the confirmation of the payment transaction (4) and can deliver the service or the product (5). In such mPayment procedures, it jumps to the eye that different sub-transactions are carried out online between different partners and there are high demands made on data protection and security.

*Complex mPayment process*

The market for mPayment has, up to today, stayed behind the exaggerated expectations of the solution providers. One reason might be the fact that in most cases, mPayment comprises a complex value creation chain with different partners (mobile phone providers, network operators, banks, financial institutions, credit card providers, etc.) and interfaces (see Fig. 6.2). Another difficulty is that in mPayment, cross-border transactions are initiated. Standardization in worldwide economic areas is necessary.

*Damp market prospects*

In Europe, a standardized area for electronic payment transactions was created under the acronym SEPA[6] (single euro payments area). To that end, legal norms and interbank agreements had to be found, technical and organizational standards created, clearing houses appointed and software solutions developed. In the mid-term, it is to be expected that SEPA will replace the national, and partly the regional, payment transaction systems.

*Successful SEPA implementation*

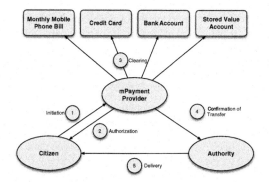

**Fig. 6.2:** Sub-steps of mPayment, adapted from Taga et al. (2004).

---

[6] see European Payments Council under www.europeanpaymentscouncil.eu

## 6.3   Online Versus Offline Distribution

Choosing and shaping a distribution system is an important task for the governmental in-stitution, and comprises picking the distribution channels and the distribution logistics. The distribution channel determines direct and indirect ways of distribution. The choice of the distribution channel depends on the particularity of the product or governmental service. In distribution logistics, it is necessary to pick storage systems, chose the trans-portation network and determine service features. For digital products like documents, software, financial, and insurance services, digital storage media are used.

Under online distribution, or eDistribution, we understand the dispensation of a dig-ital product or a digital service with the help of electronic communication networks. The online distribution can play a role in both direct and indirect distribution channels (see Fig. 6.3), taking into account the respective distribution logistics and service quality.

In the direct distribution, the governmental institution is connected directly to the citizen via an electronic communication medium. In the indirect distribution channel, individual or all sub-steps on the side of the producer, intermediary or buyer can be designed online.

Figure 6.3 illustrates the main characteristics of online distribution. The producer or provider is connected to the citizen in case (a) or to the intermediary in (b) via an electronic transmission medium. As a precondition, the consumers need to have access to the communication system, or Internet access. The advantages of online distribution are as follows:

- The buying desire of the consumer (citizen) can be fulfilled immediately and any-time.

- The governmental institution of the producer has direct contact to the citizens.

- Supply shortfalls in the reproduction of digital goods and longer delivery times cease to exist, if the computer system of the provider and the public or private communication network provide the respective capacity.

- Lower costs for production, storage and distribution result into better pricing and cost advantages.

- Niche products with low output quantities can be marketed more cost-effectively with appropriate design of the distribution system.

In other words, online distribution furthers the ubiquity in the economy. This means that digital goods and services can be offered and distributed anywhere and in any quan-tity.

The eDistribution or online distribution is independent of time and place, if the con-sumer has a mobile device (electronic books, Internet-ready mobile phones, palmtops, or portable computers with communication port). If the technical pre-conditions are given, including availability and capacity of the communication network, the online dis-tribution makes it possible to distribute the goods independently of time, time zone, or whereabouts of the consumer. Naturally, there are disadvantages to online distribution, as well; the most important ones are the following:

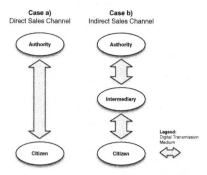

**Fig. 6.3:** Characterization of online distribution.

- In most cases, the distribution costs are passed on directly to the consumer (citizen).

- The social and interpersonal contacts during the purchase in the Internet and the delivery via online channels are often lacking.

- During distribution of digital goods, and because of capacity shortages, the products are compressed, which can lead to quality loss.

- Digital products can be multiplied and spread, because protection mechanisms like digital watermarks (see Sect. 6.5) are only applied in a few cases.

- Not all citizens have access to the communication system or the connection is too weak technically, or too unsafe.

As the online distribution is partly based on hard-to-control software and Internet solutions, it can lead to misuse in regard to copyright (pirate copies) and invasion of privacy (propagation of the citizens' preferences). For that reason, it is necessary to put special emphasis on aspects of data protection while planning and carrying out an online distribution (Sect. 6.4).

In contrast to online distribution, in offline distribution (see Fig. 6.4), the provider is not electronically connected to the consumer over the distribution channel. In-between stand a physical storage, and transportation system (bike couriers, trucks, trains, ships, and others) as well as a physical point of delivery. Of course, the distribution chain can be supported and improved by information-related channels. For example, the consumer is given updates on the delivery status via Internet, or a digital planning system orientates the citizen about the delivery process (hybrid distribution system). The citizen perhaps chooses options to accelerate the delivery by additional investments (online auctions, to sell for example licenses for highly demanded governmental services). *Functionality of offline distribution*

Digital products are not necessarily distributed over online channels, but can get to the end customer offline or with hybrid distribution structures. The immaterial goods are stored on digital data carriers like CD, DVD or further storage media and distributed with adequate means of transportation. *Hybrid distribution types*

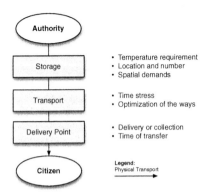

**Fig. 6.4:** Characterization of offline distribution.

The following are considered advantages of offline distribution of digital goods:

- No time is needed to download extensive data, images, audio, or movie sequences.

- The quality of digital graphic, audio, or video content can be maintained high.

- The protection of author rights (copyright) is generally better warranted.

- It is possible to keep immense quantities of data or information on new storage media (with plasma and nano-technology).

Needless to say, the disadvantages of offline distribution or a possible hybrid distribution structure have to be considered. The distribution could be chosen to be hybrid, if there is an electronic high-capacity network installed between producer and distributor. The immaterial goods are received online by the intermediary, then stored on a data carrier and passed to the citizens by conventional distribution channels.

The main disadvantages of offline distribution of digital goods are as follows:

- Defective data parts can hardly be repaired by the citizen. In most cases, the data carrier has to be replaced or the data stored freshly.

- The collection of physical data carriers may become confusing over time, and has to be organized by the user himself.

- Different formats and technical improvements of the devices affect the compatibility with existing infrastructure.

- The distribution of digital goods is not independent of time and place any more.

Despite the mentioned disadvantages of offline distribution of digital goods, this distribution alternative will have its place in the market. Particularly, it can be complemented by an online channel, when needed. With a hybrid distribution structure, the advantages of online and offline distribution can be combined. With it, flexible solutions can be offered to the citizens, depending on technical infrastructure, willingness to pay, time, or safety requirements.

## 6.4   Protection of Personal Data

The development of information and communication systems makes it possible to fit *Protection of*
vast data quantities into little space and make targeted analyses. Apart from the growing *privacy*
significance of information systems and databases, it is important to ask about the rights
that the citizens have in this matter. The main concern in this is personal data, thus data
that is stored in direct relation to a person. Such personal data are last name and given
name, date of birth, sex, civil status, information on health profile and record, among
others. Data protection laws aim at protecting the privacy and basic rights of people.
This includes both data protection and data security matters.

Under data protection, we understand the protection of data from unauthorized ac- *Definition of*
cess and utilization. Protective measures are procedures to clearly identify persons, to *data protection*
grant user rights for specific data access instances, but also for cryptographic methods
for storing and passing information (see encoding procedures in Sect. 5.4). In contrast *Definition of*
to data protection, the term data security comprises technical and software-aided mea- *data security*
sures to protect the data from falsification, destruction or loss (see Sect. 6.6 and case
studies on electronic data exchange in this chapter). It is about securing stored data with
the help of archiving methods, recovery of stored data after faults, and protecting data
against viruses and other malware.

The following information on people or members are considered particularly worthy *Protection-*
of protection: *worthy*
*characteristics*

- Ideological or religious views or activities

- Belonging to ethnical groups or minorities (ethnicity)

- Data on health, for example, specific diseases or physical handicap

- Information on felonies, criminal prosecution and penalties, respectively

- Information on a person's private sphere

According to law, personal data may only be obtained in legal ways and used in
good faith. Hence, such data may only be used for the purpose that was announced at
the time of collecting, or for purposes that are clearly understandable in the context or
are stipulated by law.

In Fig. 6.5, it is shown which rights citizens have according to data protection law. *Insight into*
They have the right to require insight into their data stock anytime, and the operator *dossier*
of the database has to explain the purpose and legal foundations of the stored data.
Personal data usually may not be passed onto third parties, unless the aggrieved party
has consented. The right to information may be restricted in exceptional cases, if a law
requires this or if it is necessary to persue the predominant interest of a third party. This
is the case, for example, if domestic and international security is in danger (fight against
terror).

Next to the right to information, every person has the right to correct false informa- *Correction of*
tion. Outdated information, or data that is not needed anymore for the intended reasons, *false information*
must be deleted according to established deadlines. Governmental institution keeps a

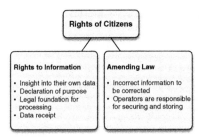

**Fig. 6.5:** Rights to information and correction according to data protection law.

register on their databases with personal data. Protection-worthy data stocks can be both electronically and manually kept databases, whenever they contain personal data.

*Tasks of Data Protection Officers*

Data Protection Officers or ombudsmen of the governmental institution counsel the citizens with regard to their rights and duties. They also can give recommendations to the legislative body, in case the regulations on the handling of personal data should be changed or adapted to the latest developments.

## 6.5   Protection of Copyright

In the distribution of digital documents or objects, it is desirable to protect the author rights and prevent unauthorized copying of data. The use of watermarks, already applied in the protection of material goods, can be transferred to digital products (software, images, video and audio sequences, texts).

*Utilization of digital watermarks*

Under digital watermarks, we understand a non-perceivable pattern, which determines the copyright holder of the digital object. The algorithm belonging to the digital watermark supports both the embedding process (watermark embedding) and the retrieval process (watermark retrieval). The embedding process, or marking process, inserts the digital watermark into the data material as a non-visible pattern. The retrieval process, or query process, makes it possible to recognize the copyright holder of a digital object.

*Tasks of steganography*

Steganography means hidden communication; it is concerned with embedding and retrieval processes which guarantee the author's authenticity in digital objects. The watermark is a secret message and holds important information about the carrier document, while being itself invisible.

*Content of digital watermarks*

Depending on the particular use case, digital watermark can involve the following tasks described bellow.

- Indications on copyright

- Indications on authentification (authenticity of the digital object)

- Keywords to characterize the carrier document (annotations)

- Date and time of creation

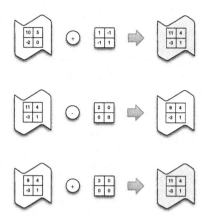

**Fig. 6.6:** Bob attacks Alice's author rights, according to Qiao & Nahrstedt (1998).

- Serial number of the recording device.

In the research literature, one can find a discourse on attacks against watermarking procedures. One known type of attack regards the author's uniqueness and is known under the name of Rightful Ownership Problem, or Invertibility Problem. Figure 6.6 illustrates an example with a non-blind watermark procedure.

Digital watermark procedures allow for repeated marking of the data material. Indeed, a document with several watermarks makes sense. For example, a digital document can be equipped with watermarks for the author, producer or publisher. If the attacker equips the already marked data material with his own copyright information, the Invertibility Problem can occur. *Problems during attacks*

According to Fig. 6.6, Alice embedded a watermark into her original document and puts the marked document at public disposal. The attacker Bob finds Alice's marked document on the Internet. He creates his own watermark and extracts it from Alice's marked document. Bob complements his simulated original with his own watermark and thereby creates a marked document, which is identical to Alice's marked document. Now, it cannot be told which one of the two marked documents represents the original one. To resolve the Invertibility Problem, the watermarks have to be rendered dependent from the original in a non-invertible way. This is difficult especially for blind watermark procedures, because complex time stamp system is necessary for solving the problem. *The Invertibility Problem*

Digital watermark procedures were developed mainly for identification of author right holders, but in the meantime are used for other purposes, as well. In case of digital fingerprints, not only the name of the copyright holder is embedded non-visibly into the document, but also the name of the respective buyer. This is meant to prevent that the buyer passes along or sells unauthorized copies. Due to the hidden watermark, he could be identified and brought to justice in case of abuse.

## 6.6   Security Management

*Formulating security goals*

The security and catastrophic management aims to prevent actual damages to the information infrastructure, information systems and databases, and furthermore to prevent the economic damages resulting from it. In order to run an effective security management, a risk analysis must be carried out, security goals must be formulated and suitable measures must be taken.

*Classification of security systems*

Under security , we understand the degree of confidentiality, integrity, and availability of the infrastructure, the application systems and databases. A classification of security systems, sorted by components, distinguishes the following groups: Personnel, buildings and premises, computer systems, communication systems, system software, application systems, databases and data warehouse. Computer experts in the administration have to collaborate with the responsible contact people in the eGovernment, in order to adapt the different protection mechanisms of the security systems to each other and to evaluate and carry out the whole security plan.

*Functionality of the firewall*

A firewall is a security system, which prevents hackers or malware from entering your own network or the information systems and databases of the administration. The complete data traffic from the outside to the inside, and from inside to outside, is conducted over the firewalls. The security system acts as a filter, checks and logs all accesses. The firewall can also contain a spam filter, in order to stay prepared against mass advertising in the Internet (see Sect. 10.5).

*Architecture with firewalls*

In Fig. 6.7, an exemplary architecture with firewalls is illustrated. Citizens send their messages to the Web server, which passes it along to the application server. When needed, inquiries are made to the in-house information systems and databases. In total,

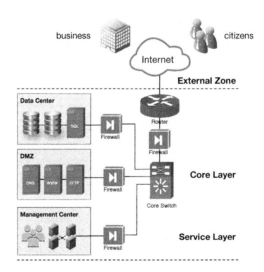

**Fig. 6.7:** Securing applications and data through firewalls.

two firewalls with corresponding checking routines have to be overcome. The following questions have to be answered when dealing with an architecture with firewalls:

- Which user, or citizen, may pass which firewalls?

- How is a user authenticated by the Web server, that is, how is the authenticity of the user verified?

- Who has access to which resources of the Web server and application server, respectively?

- Which network users may access the in-house information systems and databases?

- What is to be done if hackers or malware are discovered?

- How can different rights be administered consistently in the different systems?

The security management of the administration has to ensure the security of the infrastructure, and apart from that, keep the information systems and databases protected and guarantee a workflow without interruptions.

## 6.7   General Data Protection Regulation

The European Commission introduced the so-called General Data Protection Regulation (GDPR) as one set of data protection rules for all companies operating in the EU, wherever they are based. It includes stronger rules on data protection aiming people to have more control over their personal data and businesses benefit from a level playing field, simplifying the regulatory environment for international business by unifying the regulation within the EU[7].

The GDPR was adopted on April 14, 2016 and became effective as of May 25, 2018 in the European Union. Taking into account that the GDPR is a regulation, not a directive, it is not required that the national governments approve any enabling legislation being this directly binding and applicable. There are strong penalties for infringing the GDPR. In the case of existing offenders, they can receive a fine of up to 20 million euros or up to 4% of the annual global turnover of the previous financial year in the case of a company, whichever is greater.

The European Commission defines personal data as "any information related to an individual, whether it relates to his private, professional or public life. It can be anything from a name, a particular address, a photo, an email address, bank details, publications on social networking websites, medical information or the IP address of a computer.[8]"   *Definition of Personal Data by the EU*

The GDPR does not apply to the processing of personal data in cases of national security activities or the application of EU law. This also includes a different Data Protection Directive for the police and criminal justice sector that provides rules on exchanges of personal data at national, European and international level.

---

[7]https://ec.europa.eu/info/law/law-topic/data-protection_en
[8]http://europa.eu/rapid/press-release_IP-12-46_en.htm

To understand the levels of responsibility and accountability in the application of the GDPR, first we need to define the main actors as follows: the data controller (an organization that collects data from EU residents), processor (an organization that processes data on behalf of a data controller like cloud service providers), and data subject (person). These actors should be based in the EU.

In order to comply with the requirements of the GDPR, first, the data controller must implement measures that comply with the principles of data protection by design and by default (Article 25 of the GDPR). This article indicates what are the necessary measures for the protection of data for the development of commercial processes for products and services.

*User rights by GDPR*    When collecting user data, stakeholders should be clearly informed about: scope of data collection, legal basis for data processing, time the data will be retained, if the data is transferred to a third party and / or outside the EU, and disclosure of any automated decision making that is made on an exclusively algorithmic basis. Users must be informed of their privacy rights under the GDPR, including:

- The right to revoke consent for data processing at any time
- The right to see their personal data and access a general description of how they are being processed
- The right to obtain a portable copy of the stored data
- The right to erase data under certain circumstances
- The right to challenge any automated decision making that has been made on an exclusively algorithmic basis, and
- The right to file complaints with an authority Data Protection.

Based on Article 35 Impact evaluations of data protection must be carried out when specific risks occur to the rights and freedoms of the interested parties. Risk assessment and mitigation is required and the prior approval of data protection authorities is required for high risks. A *right to be forgotten* was replaced by a more limited *right of erasure*[9] adopted by the European Parliament in March 2014.

## 6.8   Bibliographical Notes

*Literature on supply chain management*    There is extensive literature on the supply chain management, which feature aspects of information and communication technologies more or less prominently. Chopra's and Meindl's standard work (Chopra & Meindl (2007)) dedicates a chapter to the coordination of supply chain management and electronic business. Hässig (2000) textbook describes the performance of networks and contains a chapter on supply chain management, virtual organizations and electronic commerce. The edited volume of Lawrenz et al. (2013) describes strategies for building and managing a supply chain and gives concrete instructions on how to act by real-life examples. The Supply Chain Operations

---

[9]https://gdpr-info.eu/art-17-gdpr/

Reference (SCOR) model was published in its 5.0 version by the Supply Chain Council and is available on the Internet under SCOR (2004).

Herwig (2001) doctoral dissertation is dedicated to the distribution of goods and services in public institutions and in the eGovernment, respectively. To this end, influence factors for the production and distribution process are studied and legal framework conditions discussed. The eBusiness handbook for small and medium-sized businesses by Bullinger & Berres (2013) deals with online distribution in one chapter section, and describes possible solutions for software distribution. The book by Piller (2004) is dedicated to customized mass production. Helmke & Uebel (2003) have compiled a compendium on online distribution. The remarks on online and offline distribution are taken from the book by Meier & Stormer (2009).

*Online and offline distribution*

The manual by Lammer (2006) describes up-to-date ePayment procedures and analyzes the legal framework conditions. In this edited volume, you can also find an article on mPayment in the international context, written by Karlsson & Taga (2006).

*ePayment procedure*

The book by Dittmann (2013) compiles the most important procedures for digital watermarks and describes open issues. The Invertibility Problem stems from the research work of Qiao & Nahrstedt (1998).

*Digital watermarks*

A security measures plan with risk classes was created by Krallmann (1989). More recent methods and techniques for security management are dealt with in the book of Müller (2008).

*Works on security management*

The EU introduced the General Data Protection Regulation (GDPR) as a regulation in EU law on data protection and privacy for all individuals within the European Union (EU) and the European Economic Area (EEA). The full regulation can be download at European Comission (2018).

*GDPR*

## 6.9   Case Study—Safeguards on Data Exchange of Salzburg Research

### 6.9.1   Background

Univ.-Doz. Dr.
Siegfried Reich,
*Salzburg
Research
Forschungsge-
sellschaft
m.b.H.*

Being a research society the country of Salzburg, the Salzburg Research Society con-
ducts applied research projects in the area of information and communication technologies for the benefit of companies and public institutions. For the last decade, the "Advanced Networking Center" of the Salzburg Research Society has been dedicated to the
evaluation and improvement of the quality of telecommunication networks and services,
especially of the Internet and its services. One of the recent projects (Privacy-aware Secure Monitoring (PRISM)[10]) is concerned with the conflict between operating security
and data protection in the surveillance of electronic communication.

### 6.9.2   Case Study—Disregarding of Data Protection and Defense Measures

Felix
Strohmeier,
*Salzburg
Research
Forschungsge-
sellschaft
m.b.H.*

More and more, governmental institutions and public administrations see the Internet as
a medium with which they can not only inform, but also ease and accelerate administrative procedures. Though, handling personal data is delicate by nature, and there have
been repeated reports of minor and mayor mishaps.[11]

As with all Internet applications, the handling of services over the Internet implies
several providers that act as communication mediator. Usually, the communication partners neither know the communication path, nor can they influence it actively. Although
in the eGovernment all communication between communication partners tends to be encoded, the intermediary providers can observe personal data. Among other things, it can
be determined who communicated with what service for how long. If weak encoding
procedures are applied (see online article "Schwache Verschlüsselung in weit verbre-
iteten Linux Distributionen",[12]) the whole communication can be decoded. As shown
schematically in Fig. 6.8, there are always several organizations involved in the transmission of data when an Internet service is used. These have the technical possibility to
observe and record the traffic. Recently discovered scandals show that these possibilities
were indeed used, violating data protection laws.[13]

Nevertheless, appropriate traffic monitoring in communication networks is indispensable for the network operation; for smaller, local providers as well as for multinational ones. Comprehensive data recording is necessary for electronic payments or in
order to check whether contracts (service level agreements) were fulfilled. The security
of the network infrastructure and its users must be guaranteed. To this end, it is necessary to apply mechanisms to detect network attacks (e.g., distributed denial of service

---

[10]PRISM: http://www.fp7-prism.eu/

[11]Data mishap in the municipality of Potsdam, reported on June 24, 2008 at: http://www.heise.de/
newsticker/Gut-dass-es-passiert-ist-Datenpanne-zwingt-zum-Umdenken--/
meldung/109933

[12]Published on May 13, 2008. http://www.heise.de/security/meldung/Schwache
-Krypto-Schluessel-unter-Debian-Ubuntu-und-Co-207332.html

[13]Bugging operation at German Telekom and Greek Vodafone.

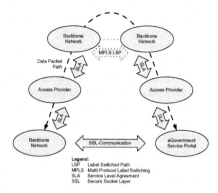

**Fig. 6.8:** Organizations involved when Internet services are used.

attacks), computer viruses or other anomalies. In order to trace such attacks back to the origin, IP addresses must be filtered from the data traffic stream. It is therefore essential to analyze the whole network traffic.

**Variety of Regulations**

Basic concepts of data protection are defined in the European Data Protection Directive 95/46/EG (see literary quote listed under EU-DSRL). According to the directive, personal data comprises all information on an identified or identifiable natural person, that is, if the person can be identified directly or indirectly (e.g., name, capacity, and so on). When electronic communication occurs in applications (e-mail, electronic governmental services, among others), this generates not only process-related data, but also other personal data (see literary quote DGEGOV). This is, for example,

- Inventory data (e.g., bank connection)

- Usage data (e.g., bank account information) and

- Connection data (e-mail addresses, time of delivery, among others).

The processing of personal data is the application of automatized procedures of any kind. The Working Group for data protection, instituted by article 29 of this directive, recommends in a statement on the term "personal data," that all IP addresses should be treated as such, too. For this reason, data protection regulations must be considered when monitoring the traffic (bibliographical notes, Gaudino, 2008).

In Germany and Austria, this directive was put into practice by means of the Federal Data Protection Law ("Bundesdatenschutzgesetz," see DE-DSG in bibliographical notes), and the Federal Law on the Protection of Personal Data ("Bundesgesetz über den Schutz personenbezogener Daten," see DAT-DSG in bibliographical notes), respectively. In Switzerland, the corresponding law is the Federal Law on data protection ("Bundesgesetz über den Datenschutz," bibliographical notes under CH-DSG), which in contrast to the EU directive includes legal persons as well as natural persons. This law was declared appropriate for the transmission of personal data to third countries by the European Union.

In addition to the Data Protection Directive 95/46/EG, the EU passed the Directive on privacy and electronic communications 2002/58/EG in the year 2002 (see literature under EU-DSEK). The directive harmonizes the individual legal implementations in the member states and complements them to make them applicable for legal persons. In Austria, the implementation was carried out by means of the Telecommunication Act ("Telekommunikationsgesetz," see AT-TKG), and in Germany by the Telemedia Act ("Telemediengesetz," see DE-TMG) and the Telecommunication Act ("Telekommunikationsgesetz," see DE-TKG).

Not included in the above-mentioned directives are all activities concerning public safety. This exception was added to the 2006 directive 2006/24/EG (see EU-VDSP), demanding from all Internet service providers and network carriers to retain personal telecommunication data. The stored data is to contain traffic and location data. Nevertheless, it is not to contain content data that is transmitted via fixed line networks, cellular phone networks, Internet access, e-mail or Internet telephony. The data to be stored are: source, destination, date, time, duration and type of communication, as well as identification of the end user device and its location in case of mobile devices. For the source and destination of the communication, the IP address and telephone number, respectively, are stored. Both must be relatable to the name or address of the participant. With anonymous services like prepaid card systems, date and time of its first activation must be stored. The retention deadline is at least six months and two years at most.

In some countries, it is doubted that the directive is constitutional with regard to data protection. A claim against this directive was taken to the European Court of Justice by Ireland, although the claim is not against its contents, but rather against its formal realization. Therefore, most countries have not completely implemented the directive yet, and the permitted deadline prolongation until March 15, 2009 was utilized by many member states.

**Data Storage and Protection of Personal Data**

The problem of retention of personal data was taken up by the PRSIM project. In order to prevent abuse of the retained data, an infrastructure is to encode all stored data directly after collecting it. After that, people with access authorization may only access the data after respective authentification. Four different application categories of traffic monitoring were identified (see bibliographical notes, Strohmeier et al. 2008):

- **Performance monitoring** This service makes it possible to monitor continually the network status and to optimize network operation and planning. It does not contain any personal data and usually is strongly aggregated. Some providers of public networks, like research and educational networks, publish performance statistics of their main links on the Internet. Some examples of performance monitoring are measuring link traffic or distribution of the traffic regarding its source and target networks. In both examples, the monitoring can be done anonymously and therefore does not constitute a violation of data protection. When analyzing each IP address, for example in order to recognize those clients who produce disproportionately high traffic in fair-use contracts, the procedures must be evaluated with regard to data protection.

- **Systems for detection of anomalies and trespassing** Detection systems not only serve to discover anomalies and trespassing, but also for prevention. As early warning systems, they protect the network or individual services. Recognition procedures are based on identifying known patterns of former intrusions and removing the originator from circulation. In contrast to that, anomaly recognition tries to detect unusual fluctuation in the network traffic. It is based on self-learning systems and is able to fend off new kinds of attacks, whereas the pattern recognition can only recognize already known trespassing methods. In order to further develop these systems, it is necessary to have up-to-date data available. The anonymization strategies applied in PRISM are thought to make it possible to provide traffic data in anonymized form for research.

- **Classification of traffic by applications** Application analyses allow for prioritization, for example, preferring real-time critical telephone communication over e-mail data traffic. Apart from that, long-term statistics help to predict the further development of Internet traffic.

- **Tapping service** This service serves the public safety (lawful interception). While originally being limited to telephone conversations, in the future it is planned to amplify the service to cover all Internet traffic by means of the above-mentioned EU directive. To this end, the European Telecommunications Standards Institute gives standards[14] that have already been implemented by some commercial software producers.

While monitoring, all personal data should be protected from unauthorized access; that is why anonymization and encoding procedures are applied (bibliographical notes under Schmoll 2008). Anonymization has the purpose to render data unrecognizable. With encoding, on the other hand, the original data can be restored with the help of a valid key.

Anonymization procedures may have flaws. For example, in pseudonymization[15] there is a chance that original data can be restored if its allocation is known. Even if the pseudonymization is random, that means the pseudonyms are allocated without known correlation, there is still a chance to trace back the original data by means of pattern recognition (fingerprinting) over other characteristics of the data stream (e.g., packet length). As a consequence for applications in the eGovernment, it is recommended to utilize anonymization instead of pseudonymization.

Nevertheless, it is not possible for the providers to abandon traffic monitoring completely for the sake of data protection. It is necessary to recognize, ward off and trace back attacks on the service or abuse of it. Apart from that, providers are legally obliged

---

[14]http://portal.etsi.org/li/Summary.asp

[15]In pseudonymization, the identification of the actual user is prevented or distinctively complicated by using a code. In contrast to anonymization, there are still correlations between the data sets.

to record the data traffic. This is were PRISM comes in to enable the providers of services and communication networks to keep operating by targeted traffic monitoring, without violating the users' privacy at the same time. It is also necessary to enable the providers to monitor the fulfillment of contracts with neighbor providers. Apart from that, it is intended to create transparency for the user, this means it should be traceable who stored what data for what reason, and for how long.

One of the contributions of PRISM to the scientific community is to provide the possibility to access real and up-to-date traffic data for recognition of new network attacks, viruses or worms and for the design of new traffic models. The project also has a share in creating awareness of data protection in producers of measuring systems, providers of Internet services, network providers and, hopefully, in the citizens as well.

### 6.9.3   Opportunities and Risks

In the eGovernment, streams of communication, exchange and payment in the Internet always run by an access provider and, in most cases, also with backbone networks. These providers are legally obliged to store personal data for a certain time. This results into several opportunities, but also risks.

One of the new opportunities is the possibility to monitor the network without violating data protection. Apart from that, by monitoring and temporarily storing data it is possible to obtain better recognition results of cyber attacks and intrusions and to discover viruses and worms. The necessary systems are technically and organizationally complex, and they therefore contain security risks, also there are persisting questions about the performance and maintainability. As the installation of advanced systems means an additional effort for the Internet service providers, its application is only cost-effective if the systems are amortized after a certain operation time.

### Further Reading

- AT-DSG: Datenschutzgesetz 2000 (DSG 2000), BGBl. I No. 165/1999

- AT-TKG: Telekommunikationsgesetz 2003 (TKG 2003), BGBl. I No. 70/2003 idF. BGBl. I No. 133/2005

- CH-DSG: Bundesgesetz über den Datenschutz (DSG), June 19, 1992 (version of January 1, 2008)

- DE-TKG: Telekommunikationsgesetz, June 22, 2004 (BGBl. I p. 1190), last changed by article 2 of the law of December 21, 2007 (BGBl. I p. 3198)

- DE-TMG: Telemediengesetz, February 26, 2007 (BGBl. I p. 179)

- DGEGOV: Datenschutzgerechtes eGovernment. Handreichung zur Konferenz der Datenschutzbeauftragten des Bundes und der Länder am 8./9. Accessed 03-2001, from http://www.lfd.niedersachsen.de/master{/ -}C27872_N13151_L20_D0_I560.html

- EU-DSEK: Richtlinie 2002/58/EG des Europäischen Parlaments und des Rates vom 12. Juli 2002 über die Verarbeitung personenbezogener Daten und den Schutz der Privatsphäre in der elektronischen Kommunikation (Datenschutzrichtlinie für elektronische Kommunikation)

- EU-DSRL: Richtlinie 95/46/EG des Europäischen Parlaments und des Rates vom 24. Oktober 1995 zum Schutz natürlicher Personen bei der Verarbeitung personenbezogener Daten und zum freien Datenverkehr

- EU-VDSP: Richtlinie 2006/24/EG des Europäischen Parlaments und des Rates vom 15

- EU-VDSP: Richtlinie 2006/24/EG des Europäischen Parlaments und des Rates vom 15. März 2006 über die Vorratsspeicherung von Daten, die bei der Bereitstellung öffentlich zugänglicher elektronischer Kommunikationsdienste erzeugt oder verarbeitet werden, und zur Änderung der Richtlinie 2002/58/EG

- Gaudino, F. et al.: Assessment of the legal and regulatory framework. PRISM - Privacy-Aware Secure Monitoring, Deliverable D2.1.1. Accessed 14-09-2018, from http://www.fp7-prism.eu

- Schmoll, C. et al.: State of the art on data protection algorithms for monitoring systems. PRISM - Privacy-Aware Secure Monitoring, Deliverable D3.1.1. Accessed 14-09-2018, from http://www.fp7-prism.eu

- Strohmeier, F. et al.: State of the art on monitoring applications. PRISM - Privacy-aware Secure Monitoring, Deliverable D3.2.1. Accessed 14-09-2018, from http://www.fp7-prism.eu

## Contact Details

Salzburg Research Forschungsgesellschaft mbH
Jakob Haringer StraSSe 5/III
A-5020 Salzburg
Internet: http://www.salzburgresearch.at/
eMail felix.strohmeier@salzburgresearch.at;
siegfried.reich@salzburgresearch.at

## Profile of Authors

### Univ.-Doz. Dr. Siegfried Reich

Siegfried Reich studied Business and Administration Informatics at the Johannes Kepler University Linz and in 1995 obtained his doctoral degree with distinction at the University of Vienna on the topic of interoperability of workflow systems. Between 1996 and 1999, he worked as a lecturer and researcher in the Department of Electronics and Computer Science at the University of Southhampton, the main subject of his work being hypermedia systems. In 2000, he habilitated in the subject of applied informatics at Linz University. Since 2002, he is academic director and manager of the Salzburg Research Society. Salzburg Research does applied research in the areas of intelligent mobility, eTourism, knowledge and media management, eCulture and reliable network technologies, among others things.

## Dipl.-Ing. (FH) Felix Strohmeier

Felix Strohmeier is a scientific assistant in the Advanced Networking Center at Salzburg Research. He collaborates in Austrian and European research projects with focus on measuring and monitoring in the Internet. Before that, he studied telecommunication technology and systems at the Salzburg University of Applied Sciences and wrote his diploma thesis at Siemens Austria. He teaches at Salzburg University of Applied Sciences and represents Austria in the management committee of the COST Action IC0703 on the topic of " Data Traffic Monitoring and Analysis: Theory, Techniques, Tools and Applications for the Future Networks."

# 6.10   Case Study—Consent Management System: A Case Study of BitsaboutMe Platform

While entering a new era of digital societies a vast number of digital footprints left by users becomes a new source of economic wealth. With that personal data has become a valuable asset for the operation of companies, which require different levels of access. Companies in the past often tried to get access to more than is needed for correct operation of their product or service (Big Data paradigm). As past legislations did not sanction extensive collection of personal data and selling to third parties, many companies practiced and continue to apply this model of operation. This model used to be considered legal, albeit unethical, because citizens have allowed it by agreeing or signing the terms and conditions of use. These terms and conditions were often written in a way that citizens can only choose between accepting all of it, or accepting none which means compromising their data and privacy for use of the product or service, without having a choice in between. This lack of choice can cause citizens to feel discomfort when sharing their information and even go as far as refusing from using the product or service all together. Others may choose to provide false information in order to protect themselves from this behavior of companies that can be described as predatory. Situations like these are not beneficial for both, citizens and companies. The former ones do not have access to services that would improve their lives, and the latter ones losing profit and influence. It becomes evident that there needs to be a change that would establish a greater trust between citizens and companies. The introduction of new General Data Protection Regulations (GDPR) was a major step towards building the trust and provide citizen's rights of data protection and privacy. Another way to establish the trust is by giving citizens control over their data and informing them how the collected data is used in a more transparent way. Then, it becomes important to have a clearly documented consent from citizens where this process can be facilitated through implementation of consent management systems.

Christian Kunz,
*BitsaboutMe AG*

Luka Hamza,
*BitsaboutMe AG*

Andreas Meier,
*University of Fribourg*

## 6.10.1   Background

When reading the text of the GDPR regulations, one can find that there are a lot of new terms and ideas introduced which are not always clearly defined in a form of the final implementation guidelines. For example, conditions for a valid consent are defined in the regulation, but still, there are no explicit technical directions in which form each request for processing of personal data has to be presented. Undefined standards and requirements in the regulation would present a significant problem for both, citizens and the companies alike.

Aigul Kaskina,
*University of Fribourg*

From a company's perspective, each company has to invest significant resources to become GDPR compliant, and that has to involve a multi-disciplinary approach: computer science, legal professionals, design professionals, marketing, and economists. This proves to be a very expensive change, especially for small businesses. In some cases, small businesses are threatened to shut down because of their inability to implement GDPR in an affordable way. Another challenge is the compatibility issues when com-

panies have to communicate and exchange data about users, because of different inter-organizational standards and procedures defined and used.

From citizens' perspective, if they encountered a different user interface for each service they want to use, they would not be able to adapt very quickly and make clear, informed and independent decisions which is not permitted under GDPR. This problem is not eased by the fact that most users would encounter something that they are not familiar with, concepts that they do not understand, but would be under pressure to make a decision.

GDPR brings some changes in user interface requirements, like the need for the users to opt-in instead of opt-out, need to have certain aspects of the system accessible with the same level of complexity, still having a need for a completely new set of specifications for new additions with GDPR – well defined consent request for accessing the citizens' data. After identifying the problems that currently exist and which would most likely be encountered once GDPR application became mandatory, it seemed like a logical solution to try to create, if not standards, then at least guidelines on how to design certain aspects of the consent management system.

This case study describes the approach of implementing a consent management system for use in personal data marketplaces and describes the solution implemented by the company BitsaboutMe AG [16] which offers intuitive way for users to have overview of their personal data and receive compensation for exchanging that data with interested parties. The proposed system attempts to standardize many aspects of GDPR requirements as they have to be implemented in all GDPR-compliant businesses. Aspects addressed in this case study include consent management systems, consent framework, consent requests, design of a consent request, required parts and fields in a consent request, optional parts of the consent management systems (e.g., reports).

### 6.10.2   EU Data Protection Regulation

GDPR is a regulation that was adopted in 2016 as a replacement for Data protection directive (EU Parliament, 1995) that was applied in European Union and came into force on 25 May 2018. Territorial reach of the regulation covers countries belonging to European Union and European Economic Area. Regulation protects all natural persons, whether they are nationals, residents or just traveling through. Regulation also protects individuals that are nationals of an EU country, but are not within its territorial scope. In principle, that means that any company or entity that operates with personal data of EU citizens has to alter its operations to become GDPR compliant towards all individuals that GDPR protects – in effect, businesses will have to apply the same data and privacy protection standards to all its users, whether they are under jurisdiction of GDPR or not.

The aim of GDPR is to bring vastly improved protections for citizens in terms of personal data, privacy and data breach prevention. Although the principles of the older data protection directive remain, improvements to the regulation are implemented to combat new ways of infringing upon person's rights, ones that appeared since the introduction of last directive. One aspect of GDPR that is important to person's rights are changes to how companies must obtain consent from users for using a service or product. Informed

---

[16]https://bitsabout.me/en/

consent is required so that personal data can be collected and processed, must be voluntarily given, must be clearly communicated and defined. This requires great investments from business side, to develop an effective and legal way of obtaining consent, providing interface to users to change their privacy preferences, or even revoke their consents. It would also take great effort for citizens to adapt to all the variations of systems that they would have to use – in worst case as many systems as there are services that they are using.

*Consent*, as defined in GDPR text (Intersoft Consulting, 2016), is "Any freely given, specific, informed and unambiguous indication of the data subject's wishes by which he or she, by a statement or by a clear affirmative action, signifies agreement to the processing of personal data relating to him or her."

*Consent request* is part of a consent management system in charge of presenting incoming request for access and processing of personal data from interested entities to users. Since processing of personal data requires informed consent from data subject, consent request needs to present all relevant information to that request to the user.

While GDPR regulations have positive changes on the side of citizens, they are still novel concepts for citizens to grasp and actively use them. This presents a huge challenge from the point of educating consumers about consent and their rights. Another very important challenge is a design of the system that consumers would use to manage their privacy settings under these new laws. Currently, there is no universal template for privacy management and consent management systems. This subject is very complex as it encompasses multiple areas including consumer trust, user interface design, permission management, and technical system architecture.Therefore, opportunities emerge for services that can manage user consents in a centralized way and further research into these topics in the context of consent management system is required.

### 6.10.3  Case Study – BitsaboutMe Platform

Personal Information Management Services (PIMS) offer one central system from which users are able to manage their personal data and how interested parties can access it. PIMS is an emerging market, enabled by GDPR, and that mature PIMS market will be worth £16.5 billion (Ctrl Shift, 2014). However, PIMS model is at an early stage of development and because of it is still unexplored in terms of practical use and impact on the processing of personal data (European Data Protection Supervisor, 2016). Moreover, PIMS face significant challenges to become mainstream for personal data management in a market dominated by a small number of operators that may often not be interested in creating synergies with them. It concludes that effective and user-friendly mechanisms would be needed for providing or withdrawing consent, keeping users data accurate and up-to-date, and exercising other data and privacy rights enabled by GDPR. Standardization of how personal information management systems should look like, which vocabulary should be used in them, which elements ought to be present and which other measures could be taken in order to ease user transition to a new paradigm of data and privacy control.

BitsaboutMe AG is a startup company located in Bern, Switzerland that offers its users personal information management services. The BitsaboutMe's PIMS solution is

based on three components: Personal Data Storage (PDS) for individuals to store encrypted data and information provided by third parties and themselves; a Personal Data
Marketplace (PDM) to which users can send some of their data so that such data can
be requested by third parties; and a Consent Management System (CMS) which is how
users can choose what sort of data requests they see and whether or not they consent to a
given data request, thus allowing third parties to read that data from the PDM. A consent
request can include a specific monetary reward that will act as an incentive for citizens'
to accept. BitsaboutMe does not own the data, and collects commission of typically 20%
on successful data trades. In addition BitsaboutMe provides a Salesforce integration App
for third parties to easily participate in Personal Data Marketplace.

The CMS requires that consent requests categorize the type of data they are requesting, what type of processing will take place on the data, for what purpose the data request
will be made, and the duration of the data access requested. When participating in the
marketplace, citizens enter their privacy settings or preferences: they select which data
types are offered on the marketplace, and for which purposes and processing they can
be requested. It is stated in BitsaboutMe AG's terms of service that user owns the data
and is the only one who can access it, while BitsaboutMe AG is offering a mechanism
to connect interested third parties with citizens that might be willing to sell their data.
Management of consent requests and consent receipts is now a critical feature for such
a product, because of the obvious need to provide users with a user interface to manage
incoming consent requests (offers), and revoke the consent if they would like to do so.
This consent management system needs to be in line with GDPR, and since this has not
been done before, there are no guidelines on how to proceed with designing it.

### 6.10.4   Consent Management System

Consent management system (CMS) is a system that enables users to manage access
to their personal data by interested entities and must be compliant with GDPR privacy
protection directive. The CMS that was designed for BitsaboutMe AG consists of several
parts related to new offers, overview, reports, marketplace settings, and consent request.

**New offers** is a page for users to see consent requests that they still have not made
any decision on. Requests shown on this page would be in line with users' marketplace
settings – for example which data users are willing to give consent to use, or for which
purpose. These are essentially filters, and can be found on "Marketplace settings" page,
along with the complete list of possible categories on which filters can be applied.

**Overview** page is a place that enables users to manage the consent requests that
they have made a decision on in the past. This means that users will be presented with
a history of accepted or declined consent requests on this page, from where, by clicking
on the chosen request, can reevaluate it and reverse their decision on it. That means that
accepted requests, where users have given their consents in the past, can be revoked
at later stage. For declined consent requests, users can go back to those requests and
change their decision, accepting them. As required in GDPR, revoking one's consent
is as easy and uncomplicated as giving consent. Beside providing users with a basic
overview of accepted, declined and revoked consents, users should also be able to see

more advanced information, like exact time and date when the decision was made and how much money or other rewards they earned from that consent request.

**Reports** page lists all accesses to users' personal data by entities to whom the consent was given to. Entries in the list are kept simple, presenting only the most necessary information: logo of the company; time and date when the entity accessed the data and how much did the user profit from that access (based on the reward that was agreed upon in the consent request); icon representing which of the categories of personal data was accessed.

**Marketplace settings** is a part of the CMS where users can control their participation on the data marketplace, in particular, to choose which consent requests to receive, to stop or start participating in the marketplace. Settings that users can adjust are the following: participation on the personal data marketplace; filters for incoming consent requests based on personal data being requested (personal information, demographic information, interests and behaviors); filters for incoming consent requests based on purpose for processing; filters for incoming consent requests based on processing type performed; filters based on personal data being requested in a consent request can be adjusted for each piece of personal data that users have entered in the system or system holds about them (see Figures 6.10, 6.11).

**Consent requests** are handling incoming requests for users' consent to use their personal data. Consent as a lawful basis for processing personal data has been introduced and defined with GDPR and while the legal framework is outlined, the very specifics of how the request is going to be presented to users is not defined in the legal text. This was an obvious problem that had to be solved. After researching the literature and competitive solutions, a certain structure and elements were selected as essential, and described with an example displayed on Figure 6.9. There are marked sections of the consent request. Section marked with (1) is the creative picture, supposed to attract users to consider the consent request and is supposed to visually be related to the offer. Section marked with (2) is the logo of the entity requesting the consent. It is included in the design because people are used to seeing logos and associating them with brands they are representing, their trustworthiness and public image. The idea is to invoke the established feelings about the company and then hopefully the user will be willing to read what the company is requesting from them and offers in return. Section marked with (3) is a placeholder for rating of that consent request. The rating would be given by any user on the marketplace, and would rate the quality of that consent request. There are no guidelines on what is supposed to be considered when giving the rating, but would let users to rate the consent request on based on their own preferences. For example, it could be if the amount of data requested is large, for the purpose that may be considered too invasive for the sensitivities of the citizen but the reward is not appropriate, rating for that consent request could be low and vice versa. If the offered reward is relatively high to what of personal data is being asked in return, that consent request would be rated favorably.

Another parameter that is expected to be of significant impact to the rating is the public opinion of that company. For example, if the company recently had data breach, that would also reflect negatively on their rating. Rating system is expected to be a very effective way of persuading companies to offer high quality consent requests, because

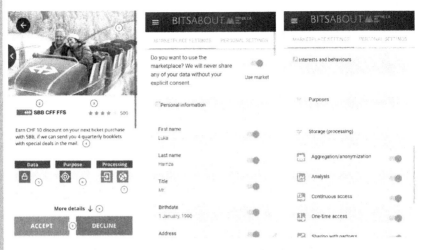

**Fig. 6.9:** Consent request.    **Fig. 6.10:** Marketplace settings (1).    **Fig. 6.11:** Marketplace settings (2).

otherwise their public image would deteriorate. Section marked with (4) is a brief textual description of the consent request, what is being asked from users, for which purpose, and what the reward would be. This is supposed to be a very informative marketing line, used to attract the users to consider the consent request laid before them. It is supposed to be short, no longer than 4 lines of text when viewed on a typical mobile phone. If the text was any longer, it could not be guaranteed that sections (5), (6) and (7) would be initially visible when the page loads on a typical phone.

Sections marked (5), (6) and (7) are symbolic (icon) representations of consent dimensions designed to transfer information about key questions that have to be answered in order to have an informed consent by law: which personal data is being used, for which purpose and how it is going to be processed. Section marked with (8) is a downward facing arrow, used to indicate that more information can be found on the page below. Section marked with (9) contains two buttons, "Accept" and "Decline", used to accept or decline that particular consent request. After making a decision about the particular consent request by clicking one of the buttons, user will be redirected to the page from which they came from.

## 6.10.5   Lessons Learned

Two evaluations on the implemented CMS were performed, in particular, the evaluation of citizens' acceptance and perceptions of the consent management system (tested on 17 subjects). Additional user study was conducted to determine the needs of current and potential users of BitsaboutMe platform (involved 80 subjects). Based on the questionnaire responses, the results of the first study showed that testers were able to understand the concept of personal data marketplace and use CMS in accordance to their needs. Overall, the system was considered to be easy to use and with adequate explanations. However, not all visual elements were considered to contribute to the general understanding of the new concepts and were, based on the opinion of some testers, harming the appeal of the website. Therefore, the interface of the system can still be improved by using less icons and changing the design of some. Being the foundation of the CMS, control and transparency traits are of particular importance. In 41.1% of responses, testers were indifferent about the level of control, transparency and the trust that they have in the system. As users are supposed to trust the system with their personal data, it is important to find the ways to incite trust in users. Therefore, further detailed research would be needed to improve this aspect of the system. A general idea of managing personal data from one place was well accepted, and most of the testers agreed that reward is the biggest incentive for using a CMS.

The survey of the second study showed that most survey participants are already BitsaboutMe users. The majority of them are globally satisfied with BitsaboutMe in terms of design, instructions, data import, user-friendliness and features of the platform. This may imply that registered users log in to their BitsaboutMe account only sporadically. To conclude, consent management system presented in this case study can be considered as a good starting point for further development. Testers could grasp new concepts of consent management system easily and could associate purpose and reason for using it. The implemented system showed weaknesses when performing advanced actions that needed previous knowledge of the system. This means that more complicated ideas present in the consent management systems need better explanation or completely different design that would be better suited to the non-technical user mental model.

## Further Readings

- Ctrl Shift (2014). Personal Information Management Services: An analysis of an emerging market. Accessed 14-09-2018, from `https://www.ctrl-shift.co.uk/insights/2014/06/16/personal-information-management-services-an-analysis-of-an-emerging-market/`

- European Data Protection Supervisor (2016). EDPS Opinion on Personal Information Management Systems. Accessed 14-09-2018, from `https://edps.europa.eu/sites/edp/files/publication/16-10-20_pims_opinion_en.pdf`

- Intersoft consulting (2016). General Data Protection Regulation. Accessed 14-09-2018, from `https://gdpr-info.eu/`

- The European Parliament and the Council of the European Union (1995). Directive 95/46/EC. Accessed 14-09-2018, from`https://eur-lex.europa.eu/legal-content/EN/ALL/?uri=CELEX:31995L0046`

- L. Hamza (2018). Consent Management System for A Personal Data Marketplace: Case of Bitsabout.me. Master's thesis, University of Fribourg, Switzerland.

- A. Kaskina (2018). Fuzzy-Based User Privacy Framework and Recommender System: Case of a Platform for Political Participation. PhD thesis, University of Fribourg.

- A. Kaskina (2018). Exploring nuances of user privacy preferences on a platform for political participation. In eDemocracy & eGovernment (ICEDEG), 2018 International Conference on (pp. 89-94). IEEE.

## Contact Details

BitsaboutMe AG, Bollwerk 4
3011 Bern, Switzerland
Internet: https://bitsabout.me/en/about/team/
eMail info@bitsabout.me

## Profile of Authors

### Christian Kunz

Cofounder & CEO, is a web veteran and data enthusiast. He is convinced that only user centric data models can protect privacy and guarantee that consumers get a fair share of the value generated from their data. He holds a Ph.D. in Nuclear Physics from MIT and has spent his corporate career with McKinsey & Company, at eBay where he was responsible for the global advertising business and most recently as CEO of ricardo.ch.

### Luka Hamza

He accomplished his Master in Computer Science at University of Fribourg. His Master thesis titled "Consent management system for a Personal Data Marketplace: Case of BitsaboutMe" studies how the legal text of GDPR can be translated into easy to understand consumer rules based on which a standardized framework for consent management systems can be created.

### Andreas Meier

He is a professor of computer science at the business of economic and social science faculty of the University of Fribourg. His research areas include eBusiness, eGovernment and information management. After music studies in Vienna, he graduated in mathematics at the ETH in Zurich, doctorate and his habilitation at the Institute for computer science. He conducted research at the IBM Research Lab in California, a systems engineer at IBM Switzerland. He was director of the UBS bank and executive member of the CSS insurance.

### Aigul Kaskina

She is a PhD student at the Information System Research Group, University of Fribourg. In 2010, she finished a M.Sc. in Computer Science at the Oxford Brookes University, Oxford, UK. In 2009, she obtained a B.Sc. in Computer Science from Aktobe Regional State University, Aktobe, Kazakhstan. Her research focuses on privacy, recommender systems and fuzzy logic.

# Chapter 7

# eCollaboration

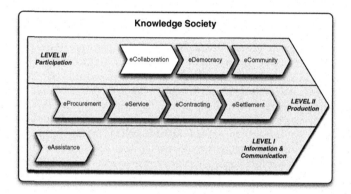

Chapter 7 describes important procedures and systems for computer-aided collaboration. Section 7.1 analyses the components of a Web-based information system and deals
with document administration. The architecture of a content management system is the
topic of Sect. 7.2. Section 7.3 discusses the use of wiki tools in the eGovernment. Weblogs
are in the cross-hairs of communication media; their application in the administration
is discussed in Sect. Sect. 7.4. Group-ware systems in Sect. 7.5 are technically mature
products for information exchange, work-flow control, collaboration, and data management. Depending on the complexity of the services, the administrative units must rethink
their organization (Sect. 7.6). Section 7.7 contains bibliographical notes. The case study
about virtual campus is brought in by the distance teaching University of Hagen, in
which over 50,000 students of the areas culture and social studies, computer science,
business administration, and law are registered. Additionally, a second case study about
the implementation of accessibility in Massive Open Online Courses, is presented.

© Springer Nature Switzerland AG 2019
A. Meier, L. Terán, *eDemocracy & eGovernment*, Progress in IS,
https://doi.org/10.1007/978-3-030-17585-6_7

## 7.1   Document Management

*Web-based*
*information*
*systems on the*
*advance*

The World Wide Web (WWW or Web) has undergone a fast-paced development over the past years. More and more, the information and database systems are embedded into the Web in order to make the respective information accessible to both open and closed user groups. Apart from that, it is attempted to include the existing information systems with the help of database and application servers.

*Information*
*exchange and*
*relationship*
*management*

In a Web-based information system, important documents and information are put at disposal online. Such systems not only serve to exchange information, but they are also used to maintain relations with the citizens (citizen relationship management, see Chap. 9) and for handling electronic services. Apart from that, it is more and more common to organize offerings, forms, contract agreements, distribution, and payments online, mostly as part of the value creation chain between administrative units, with the suppliers (supply chain management) and more and more with the citizens (see electronic governmental services in Sect. 4.2 and electronic votes and elections in Sect. 8.3).

*Gross*
*architecture of*
*Web-based*
*information*
*systems*

In Fig. 7.1, the gross architecture of a Web-based information system is depicted schematically. Its main element is the WWW server, which provides information in hypertext documents over a communication protocol (HTTP = Hyper Text Transfer Protocol). Such documents are mainly composed in HTML language (Hyper Text Markup Language) or in the continuative XML (eXtensible Markup Language).

Normally, it is possible to access the information provided by the WWW server around the clock, and from anywhere. The precondition for that is a device (client) with a WWW browser. Such devices do not have to be stationary, but can be used when on the move, for example, laptops, palms, eBooks, mobile phones, or digital assistants.

*Dynamical*
*document*
*generation*

The hypertext documents are located either statically in the file system of the WWW server, or are generated dynamically by the server when accessed by a user. There are numerous methods and techniques available for dynamical document generation. Nor-

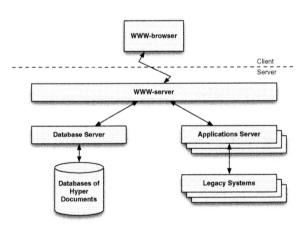

**Fig. 7.1:** Components of a web-based information system.

mally, the information needed for document generation is located on the database server. Apart from that, data can be retrieved from existing information systems (legacy systems) with the help of special interfaces. The so-called application servers process incoming assignments and fall back to the database server or the existing information systems, as well.

The operators of Web-based information systems or Web sites are confronted with an enormous amount of hypertext documents. For this reason, they utilize database servers in order to store hypertext documents permanently. A forward-looking storage option is to manage the semi-structured data in XML databases. We will take a closer look at this approach. The markup language XML (eXtensible Markup Language) was developed by the World Wide Web Consortium (W3C). The contents of hypertext documents are marked with tags, just like in HTML. An XML document is self-descriptive, as it contains not only the actual data, but also information on the data structure:

```
<Address>
<Street> Boulevard de Pérolles </Street>
      <Number> 90 </Number>
      <Postcode> 1700 </Postcode>
      <City> Fribourg </City>
 </Address>
```

The basic modules of XML documents are the so-called elements. They consist of a start tag (in angle brackets <Start>) and an end tag (in angle brackets with slash </End>), embracing the content of the element. The identifier of the start and end tag must coincide. *XML documents*

The tags give information on the meaning of particular values, thereby revealing something about the data structure. The elements can be nested arbitrarily in XML documents. In order to illustrate such hierarchically structured documents, a very useful graph is utilized; Fig. 7.2 gives an example.

Figure 7.2 shows a fragment of an XML document, namely the description, post address and Web site of an organizational unit. As can be seen here, the XML documents contain implicit information on the structure of the document. As it is important for many applications to know the structure of the XML documents, explicit types of display (DTD = Document Type Definition or XML Schema) have been proposed by the W3C. An explicit schema determines which tags occur in the XML document and how they are arranged. This allows locating and repairing errors in XML documents, among other things. *Example of an XML document*

Different XML editors have been developed, which are able to display the XML document or the XML Schema graphically. These editors can be utilized both for the declaration of structural characteristics and for entering the data content. As the different parts of the structure can be shown or hidden, comprehensive XML documents or XML Schemas can be arranged clearly. *Use of XML editors*

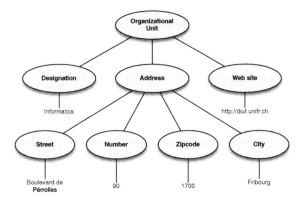

**Fig. 7.2:** Representation of an XML document fragment.

*XQuery*
*language* It is of interest to analyze XML documents or XML databases. In contrast to traditional query languages, the selection conditions are not only tied to values (value selection), but also to element structures (structure selection). To that end, the W3C proposed XQuery, influenced by SQL (Structured Query Language), different XML languages and object-oriented query languages.

## 7.2   Content Management

*Tasks of the*
*content*
*management*
By content, we understand preprocessed digital information (text, graphics, images, audio, video, etc.), which is put at disposal on the Internet or intranet in different forms of display. The content management aims at planning and coordinating all activities for the supply and use of content. To that end, an architecture with appropriate software components must be built and maintained (see Fig. 7.3).

*Information*
*supply*
Contents are procured externally by information brokers in digital form, e.g. traffic news, update on public projects or information on votes and elections (see Chap. 8). Specialized providers offer not only content, but also services related to it. In most cases, the structured contents are captured with the ICE protocol (Information and Content Exchange) and exchanged; this protocol is based on XML and offers exchanges formats and technically mature subscription services.

Apart from external procurement of structured content, internal content editing processes prepare data and documents. To that end, information objects with different attributes are created. It is necessary to describe the information objects with descriptors, so that they can be found and processed efficiently. The centerpiece of a content management system is the tool for describing and structuring content. These tools primarily draw on databases, which contain both structured data and arbitrary documents and multimedia objects.

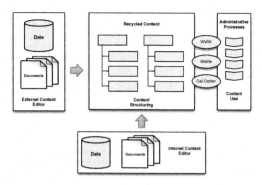

**Fig. 7.3:** Architecture of a content management system, according to Christ (2013).

The layout principle of content management systems is the separation of structure, content, and layout:

*Separation of structure, content and layout*

- **Structure:** The arrangement of individual content parts is determined independently. This regards the sequence of paragraphs, the placement of headlines or the positioning of images. The structural characteristics can be described hierarchically, which is why XML is used as markup language. It is of great practical interest to create structure templates for different application purposes. In order to display different contents with one and the same structural description, wildcards are shown with special tags.

- **Content:** The desired content is inserted at the places of structural description that where marked by the corresponding wildcards. For this reason, the contents are split into its individual elements (assets). The granularity of these assets varies from individual words, images, or reference lists to structured content sections. Editors assign an asset to each wildcard of the structural description, so that the same content can be used again in different structures. In public portals (see Sect. 2.4), e.g. different information offers and other services can be displayed with the same structure, but with different characteristic values.

- **Layout:** The layout of a document is specified by style sheets. These determine the rules for transforming the data into the desired output format.

Several communication channels combine the content management system with the diverse administrative processes. Apart from using the Internet as a communication channel, mobile devices and communication centers (see case study in Chap. 9) put the contents for processes in the administration at disposal. Depending on the degree of maturity of the content management system, workflow management systems are utilized.

Figure 7.4 shows the value creation chain of content applications in the administration. Contents of a governmental or administrative unit have a value, if citizens or companies and organizations request them. For that reason, it is necessary to provide

*Value creation chain*

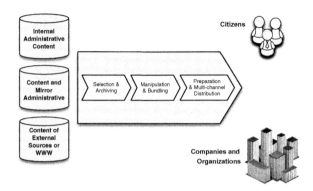

**Fig. 7.4:** Steps of the value creation chain in content applications.

qualitative content at the right time in a secure and efficient way for the respective target groups.

Sources from inside and outside of the administration are opened up and evaluated in a selection process, before storing them in a document or content management system. If needed, the content must be adapted to different user groups (households, citizens, adolescents, companies, organizations). In the third step, again supported by the content management system, the content is processed and allocated to the desired distribution channels and media.

*Using distribution channels*   By multi-channel or cross-channel publishing, we understand the process of putting at disposal identical raw content over different distribution channels (see Sect. 9.2), adapted to the capacity and display possibilities of the respective channels and devices. Once again, the main principle here is the strict separation of raw content, layout concerns and device-specific or media-specific characteristics. After choosing a particular channel and medium, the necessary meta-information is added and the distribution and layout is obtained.

## 7.3   Wiki Tools

*What is a wiki?*   Ward Cunningham calls his invention, the wiki,[1] "the simplest online database that could possibly work." With the help of the wiki tool, Internet users can create, edit and link individual entries to a topic or document easily and quickly. Furthermore, it is possible to add to other users' entries, change, or delete them. Apart from these editing functions, a wiki tool comes with a user administration, an option of notification for each change of content and log of changes. It is important that the users themselves do not need specific knowledge about the Internet or HTML.

For wiki applications, in most cases free software with a specific syntax is procured. In order to format and insert text, no more than simple control instructions are needed. The most important functions of wiki software systems are:

---

[1] The word wiki wiki means "quick, quick" in Hawaiian and aims to point out that wikis facilitate different users to edit entries quickly and easily.

| Topics | Potential Benefits | Opportunities and Risks |
|---|---|---|
| Project Management | • Project Manual<br>• Reviews<br>• Reporting<br>• Information Exchange | • Transparency<br>• Relevance<br>• Controlling<br>• Copyright |
| Employee Suggestion Sysmte | • Collection of Ideas<br>• Discussion Forums<br>• Reviews online | • Creativity and Exchange<br>• Motivation<br>• Access barriers<br>• Rewards |
| Document Management | • Protocols<br>• Manuals<br>• Reports | • Relevance<br>• Simplicity<br>• Quality |
| Product Development | • Participation<br>• Consultation<br>• Pretests | • Goal Conflicts<br>• Confidentiality<br>• Patent Protectio |
| Community Building | • Relationship Management<br>• Involvement<br>• Participation<br>• Creativity | • Leeway<br>• Emotions<br>• Interactivity |

**Fig. 7.5:** Possible uses of wiki applications in the administration.

- **Search function:** The automatic search for terms, headlines or text parts is supported by different retrieval functions.

- **Editing:** Every wiki comes with a change service. Only in exceptional cases, specific pages or headlines are excluded from the editing possibility.

- **Association:** With the help of links, entries can be connected to each other. This way, hypertext structures can be created or amplified.

- **Log:** Versions and changes of individual pages are kept in a log. This makes it possible to follow back the development of a document or working paper, if required. Specific history functions enable the user to open previous versions and, if needed, publish the original content. Furthermore, there are difference functions, which compare different versions of documents with each other.

- **Observation service:** With specific functions, it is possible to gain an overview over the last changes applied to a document, if needed restricted to a limited time frame. Change or observation lists are generated automatically and cannot be altered by the users.

Figure 7.5 lists important wiki applications for the administration. In its practical use, potential benefits and opportunities have to weigh against risks. Wiki applications appear suitable for the case that employees of the administration or citizens work together in a project, but are separated by time and place. Thanks to the simple and quick updating mechanisms for reports and results, all project members have the same information available. Apart from that, they are able to give their opinion anytime, and carry out improvements or changes to individual passages. Absences due to sickness or vacation have less influence on the work, if access barriers are kept low for all participants. Nevertheless, it has to be pointed out that it is more difficult to put into practice competence and responsibility in administrative projects. This is especially the case when realizing citizens' initiatives or projects that go beyond administration.

*Using wikis in project management*

*Problems in*
*application*

The biggest problems for the application of wiki tools are the following:

- **Copyright:** Different authors work on an electronic document or report at different times. It is difficult to verify or guarantee the author rights of individual text sections or entries.

- **Quality standards:** Normally, there is no one who answers for the completeness or correctness of a document. The quality of individual entries is hard to control.

Despite these flaws, wiki applications are becoming more and more accepted, especially as a replacement of elaborate Intranets. As it is possible to limit the group of users and to retrace the evolution of a document anytime, wiki applications are suitable for application inside administrations, and in specific cases as well beyond them.

## 7.4   Use of Weblogs

*Definition of*
*Weblogs*

A Weblog, or short blog, is a frequently updated digital journal, whose entries are displayed in a chronologically descending way. The editor (blogger) of a Weblog is either an individual person (private blog) or a group of people (corporate blog). A Weblog can be a textual or multimedia journal or its content can be a link collection dedicated to different matters and topics. Normally, the readers of a Weblog comment on the content.

*Weblogs are*
*situated between*
*push and pull*

According to Fig. 7.6, Weblogs can be situated between push and pull techniques (see Sect. 9.1). In a push medium like instant messaging (message transmission over the Internet) or e-mail, the communication flow is unidirectional, from sender to receiver. The sender "pushes" his content to the receiver, who, in same cases, cannot evade the reception (spam or bulk mailing of e-mails). In a pull medium like the WWW or discussion forums, the interested user must become active and "pull" the information out of the information offered.

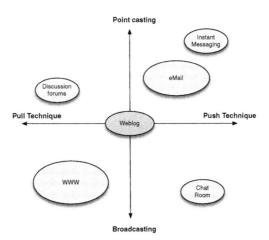

**Fig. 7.6:** Weblog in the cross-hairs of communication media, adapted from Picot & Fischer (2006).

Weblogs, e.g., have pull character, if the users put together their own news pages      *Use of RSS*
from existing Weblogs with the help of aggregators. As an example of a push alternative
serve the moblogs, which feed mobile devices like cellular phones or PDAs with content.
In most cases, Weblogs have a simple syndication with which other users can subscribe
to the Weblogs. Technologically speaking, this option is based on Really Simple Syndication (RSS) functions, which is available in most browsers for free. Users can put
together individual blogs in their news feeder with RSS. They are notified automatically
when new input appears in the Weblogs.

Figure 7.7 shows roughly the process for creating and using Weblogs. In Step 1, a      *Setup of Weblogs*
blogger opens his Web browser, goes to this Weblog system and creates a new entry.
If the blogger wants to publish his news, the Weblog system takes on his entries and
integrates them chronologically in the respective journal (Step 2a). At the same time,
the Weblog system updates the RSS feed in Step 2b, so that later on, RSS aggregators
can draw on the new input. Apart from that, during blogging, also ping servers (Packet
Internet Gopher) are utilized (Step 2c), in order to inform other pages about the updated
content. The occasional Internet user or surfer can get an overview on up-to-date topics
in Weblogs via search engines (Step 3). The search engines check the ping server on
a regular basis, so that they can index the Web sites of the updated Weblog in case of
changes. As a result, Weblogs get high page ranking in search engines because of their
topicality.

If an Internet user is interested in a certain topic over a long time, he uses an RSS      *Using RSS*
reader as another option (Step 4). With it, he can have several Weblogs checked for      *aggregators*
updated content. In fact, the RSS reader trawls the Weblog systems specified by the user
via RSS feeds and continuously informs about the updates.

As a third and most laborious option, the Internet user can trawl the interesting Weblog systems by himself (Step 5). In this case, he abandons the help of a search engine
or an aggregation function.

The possible uses in the eGovernment are versatile, because Weblogs can be used      *Risks with*
in and outside of administrations, both as push and pull medium. Nevertheless, the risks      *Weblogs*
for individual application areas must be discussed and weighed beforehand:

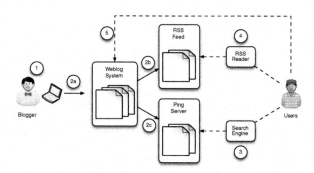

**Fig. 7.7:** Functioning of Weblogs, adapted from Przepiorka (2006).

- **Copyright:** In Weblogs, external Web sites are cited and external content is reused. Additionally, the user's entries are commented by bloggers and newly put together for their own purposes. This way, networked hypertext documents are generated, created by different authors and stored on different servers. It is, therefore, difficult to verify or protect the copyright in each case.

- **Subjectivity:** The Weblogs usually divulge personal estimations and opinions. Actual facts are rare and often only found through further links. Comments and estimations are subjective and only in rare cases can be utilized to acquire knowledge or to get objective news.

- **Privacy:** Blogger comment on certain topics quickly and from a personal point of view. With modern search engines and RSS options, it is possible to create personal and behavioral profiles of these authors. These profiles can be misused in situations like job applications, political or administrative elections and promotions.

*Advantages of Weblogs*    Next to risks and dangers, Weblogs have advantages for the administrative work, too. Weblogs inform quickly and inexpensively, because with the linking of constantly updated content, the so-called news tickers are created and operated. Trends and estimations can be discussed and commented early in the communities, which is applied directly by members of the administration in different phases of the project. Thanks to the independence of time and place, the administrative units are more involved into the opinion-forming process in geographically less accessible regions.

## 7.5   Collaborative Working Environment

*Computer supported cooperative work*    For efficiency of organizations and administrative units, computer-supported coordination, cooperation and communication are more and more important. Software systems for computer supported cooperative work (CSCW), often called groupware, support members of administrative units and, increasingly, also citizens independently of time and place, in order to reach the goals of common projects.

*Differentiation of groupware*    The terms computer supported cooperative work or computer supported collaborative work stem from a scientific field with representatives of information management, occupational psychology and organizational studies. Its purpose is to increase effectiveness and efficiency with the help of computer supported information and communication systems. There are a lot of possible applications for groupware, as can be seen in Fig. 7.8.

The type of interaction can be distinguished in a temporal or local dimension, depending on whether the participants collaborate in the same or different places, or at the same or different times. Empirical studies show that using groupware can ease critical factors of teamwork. The following factors are important:

- In the process of coming up with ideas or brainstorming, uniformity in the group should be prevented, for instance by asking for anonymous input or by controlling the participation in order to prevent individual group members to dominate the discussion.

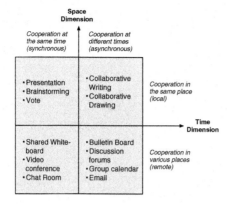

**Fig. 7.8:** Groupware supports different kinds of collaboration.

- The high expenditure of time for group decisions and project results can be lowered by creating sub-groups or parallel activities.

- In order to achieve agreements more quickly and to avoid risky decisions, a transparent information policy should be aimed at.

- Publishing partial results and laying open timetables and status reports increases the motivation of the group members and constitute a strong controlling instrument.

A group work comprises the sum of all task-related activities that have the purpose to reach the project goal and accomplish a final result or product of high quality. The group processes needed for that purpose could be divided into processes of communication, coordination and cooperation. The necessary supporting technology functions are listed in Fig. 7.9. According to Fig. 7.9, groupware systems include different system components, that can be classified as follows:

- **System Class 1—information exchange:** It is one of the central tasks of groupware to support the communication. It is distinguished between textual communication, audio communication (hearing) and video communication (hearing and seeing). Therefore, system Class 1 comprises e-mail systems, conference systems for audio and video and bulletin board systems.

- **System Class 2—process controlling:** A workflow is a chain of activities, which is started, changed and ended by incidents. Its processes have work-sharing character, involving different protagonists and organizational units. A workflow management system makes it possible to model the processes, simulate, optimize, control, and take minutes (quantity structure, throughput time, standby time). Apart from process control, workflow management systems come with data storage components and notifications functions.

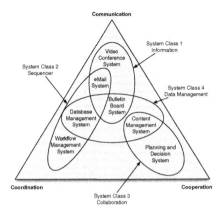

**Fig. 7.9:** Supporting technology for group work, according to Bauknecht et al. (1995).

- **System Class 3—collaboration:** The core of groupware systems consists in supporting functions for the actual group work. An important factor is the cooperation of group members in tasks, which are characterized by low structural complexity and low repetition frequencies. Therefore, this system class contains systems for schedule administration and planning, agreement components, group editors, software for support of meetings and decision-finding systems.

- **System Class 4—data management:** This class manages data and documents and disposes of suitable access mechanisms and interpretation components (information retrieval). The class comprises database systems, document systems, hypertext administration systems or content management systems and bulletin board systems. An important aspect is that the users of groupware must be able to process and update the information stock or documents at the same time, without causing a conflict by this multiple-user operation.

Groupware systems allow different administration members to carry out processes and activities independently of time and space in different organizational units effectively and efficiently.

## 7.6   Virtual Organization and Forms of Cooperation

*Changes in*
*organization*
Organizations and administrative units are undergoing a change due to market alterations and social developments. The following changes can be observed:

- **Process orientation:** Citizen expect service-oriented actions from the administrative units. The latter are requested to rethink their processes and services and to lay more stress on the management of administrative processes.

- **Dissolving functionally defined limits within the organization:** Due to the above mentioned process orientation, and the decentralization of administrative

tasks, traditional organizational units are dissolved. The use of groupware systems allows overcoming the local and temporal distance in the changed workflow
and services.

- **More cooperation projects and outsourcing of administrative tasks:** Limits
  are altered not only within the administration, but also beyond individual administrative units (New Public Management, see Sect. 10.1). As a consequence, administrative units search horizontally and vertically for new forms of collaboration or
  outsource parts of their line of activity.

These changes result in administrative units reorganizing themselves. Figure 7.10     *Change*
illustrates four different options, depending on the complexity of the service and the     *Management*
dimension of the economical and social change.

Modularization means to restructure organizations with the goal of integrated and     *Restructuring*
clear administrative units (modules). Decentralized decision-making authorities and ser-     *organizations*
vice responsibility characterize modular administrative units. The coordination between
administrative units more and more has a non-hierarchical character. The main interests
are transparent and citizen-friendly services and processes, also past service hours.

A virtual organization has the potential of traditional organizations, while lacking     *Potential of*
a comparable institutional background at the same time. Such an organization appears     *virtual*
as an "as-if organization." In their possibilities, virtual organizations surpass reality and     *organizations*
dissolve internal and external barriers of the organization. Virtual organizations optimize
their added value and try to be of great benefit for the citizens.

Normally, virtual organizations agree to temporally limited, network-like partnerships. Based on a culture of mutual trust and the task they have in common, the cooperation partners (administrative institutions, NPOs, NGOs, companies, expert teams,
individual persons) put their core competence at disposal. The constituent characteristics
of virtual organizations are:

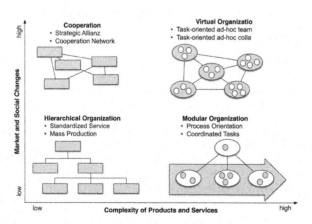

**Fig. 7.10:** Strategies of organizational development.

- **Voluntary cooperation of several independent network partners:** The fusion of organizations to a virtual organization network is voluntary and requires that the individual group members and management body trust each other.

- **Common goal:** Every virtual organization formulates a common organizational goal and comes to an agreement regarding task sharing and collaboration.

- **Bundling of core competences:** Virtual organizations try to obtain the required expertise through their network partners.

- **Utilization of information and communication technology:** Virtual organizations consequently use the possibility of electronic communication and the electronic exchange of service, for example, by running a collaborative portal. Such a platform is needed for information, communication and handling of projects of the virtual organization.

The mentioned characteristics of virtual organizations differ in some cases from the characteristics of traditional forms of alliances (see Fig. 7.10). For instance, strategic alliances have the intention to cooperate for an unlimited time span, and therefore have little flexibility to exchange partners.

*Fractal organizations*    Other alternatives for building organizations are fractal organizations and outsourcing task areas to third parties. Fractals are self-organizations in which the administration members aim for self-regulation, self-determination and self-administration in groups. Fractal organizations normally do not bundle their competences with third parties.

*Outsourcing*    In outsourcing, on the other hand, there are long-term commitments to selected partners, in order to source out integral parts of the organization. For example, administrative units delegate task areas or services to a non-profit organization, non-governmental organization, or private companies.

## 7.7    Bibliographical Notes

*Literature on New Public Management*    Administrative and governmental units have launched different projects to increase their efficiency. Under the headline of New Public Management (Schedler & Proeller (2000); Norbert & Adrian (2006)), all tasks and duties were examined closely and adapted more accurately to the needs of an information and knowledge society. The goal is to try to carry out corresponding reforms of the administration and programs to modernize the state.

*Literature on different software systems*    An important subarea of the eGovernment is the use of information and communication techniques for an improved collaboration between the administrative units and beyond them. An important aspect of this are document management systems (Götzer et al. (2004); Limper (2001); Meier (2010)), content management systems (Büchner, 2001), workflow management systems (Gadatsch (2013); Jablonski et al. (1997)) and groupware systems (Borghoff & Schlichter (1998); Schwabe et al. (2012); Bauknecht et al. (1995)).

*Web 2.0 and social software*    Enhancements under the headline of Web 2.0 (Beck, 2007) and social software (Hildebrand & Hofmann (2006); Szugat et al. (2006)) have great influence on the forms of collaboration. Wiki tools (Picot & Fischer (2006); Przepiorka (2006); Richardson (2010)) constitute a possibility to take minutes of recent findings and results in the Internet without much trouble. For online communication (Misoch, 2006), Weblogs (Picot & Fischer (2006); Przepiorka (2006); Richardson (2010)) are adequate instruments, among others, as they allow push and pull mechanisms.

The changes in society and the increasing complexity have consequences for the organization of the administration. It is highly recommendable to consider virtual forms of organization (Gora & Bauer (2013); Warnecke (2013); Wüthrich et al. (1997)) and to evaluate shared forms of work and organizations (Reichwald et al., 2013), especially if the administration wants to use Web-based technologies (Picot & Quadt, 2001).

*Literature on virtual organizations*

## 7.8   Case Study—Learning Environment Virtual Campus at the University of Hagen

Birgit Feldmann
M.A.,

*University of Hagen*

### 7.8.1   Background

The University of in Hagen is the first and only public distance university in the German higher education area and constitutes a real alternative to on-campus programs, including full-fledged university degrees (bachelor, master, German Diploma, and doctorate) in the areas of cultural sciences, social sciences, computer science, business studies and law. At the moment, about 50,000 students are enrolled at the University of Hagen. With typical issues of distance teaching in mind, like isolation, motivational problems, lack of communication possibilities, eLearning became a topic at the University very early. In 1996, the subject area of information systems and databases, headed by Professor Dr. Gunter Schlageter, designed and developed the first German virtual university.

The purpose of the project was, and still is today, to develop and test scenarios, applications and tools for eLearning: Aiming for temporally and locally independent learning that is flexible, customized and demand-oriented, through consequent use of new media (multimedia and communication technologies). The students with their individual needs are the main concern. The functionalities answer to the actual requirements and not the organizational build-up of a university. Although the projected started at the Faculty of Mathematics and Computer Science, it has always been open to other faculties. In the year of 2001, the project of a virtual university passed from project status to regular operation and was completely revised in 2004. More than 70,000 users up to today demonstrate the success of the system. Since the virtual university was launched, several 1,000 different courses have taken place. The experiences are mostly positive.

### 7.8.2   Case Study—Characteristics of a Virtual Campus

The build-up and structure of the virtual university have not changed much in the first 5 years. The biggest changes took place on a technical level; apart from that, the interface for lecturers was thoroughly revised due to altered requirements, until the current platform "Lernraum Virtuelle Universiät" (Learning Environment Virtual University) took up operation in 2004 (see Fig. 7.11). Today, the Learning Environment Virtual University permits the students to participate in the following activities:

- Access to its courses and news overview

- Re-enrollment and reservation of courses

- The possibility to change the address, telephone number, e-mail address, and password registered at the University

- Attribution to a center of studies and access to the contact lists

Apart from that, the students can also use groupware, access newsgroups and submit their assignments with the help of an electronic exercise system.

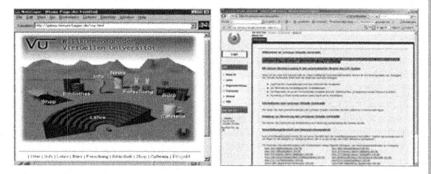

**Fig. 7.11:** The virtual university in 1996 and today.

### 7.8.3   Changes in Learning and Teaching

The majority of students consider the intensity of contacts and discussions reasonable. The evaluation of Web-based learning and working groups obtained similar results. Another trend is the decrease of course dropouts. For example, the number of people who dropped out of virtual seminars is significantly lower than in comparable face-to-face classes (see literature under Feldmann 2003, 2006).

Changes are not limited to the students, also the lecturers experience some changes. Their role is increasingly changing from a mere provider of teaching material to a counselor, supervisor and learning manager. More than in the traditional distance and on-campus teaching, it is now the task of the lecturers to organize the learning process and support the learners actively. Induced by this structural change in the lecturers' profile, a variety of problems come up. The acceptance of the virtual platform is still tainted with prejudices. Advantages are not always recognized and excess work is feared. A consequent support by the head of the university and the faculties might help in this area, as well as help offers for newcomers and the sensitive handling of skeptics.

### 7.8.4   Communication and Interaction

The virtual university bundles existing Web supported alternatives for communication and cooperation, and combines them with the teaching material. Parting from the teaching material, thus, a comprehensive discussion may be started. By including the library, the research process is facilitated; in a trial mode called Web Assign, the student can practice online to submit tasks, trace the correction status (tracking) and, finally, archive the revised task and sample solutions.

Our experiences show that students prefer asynchronous means of communication like e-mail and newsgroup by far, and out of the synchronous means of communications, audio conferences are most popular. This is mainly because asynchronous media are independent of time and place, and because all text based means of communication are easy to handle, whether synchronous or asynchronous. The textual chat, most popular in the first few years, has now taken a back seat and is mainly used just to solve problems of the audio channel.

The bundling and linking of network supported communication and cooperation alternatives with the teaching material roused concerns about a capacity overload in supervision. Many lecturers expect a multitude of personal requests of all kind. It is assumed that the inhibition threshold is significantly lower in electronic communication media than in conventional ones. Experience shows, nevertheless, that the students actually do not approach the supervisor directly, but rather ask fellow students for help. Apart from that, it is important to organize and delegate communication, if needed, for example point out FAQs or newsgroups to students. Discipline in communication is decisive for eLearning supervisors.

### 7.8.5   Cooperation

In virtual seminars, practical trainings and project groups, the students learn to work together on a topic or a task, process the results, publish them on the Internet and discuss them together. This way, it becomes possible for the first time to obtain a continuous communication and discussion process for both supervisors and students. Supervisors and students have the possibility to observe the students' work process and their results. This starts with the joint choice of the topic and the formation of learning groups, up to collaborative elaboration and discussion of the seminar work.

The discussions may take place simultaneously (i.e., by chat or video conference) or time-delayed (newsgroup, groupware). Typically, students prefer the more independent asynchronic techniques of communication, but nowadays enjoy the advantage of fast audio communication via Skype or Teamspeak, also. The most frequently used tools for this type of courses are: Moodle, CURE, BSCW, Skype, Adobe Connect, Teamspeak.[2] Even students at on-campus universities who take classes at the University of Hagen, feel better cared for in virtual seminars at the University of Hagen (see literature under Feldmann 2003).

### 7.8.6   Exams and Examination Regulations

Like at any other university, at the University of Hagen, too, exams have to be conducted. In contrast to traditional on-campus universities, the distance students do not necessarily have to travel to Hagen to take the exams. Written exams are held at chosen locations in Germany, Austria, and Switzerland, mainly on Saturdays or evenings, so that all students should have the possibility to come to the exam. In non-German speaking foreign countries, it exists the possibility to take the written exam in Goethe institutes or in the German embassy. Inmates of correctional facilities usually write their exams on site and are supervised by the local personnel.

---

[2]References in order of mention: `http://www.moodle.de`, `http://www.pi6.fernuni -hagen.de/CURE/`, `http://www.bscw.de/`, `http://skype.de`, `http://www.adobe -connect.de/`, `http://www.goteamspeak.com/`
More information on teaching with scenarios can be found at: `http://www.fernuni-hagen.de/ arbeiten/lehren/lehrepraktisch/szenarien_index.shtml`

For oral exams, the students either come to Hagen to meet with their examiner or they take the opportunity of videoconference exams, which is offered by most faculties by now. In this case, interested students contact their nearest study center, make an appointment and take the exam with their Hagen professor, while being monitored by the employees of the center (who are also in charge of verifying the identity). Abroad, this is possible in the German embassy or in other cooperating institutions. In special cases, the examination office helps students with residence abroad to find a suitable solution. Exams via home computers still fail for reasons of either laborious or expensive identity verifications or the problematic monitoring in order to prevent students to get personal or technological help.

### 7.8.7   Supervision Relationship

Students find suitable contact persons for all problems related to distance studies in the info area or in one of the numerous newsgroups. There already existed counseling offers on the Internet before the introduction of the University of Hagen, but only when the different offers where bundled, the number of users went up. The students themselves state the quality of supervision has improved and wish that the platform be further developed.

In qualified supervision, there must be a fun factor. Thus, lecturers experience that their work gains a new quality, too. Although there is a certain effort necessary to become acquainted with the system, it is sure that the day-to-day workload is reduced significantly afterwards. The intensive contact permits to get to know better the other person. Lecturers have vastly improved possibilities to offer help and support, to intervene into the development process, recognize misguided developments and, above all, to prevent them. Instead of being confronted with the debacle at the end, they can exert influence during the most important phases of the learning development. This of course has an effect on the quality of the results. Multiple corrections and revisions are daily routine. This means that the actual end product (whether submitted assignments, term papers or practical training assignments) is usually of higher quality than in traditional distance teaching, and sometimes even than in on-campus teaching. As a consequence, the use of the learning platform leads to more job satisfaction, which has positive consequences.

It was possible to partly counteract basic problems of distance teaching, like isolation or motivation issues, by the use of eLearning. The students are involved more than before into "their" university.

### 7.8.8   Changes in the Organization

Apart from students and lecturers, one of the biggest groups within the university organization is often neglected, namely the university administration. Next to tasks of management and leadership, it is responsible for students' affairs like enrollment, re-enrollment, subject counseling, exams, etc. In the center for media and information technology, all data is handled. The logistics center takes on printing and sending of university mail and other necessary print material. At first, administrative procedures were not included at all into the virtual university, or very little so. Bit by bit, though, the concerned departments requested more participation and succeeded thanks to the support of project and university directors.

The Rectorate of the University of Hagen realized at an early stage that, in order to persist in a changing academic landscape, innovative structural changes were necessary. With the help of the initiative Learning Environment Virtual University, a coordinating institution that works beyond faculty boundaries, it was possible to coordinate the different developments in the area of eLearning and to clear the way to a media university. Apart from that, proper resources of the university were used to further develop virtual learning, the results were bundled and synergy effects were obtained.

The extension and further development of eLearning services has become a regular part of the university tasks. Since 2001, the Center for Media and Information Technology runs the carrier system the Learning Environment Virtual University (since 2004 under regular operation in the revised version) and therefore has gained more tasks. Apart from operating the platform, this central office handles the support for lecturers. The latter can use the functions of the platform, and also groupware systems like BSCW or CURE (in-house development by the teaching area Cooperative Systems, directed by Professor Dr. J. Haake,[3]) for their courses. Today, moodle is offered and used for courses of all kind, just as audio conferences and (although not in regular operation yet) videoconferences like for example Adobe Connect.

The work of the study centers changes continuously. Mentors now can offer exercises independently from the location, they can maintain working material and make use of all possibilities of the offered platform themselves. The study centers will now, more than before, be able to offer counseling and supervision opportunities and provide technical infrastructure (i.e., for Internet access, video conferences, etc.). Mentors can be involved better into the organization and supervision of courses.

In the institute for Cooperative Systems, applications for the area of eGovernment are developed.[4] The original carrier system Virtual University is available as open source software at the CampusSource initiative of the state of North Rhine-Westphalia.[5]

## 7.8.9  Opportunities and Risks

A running eLearning platform should always be seen as a chance for further development. Precisely because of its widened use inside the organization, a further expansion of eLearning possibilities is necessary. The University of Hagen must not neglect current developments in the area of eLearning and especially the use of social software. There are no modern forms of communication and interaction like for example a proper community of the University of Hagen, the possibility to create student blogs, compile content actively, even and especially outside of limited course content. Contact lists and newsgroups are good and do work, but can and must not be the end of a promising development. The possibility to meet spontaneously and anytime in an audio or videoconference for collaboration purposes is, in our opinion, a vital part of modern eLearning institutions.

---

[3]http://www.pi6.fernuni-hagen.de/
[4]http://www.iks-hagen.de/
[5]http://www.campussource.org

There have been many positive developments on the lecturers' side, for example the content management system FUXML,[6] a powerful XML based content management system for generating and maintaining course material at the University of Hagen.

Although by now an Internet access is a precondition for the enrollment in a virtual university, apart from eLearning offers, traditional on-campus courses and text based material for self-study maintain their right to exist and keep being offered as part of a blended learning concept. Concerns that virtual communication and cooperation creates a certain lack of commitment, cannot be confirmed from our experience.

Despite all the advantages of eLearning, we recognize the danger of excluding people who are not "computer literate." Mostly elderly, handicapped and people with computer phobias or without Internet access unfortunately are often excluded. In student advisory service, we noticed that the active search for information and course content is problematic for many of our students, in spite of a multitude of help offers and step-by-step tutorials. While in the past, the information packet came conveniently to the mailbox, today, it is necessary to search actively for information or at least retrieve it. In this department, there is definitely still a need for actions.

The virtual university has accomplished to develop from a small initiative to a big movement within the university. It is a typical example for a learner-centered educational system of the future. Students, lecturers, directors, and administration have contributed to this successful development.

## Further Reading

- Feldmann, B., Schlageter, G.: Das verflixte (?) siebte Jahre - Sieben Jahre Virtuelle Universität. In: Kerres M, Voss B (ed) Digitaler Campus. Vom Medienprojekt zum nachhaltigen Medieneinsatz in der Hochschule. Medien in der Wissenschaft, vol. 24 (2003)

- Feldmann, B.: Group types in e-learning environments - study team, working team and learning team. Proceedings of the International Conference on Information Technology Based Higher Education and Training 2006, Sydney, Australia (2006)

- Schlageter, G.: E-learning in distance education - towards supporting the mobile learner. Proceedings of the international conference on information technology based higher education and training 2006, Sydney, Australia (2006)

## Contact Details

University of Hagen
Information Systems and Databases
D-58084 Hagen
Internet: http://www.isdb.fernuni-hagen.de
eMail: Birgit.Feldmann@fernuni-hagen.de

---

[6]XML based content management system for generating and maintaining course material at the University in Hagen. Currently, a print and a (barrier free) web version are implemented (cross media publishing): http://www.fernuni-hagen.de/fuxml/

## Profile of Author

**Birgit Feldmann M.A.**

Birgit Feldmann is a research assistant at the department of Information Systems and Databases, headed by Professor Dr. G. Schlageter, at the University of Hagen. Since 1998, she works on the topic of e-learning, e-communication, and communities.

# 7.9   Case Study—Implementing Accessibility in Massive Open Online Courses' Platforms for Teaching, Learning and Collaborating at Large Scale

### 7.9.1   Background

There is an increasing need of qualified workers and professionals that use e-collaboration to solve local problems with global perspectives. There is also a need to improve employability of citizens of developing countries by training them in new skills and knowledges. Massive open online courses' platforms provide the infrastructure to develop and offer online courses to millions of learners worldwide. Due to their nature, MOOCs enable for participants a great amount of collaboration experiences with instructors and peers. In this case study, we describe the Open edX implementation of the Inter-American Development Bank – called IDBx – that became the first international organization in Latin America and the Caribbean region to offer MOOCs. Nevertheless, the potential of MOOCs is imperiled for several barriers that MOOCs currently presents, such as lack of quality and affordable access to electricity, Internet and devices, digital literacy and censorship barriers, language barriers, pedagogy barriers and accessibility barriers. The results of empirical validations of the accessibility level of the platforms Coursera and edX are presented. These results show that neither of both platforms complies with the level AA of the web content accessibility guidelines proposed by the World Wide Web Consortium. This level is legally mandatory in several countries. Based on these results, an architectural extension for the MOOC platform Open edX has been designed to improve its level of accessibility.

The Web brought to the world new possibilities for teaching, learning and collaborating at large scale. In 2008, George Siemens and Stephen Downes opened an online course called "Connectivism and Connective Knowledge" that was originally intended for their 24 face-to-face students, but it was also open to the general public for free. More than 2,200 enrollments made this course the first Massive Open Online Course (MOOC) in the history of education. MOOCs differ from traditional online courses in scale – a MOOC can have an unlimited number of participants – and in access – a MOOC does not have entry requirements. Due to their nature, MOOCs enable participants a great amount of collaboration experiences with instructors and among peers during the learning process. Social media and mobile devices contribute to this approach of large scale teaching and learning in a distributed fashion where students are more connected to each other and more empowered by their own learning. By 2017, the MOOC movement included 9,400 courses (see Fig. 7.12) offered by more than 800 organizations to 81 million of enrolled students. The top five MOOC platforms were: Coursera from United Stated with 30 million users, edX from United States with 14 million users, XuetangX from China with 9.3 million users, Udacity from United States with 8 million users and FutureLearn from England with 7.1 million users.

Sandra Sanchez-Gordon,
*Escuela Politécnica Nacional*

Sergio Luján-Mora,
*Universidad de Alicante*

   As for the subjects, 19.9% of the MOOCs refers to Technology, 18.5% to Business, 10.6% to Social Science, 10% to Science and 9.5% to Humanities (see Fig. 7.13).

   The involvement of the authors of this study case with MOOCs started in 2012 when one of the authors developed "iDESWEB – Introduction to Web Development"[8]. The third edition of iDESWEB had 7,730 enrollments from Spain, Colombia, Mexico, Peru, Argentina, Venezuela, Ecuador, Chile, Dominican Republic and Guatemala, in numerical order. As of June 2018, the video-lectures of iDESWEB have 2,839,997 views[9]. Another MOOC where authors are involved is "iXML – Introduction to XML"[10]. iXML is hosted in the University of Alicante platform and it has 8,747 enrollments. As of June 2018, the video-lectures of iXML have 332,692 views[11]. Other MOOC in which authors have participated is "Learn Web Accessibility Step by Step" which is hosted in Udemy. This MOOC has 8,862 enrollments and has an average valuation of 4.5 starts[12]. There is also the pair of MOOCs "Introduction to Web Development: HTML and CSS" Part 1 and Part 2[13] hosted in the Formation Activate platform. The latest one is a self-paced

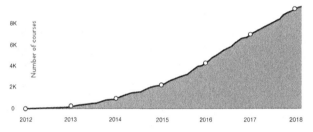

**Fig. 7.12:** Growth of MOOCs 2012 – 2017[7]

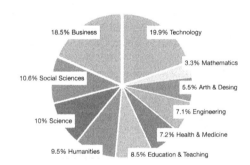

**Fig. 7.13:** MOOCs by subject[7]

---

[7]https://www.class-central.com/report/mooc-stats-2017/
[8]http://idesweb.uaedf.ua.es
[9]https://www.youtube.com/user/idesweb
[10]http://ixml.uaedf.ua.es/
[11]https://www.youtube.com/user/introxml/about
[12]https://www.udemy.com/aprende-accesibilidad-web-paso-a-paso
[13]https://cursos.formacionactivate.es/idesweb-parte-1/

MOOC called "Disabilities and active aging. Technological aids" hosted in MiriadaX[14]. This MOOC was published in 2017.

### 7.9.2    Case Description

In 2012, the Massachusetts Institute of Technology (MIT) and Harvard University founded edX as a nonprofit MOOC platform. In 2013, edX released the software of its platform as an open source project, creating Open edX. Several organizations worldwide have adopted Open edX to launch their own MOOC initiatives. In 2014, the Inter-American Development Bank (IDB) became the first international organization in Latin America and the Caribbean region to offer MOOCs. IDB created an implementation of Open edX – called IDBx – to extend its offering of face-to-face and online courses to a much wider audience of public officials, decision makers, key actors and citizens in general. As of June 2018, there are around 30 courses offered in IDBx. The MOOCs are available in Spanish, Portuguese and English. As for the topics, they cover Organizational Development, Social Development, Economics, Finance, Infrastructure, Commerce and Trade and Climate Change[15]. IDBx has 741,000 enrollments from 220 countries and territories. The five countries with more users are Colombia with 121,885 enrollments, Peru with 114,094, Mexico with 76,975, Brazil with 44,484 and Ecuador with 41,900 (see Fig. 7.14). From the total number of enrollments, men represent 53.74%, women 46.06% and others 0.2%. As for ages, the range 26-39 years old represents 55.10%, the range 40-62 represents 31.85%, the range 18-25 represents 11.1%, the range 63+ years old represents 1.75% and the range 18 or younger represents 0.21%.

The most popular MOOC in IDBx is "Management of Development Projects"[17]. In its sixth edition, there were 21,370 students enrolled. From them, 10,612 were exploring participants, i.e. enrolled users that have accessed at least once up to 50% of the learning resources; 1,998 were advanced participants, i.e. enrolled users that have earned a passing grade; 1,652 students completed the course and 1,098 paid for an official certificate. Figure 7.15 shows a summary of the total of enrollments by type.

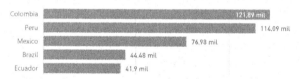

**Fig. 7.14:** IDBx enrollments – top ten countries[16]

---

[14]https://miriadax.net/web/discapacidad-y-envejecimiento-activos
-soportes-tecnologicos

[15]https://www.edx.org/es/school/idbx

[16]https://indes-idbx.org/dashboard/

[17]https://www.edx.org/es/course/gestion-de-proyectos-de-desarrollo-idbx
-idb6x-3

[18]https://indes-idbx.org/dashboard/

### 7.9.3   Barriers

On the web portal of the MOOC platform MiriadaX, philosophy section, it can be read: "Miríadax offers Massive Open Online Courses (a.k.a. MOOCs) to any interested party through an open platform without restrictions, without conditions, without schedules, WITHOUT BARRIERS."[19] However, in our opinion the expectations created by MOOC providers have not been completely met and it is not foreseen that they will be fulfilled in the short term, unless a series of important barriers that present MOOCs are resolved. These barriers have limited the extension of the MOOC phenomenon especially in developing countries.

**Electricity, Internet, Devices, Digital Literacy and Censorship Barriers.**   Access to electricity, Internet, devices and digital literacy are essential factors for the success of MOOCs towards offering education opportunities at large scale. In many developing countries, there is still limited access to electricity. For example, in countries of sub-Saharan Africa, 36% of the population does not have regular access to electricity. Around 620 million sub-Saharan Africans live without access to electricity. While in Europe, the United States and Canada, the number of users with Internet access exceeds 80%, in countries such as Burundi, Ethiopia, Guinea or Niger it is less than 2%, and there is a lack of access to affordable and quality Internet for the general population. In some cases, the downloading speeds of Internet connections are not sufficient to download large files or view streaming videos in an acceptable way. In Latin America, the situation is not as unequal as in Africa, but there is still inequality between urban and rural areas. In some developing countries, there is also a lack of access to affordable devices (computers, tablets and smartphones) for the general population. Finally, in some developing countries digital literacy levels are low. Another issue is that some governments censor access to certain web content and services. For example, in 2014, Coursera

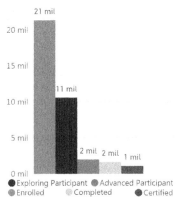

**Fig. 7.15:** MOOC "Management of Development Projects" – enrollment by type[18]

---

[19]https://miriadax.net/web/guest/nuestra-filosofia

announced that citizens from Cuba, Iran, Sudan and Syria could no longer access their platform due to a regulation of the United States government.

**Language Barriers.**   Most MOOCs are offered only in English. A quick review of edX as of June 2018 shows that of 2,192 courses, 1,817 are offered in English, representing 82.9% of the offer; Spanish is the second language with the most courses offered, 179, but it only represents 8.2% of the total. Students with different native languages might have difficulties related to their proficiency in English. Language barriers discourage many potential learners, especially from developing countries.

**Pedagogy Barriers.**   Compared with modalities of face-to-face, traditional distance and online education, MOOC mediated learning lacks a formally defined pedagogy. Their massive nature implies peer-support through intensive collaboration and self-learning as the bases of the learning process. New pedagogical approaches are needed since current ones do not fully support teaching on a massive scale. There need to be alternative credentialing mechanisms. Some options are as digital badging, micro-credentialing, noncredit training courses, noncredit certifications, blockchain academic records and learning digital passports. There needs to be adaptive and personalized learning using learning analytics and profiling. Recommender systems and curation tools can help in defining learning paths and providing educational resources based on student behavior and preferences. Current assessment mechanisms, such as automatic grading and peer review, are insufficient and new mechanisms for digital assessment at scale based in artificial intelligence are needed. In addition, there needs to be efficient use of social media, mobile technology and gamification as learning tools. Although some MOOCs have reached enrollments as massive as 370,000 students, for instance "Circuits and Electronics" offered by edX in 2012, the completion rates range from 10% to 40%.

**Accessibility Barriers.**   The accessibility of MOOCs needs to be improved, since the probability of students from diversity of contexts and situations participating in a MOOC is higher than traditional online courses, due to its massiveness and openness. Unfortunately, MOOCs are not accessible enough for citizens from developing countries with limited access to Internet, for students whose language is different from the language in which the MOOC is carried out, for students with disabilities and for elderly students. According to the United Nations Organization, more than one billion people live with some form of disability[20]. The same organization stated, "Lower income countries have a higher prevalence of disability than higher income countries."[21] It is necessary to analyze the problem and propose solutions to improve the inclusion of diverse learners – both able and disabled – in MOOCs platforms and content.

---

[20]https://www.un.org/development/desa/publications/graphic/disability-statistics
[21]http://www.un.org/disabilities/documents/COP/crpd_csp_2015_2.doc

### 7.9.4   Discussion and Evaluation

To promote web accessibility, the World Wide Web Consortium created the Web Access Initiative (WAI) to develop the Web Content Accessibility Guidelines (WCAG), Authoring Tool Accessibility Guidelines (ATAG) and the User Agent Accessibility Guidelines (UAAG). These guidelines are a good starting point to validate the accessibility of MOOCs. The WAI emphasizes that following the recommendations of the WCAG guidelines makes web content more usable for all users: "While accessibility focuses on people with disabilities, many accessibility requirements also improve usability for everyone. Accessibility especially benefits people without disabilities who are in limiting situations, such as using the web on a mobile phone when visual attention is elsewhere, in bright sunlight, in a dark room, in a quiet environment, in a noisy environment and in an emergency."[22]

We used WCAG to perform an empirical validation of the accessibility level of a sample of five Coursera courses from different world regions: "A Brief History of Humankind", Hebrew University of Jerusalem, Asia Middle East; "Climate Change", University of Melbourne, Australia and the Pacific; "Introduction to Mathematical Philosophy", Ludwig Maximilians Universität München, Europe; "Internet History, Technology and Security", University of Michigan, North America and "Be more creative", Universidad Autónoma de México, South America. The accessibility analysis included four sections that present important content for students' learning experience and are common to all the courses of the data set:

- Announcements. This is the home page. If this page is not accessible, it is very difficult for students to reach the other sections of the course.

- Video lectures. In this section, students access the learning resources.

- Quizzes. In this section, students take the evaluations.

- Discussion forums. In this section, students collaborate with each other.

We preferred human evaluation over automated testing due to accuracy. Two accessibility experts performed independent evaluations and the individual results were contrasted and decisions made when discrepancies arisen. We executed three test procedures. In Test Case 1 and Test Case 2, all the courses from the sample failed to comply with the web accessibility requirements. In Test Case 3, three of the courses failed to comply with the web accessibility requirements. Hence, we can conclude that the Coursera´s courses analyzed and the Course platform itself have web accessibility issues that need to be addressed.

In 2012, the WAI developed the WCAG Evaluation Methodology (WCAG-EM) to determine if web contents comply with the WCAG 2.0 accessibility guidelines. The WCAG-EM methodology covers five fundamental steps: defining the scope, exploring the website, selecting the sample, auditing the selected sample and reporting the results. These steps were adapted by the authors for use in MOOCs. The adaptation of WCAG-EM was used by the authors to validate the level of accessibility of "Latin American

---
[22]https://www.w3.org/WAI/intro/usable

Macroeconomic Reality" offered by the IDBx in June 2015. As a result, it was determined that this course did not reach WCAG 2.0 accessibility level.

The ATAG guidelines were used to evaluate the conformance of Studio, the Open edX course-authoring component. The version of Open edX Studio evaluated was the one available at the edX public sandbox[23]. ATAG has two parts: Part A addresses the problem of making the authoring-tool's user-interface accessible; Part B addresses the problem of enabling the authoring tool to give support and guidance in the production of content with a good level of accessibility. The authors test-drove features by re-creating a real scenario where an instructor creates a course, with sections, subsections and units. Then, the authors proceeded to add images, videos, text content, quizzes and so on, while evaluating the conformance with the success criteria. The results were as follows: Success Criterion: B.2.1.1. Accessible Content Possible: The authoring tool does not place restrictions on the web content that authors can specify or those restrictions do not prevent WCAG 2.0 success criteria from being met.

Result: Keyboard navigation is not fully implemented. For instance, the functionality of a zooming image component is not accessible by keyboard since the space bar handler is disabled. Main functions must be easily accessed using keyboard shortcuts, which are important for users that need to or prefer to use keyboard.

Success Criterion: B.2.2.2. Setting Accessibility Properties: If the authoring tool provides mechanisms to set web content properties (e.g. attribute values), then mechanisms are also provided to set web content properties related to accessibility information. Result: Use of attribute values is not fully implemented. For instance, when adding an image, there is no mechanism to use the longdesc attribute to link descriptions to complex images, such as graphs and charts. In addition, when adding a video, there is no mechanism to use the title attribute to provide screen readers with contextual information, such as author and date of creation. Success Criterion: B.2.3.1. Alternative Content is Editable: If the authoring tool provides functionality for adding non-text content, then authors are able to modify programmatically associated text alternatives for non-text content.

Result: Author does not have the option to modify programmatically generated alternative text. Success Criterion: B.2.3.3. Save for Reuse: If the authoring tool provides the functionality for adding non-text content, when authors enter programmatically associated text alternatives for non-text content, then both of the following are true: (a) Save and Suggest: The text alternatives are automatically saved and suggested by the authoring tool, if the same non-text content is reused; and (b) Edit Option: The author has the option to edit or delete the saved text alternatives. Result: When copying an image, Open edX Studio does not prompt the author to change the alternative text.

In summary, Open edX Studio does not comply with level A of the ATAG 2.0 guidelines since the content created with it does not comply with level A of the WCAG 2.0. A main concern is that authors might not be fully conscious of the accessibility problems caused by Open edX Studio in the content created. Figure 7.16 shows and architectural extension proposed to improve the level of accessibility of Open edX. The architecture has a user-side component and an author-side component.

---

[23]https://studio.sandbox.edx.org/

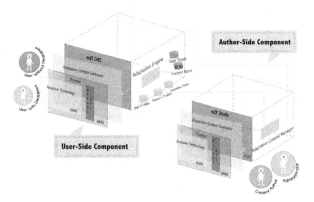

Fig. 7.16: Architecture design for improving accessibility of edX platform.

The user-side component has four layers: assistive technology, browser, adaptative content extension and the learning management system. Online learners might or might not have disabilities. Learners with disabilities might use several assistive technologies, depending on their accessibility needs and preferences. This design allows learners to manage their accessibility user profile by selecting a combination of accessibility issues that best suit their current life situation. The author-side component also has four layers: assistive technology, browser, adaptative content extension and Open edX Studio. Similar to learners, authors also might or might not have disabilities. Instructors with disabilities might use assistive technologies depending on their accessibility needs and preferences.

## 7.9.5   Conclusions

There is an increasing need of qualified workers and professionals that use e-collaboration to solve local problems with global perspectives. There is also a need to improve employability of citizens of developing countries by training them in new skills and knowledges. MOOCs are free of charge or low cost and they have no admission requirements for registration. There is a fast-growing offer of MOOCs in several areas of knowledge. MOOCs empower the creation of learning and collaborating communities around a particular topic of study. MOOCs can be used in different modalities, such as virtual courses, blended courses and as open educational resources. Many MOOCs are offered by recognized organizations and the instructors are renowned researchers in their fields. Nevertheless, the potential of MOOCs is imperiled for several barriers. MOOCs must adapt to users accessibility preferences to minimize barriers and promote a more inclusive society.

## Further Reading

- Sanchez-Gordon S., Luján-Mora S. (2018). Lifecycle for MOOCs Development and Management. In: Queirós R. (ed.), Emerging Trends, Techniques and Tools for MOOC Management, p. 24-48. Hershey: IGI Global. doi: 10.4018/978-1-5225-5011-2.

- Sanchez-Gordon S., Luján-Mora S. (2017). Technological Innovations in Large-Scale Teaching: Five Roots of MOOCS. Journal of Educational Computing Research. doi: 10.1177/0735633117727597.

- Sanchez-Gordon S., Luján-Mora S. (2016). e-Education in countries with low and medium human development levels using MOOCs. In: Proceedings of the 3rd International Conference on eDemocracy & eGovernment, p. 151-158. doi: 10.1109/ICEDEG.2016.7461713.

- Sanchez-Gordon S., Luján-Mora S. (2016). How could MOOCs become accessible? The case of edX and the future of inclusive online learning. Journal of Universal Computer Science, 22(1), p. 55-81. doi: 10.3217/jucs-022-01-0055.

- Sanchez-Gordon S., Luján-Mora S. (2016). Barreras y estrategias de utilización de MOOCs en el contexto de la Educación Superior en Iberoamérica. In: Gómez Hernández P., García Barrera A., Monge López C. (eds.), La cultura de los MOOCs, p. 141-160. Madrid: Síntesis.

- Sanchez-Gordon S., Luján-Mora S. (2015). Accessible blended learning for non-native speakers using MOOCs. In: Proceedings of the 2015 International Conference on Interactive Collaborative and Blended Learning, p. 19-24. doi: 10.1109/ICBL.2015.7387645.

- Sanchez-Gordon S., Calle-Jimenez T., Luján-Mora S. (2015). Relevance of MOOCs for training of public sector employees: enrollment, completion and web accessibility challenges. In: Proceedings of the 14th International Conference on Information Technology Based Higher Education and Training, p. 1-5. doi: 10.1109/ITHET.2015.7218016.

- Sanchez-Gordon S., Luján-Mora S. (2015). Adaptive content presentation extension for open edX –enhancing MOOCs accessibility for users with disabilities. In: Proceedings of the 8th International Conference on Advances in Computer-Human Interactions, p. 181-183.

- Sanchez-Gordon S., Luján-Mora S. (2015). Evaluation of the accessibility of educational contents for online learning based on WCAG-EM. In: Proceedings of the Iberoamerican Conference of Educational Informatics and Disabilities, p. 88-100.

- Sanchez-Gordon S., Luján-Mora S. (2014). Web accessibility requirements for MOOCs. Can MOOCs be really universal and open to anyone? In: Proceedings of the International Conference on Quality and Accessibility of Virtual Learning, p. 529-534.

- Sanchez-Gordon S., Luján-Mora S. (2013). Web accessibility of MOOCs for elderly students. In: Proceedings of the 12th International Conference on Information Technology Based Higher Education and Training, p. 1-6. doi: 10.1109/ITHET.2013.6671024.

## Contact Details

**Escuela Politécnica Nacional**
Ladrón de Guevara E11-253
Quito - Ecuador
Tel. +593 2 2976 300
Internet: https://www.epn.edu.ec
eMail: sandra.sanchez@epn.edu.ec

**Universidad de Alicante**
Carretera San Vicente del Raspeig s/n
E-03690 San Vicente del Raspeig (Alicante), Spain
Tel. +34 965 90 34 00 ext. 2962
Internet: http://accesibilidadweb.dlsi.ua.es/
eMail: sergio.lujan@ua.es

## Profile of Authors

### Sandra Sanchez-Gordon

Sandra is a researcher and professor of the Department of Informatics and Computer Sciences of Escuela Politécnica Nacional, Ecuador. She earned her PhD degree in Applications of Informatics in Alicante University, Spain and her master degree in Software Engineering in Drexel University, USA. Her current research focuses on MOOCs accessibility and including accessibility considerations in software requirements engineering and software testing engineering. Her current research work can be found at http://sandrasanchez.blog.epn.edu.ec/.

### Sergio Luján-Mora

Sergio is an associate professor of the Department of Software and Computing Systems at the University of Alicante, Spain. He has developed and executed several MOOCs in computer science. He has implemented web applications since 1997. He has also published several books related to programming and web development. His main research topics include MOOCs, OERs, e-learning, web applications, web development, web accessibility and usability and e-learning. His current research work can be found at http://gplsi.dlsi.ua.es/slujan/english.

# Chapter 8

# eDemocracy

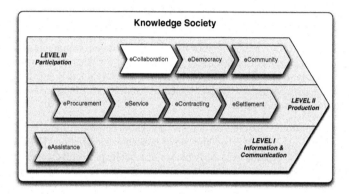

*Chapter 8 deals with Web-based processes for the participation of citizens in political events. Section 8.1 proposes a participation pyramid based on the involvement of the citizens and the complexity of public tasks. In electronic votes and elections, there is a multitude of solutions (Sect. 8.2); some especially standing out are time and place independent options via Internet. Section 8.3 explains the sub-processes for eVoting and eElection. The way in which anonymous voting works is treated in Sect. 8.4. Section 8.6 describes multi-dimensional visualization techniques for results of votes and elections. The political and cultural memory (Sect. 8.7), realized in the eGovernment by portals and digital archives, widens the options of an information and knowledge society and makes a democratic political controlling possible. Section 8.8 gives bibliographical notes. The case studies of a VAA for the 2013 Ecuador National Elections and the technical and procedural mechanisms to enhance transparency and trust in Internet voting for the Swiss elections and votes, are presented.*

© Springer Nature Switzerland AG 2019
A. Meier, L. Terán, *eDemocracy & eGovernment*, Progress in IS,
https://doi.org/10.1007/978-3-030-17585-6_8

# 8.1   Pyramid of Types of Participation

*Concept of political participation*

By the term political participation, different forms of influencing participation of citizens are understood. Among them are information interchange and discussion of topical issues and programs, giving form to political content and decision making processes or participation in votes on topical issues and collaboration in elections for politicians.

*The five steps of participation*

Political participation is always linked to a group or community of people and cannot be regarded isolated. By Fig. 8.1, it is intended to characterize both the community and the type of participation. The following five steps are relevant:

- **eGovernment portal:** The society is evolving into an information and knowledge society and makes more and more use of Web-based tools and information systems (see Chap. 10 on the Knowledge Society). It is important for government offices and institutions that no digital divide is created, which divides society in those citizens who have Internet expertise, and those who do not (see Sect. 2.5 on barrier-free web access and Sect. 10.6 on ethical rules in the Knowledge Society). For that reason, citizens can decide by themselves which governmental services they want to draw upon electronically and which ones based on paper.

- **eDiscussion:** By means of Web-based administration communication (multichannel management in Sect. 9.2) or by building a citizen communication center (Sect. 9.3), virtual communities of citizens are developed. Public project ideas and plans can be discussed and commented (consultation), in order to promote the opinion-forming process.

- **eParticipation:** If the citizens' abilities and know-how are utilized, design assignments and questions of procedure can be tackled in a joint effort. The personal involvement of the citizens in early phases of a public project increases acceptance and quality.

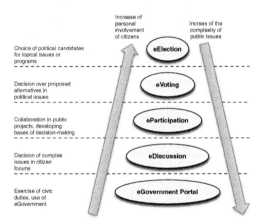

**Fig. 8.1:** Forms of participation in eGovernment.

- **eVoting:** Electronic voting must not be reduced to giving your vote in favor or against a factual issue. Rather, the eVoting process begins with putting at public disposal web-based information and discussion forums and ends with the publication of the voting results and the analysis of the voting behavior (see Sects. 8.3 and 8.6). In the participation pyramid shown in Fig. 8.1, it stands out that the complexity of factual issues is reduced when going up on the pyramid. In eVoting, people give their proper evaluation of one or several alternatives of a factual issue by announcing yes, no or abstention.

- **eElection:** On the highest level of the participation pyramid, personal involvement of the citizens is high, because it is about electing political candidates. By public information, not only through personal declarations of intentions of the candidate, but also by his or her previous electoral and voting behavior in public affairs, the citizen gains a clearer picture on the candidate's political dedication (see Sect. 8.4).

In the governmental services determined by the European Commission (see Sects. 4.2 and 4.3), it jumps to the eye that the processes on the levels of eParticipation, eVoting, and eElection are widely missing. Some first trials in electronic votes and elections have been carried out in the European area and other countries. They show that public authorities still have a lot to catch up on the development and use of web-based technologies for involvement and participation.

*Governmental services should include eVoting and eElection*

## 8.2  Variety of Electronic Voting and Elections

The application of information and communication systems allows the citizens to realize their political rights (voting, election, signing referendums and initiatives, etc.) electronically. Figure 8.2 shows the variety of electronic votes and elections.

By a web poll, we understand a Web-based inquiry about a public factual issue or a political program, the electronically obtained result of which must be considered

*No clear authentification in web polls*

| | Definition | Features | Examples |
|---|---|---|---|
| **Web Polls** | Non-biding vote or election | · No guarantee for correctness<br>· No guarantee of anonymity | Binding citizen survey |
| **Electronic Voting Systems** | Electronic voting devices in a hall | · Automatic recording<br>· Immediate display of results | Vote in Parliament |
| **Electronic Election Machines** | Electronic voting devices and ballot boxes in the polling station | · Checking the voters' entitlement to vote manually<br>· Integrating results of individual machines manually | Elections in Belgium |
| **Network Election Machines** | Networked voting devices in public polling stations | · Results determined automatically to all connected machines | Local elections in England |
| **eVoting and eElections** | Place-, and time-independent voting and elections trough devices (mobile phone, PDA, digital TV, etc) | · Non-ambiguous registration<br>· Vote or election remains confidential | Votes in Geneva and Zurich |

**Fig. 8.2:** Differences in voting and elections.

as not binding. In other words, the citizens are not clearly identified or checked for authentification through digital signatures in every case, rather it is intended to catch a glimpse of the public opinion trend concerning a factual issue or a topic.

*Electronic voting systems are restricted to a location*

Electronic voting systems can be installed in gathering places or in halls, so that each participant disposes of an electronic voting or electing device. The individual votes are counted electronically after the vote is terminated and published directly on display boards. Such voting systems usually are permanently installed in parliament halls, and apart from that can be set up ad hoc for public gatherings without too much trouble.

*Security issues with voting computers*

As another option in electronic votes and elections, so-called voting computers or electronic voting machines can be set up in public polling stations, and linked to each other if wished. With voting computers, it is possible to equip an existing PC or desktop computer with special software for votes and elections. With electronic voting machines, special devices are employed, which have been designed exclusively for electronic votes and elections. This way, it is wished to prevent that the process of entering the vote and counting the results is manipulated.[1]

*Voting and election procedures independent of time and place*

Internet based votes (eVoting) and elections (eElection) can be carried out in a determined timeframe, independently of time and place. In this case, the identification and authentification of the voters is effected with the help of a Public Key Infrastructure (see Sect. 5.6) or suitable security systems (see Sects. 8.3 and 8.4), which make any manipulation of the voting or election results impossible.

*Opportunities in eVoting and eElection*

In order to implement an electronic system for votes and elections, the necessary legal groundwork must be created. Most of the European countries have made experience with different electronic voting and election procedures. The following are considered positive aspects:

- **Ample documentation before, during and after electronic votes and elections:** On the eGovernment portal, it is possible to publish differentiated information as detailed as wished, personal profiles (see spiderweb profiles of politicians in Sect. 8.6) and decision making help by the governmental institution. In addition to that, for topical issues and elections, it is possible to load corresponding hyperlinks to political parties or important NGOs and NPOs. The citizen himself decides how deeply he wants to look into a subject or an electoral proposition. Apart from that, he has the possibility to stay up to date, using a subscription service (e.g., RSS feed, see Sect. 2.2) to follow the information phase, vote, election or analysis of results.

- **Making voting easier:** Mobility in the population increases, and there is a need for exercising political rights by eVoting and eElection. Especially handicapped people benefit from these possibilities, as they are spared the often-arduous trip to the public polling station. Additionally, citizens who are outside the country at the time of voting can exercise their rights in an easy way.

[1] In Germany, e.g., the voting computers of the NEDAP producer is utilized in municipalities. By means of surveys regarding the security and susceptibility to manipulation, it could be proven (see article by Kurz & Rieger (2007) in the bibliographical notes) which methods are used to install altered software on the voting computer and how hardware components are exchanged. Therefore, this device does not fulfill the requirements of manipulation-resistant, comprehensible and transparent votes and elections.

- **Activating the citizens:** Electronic votes and elections can be utilized to place additional questions on governmental tasks and duties. Thereby, it is not only possible to make more accurate assertions on the ongoing voting topic or an election, but it is furthermore possible to increase eParticipation of the citizens. Like with many enterprises in the eGovernment, electronic votes and elections bring along chances, but also risks:

*Risks in eVoting and eElection*

- **De-ritualization of the voting and election process:** Conventional votes and elections are linked to rituals and certain places. Exercising political rights through Internet based procedures demands a change in behavior and trust in the cyberspace. Place-centered and federalistic structures must be supported and facilitated with the help of Web-based methods and techniques.

- **Flood of Web polls and devaluation of people's rights:** Collecting signatures for initiatives or referendums is made easier by Web-based procedures. The danger in this is, that public topics and projects might not be discussed in detail, but rather evaluated and voted on spontaneously with one click.

- **Data protection and data security issues:** Although conventional procedures of voting and elections also have security risks, electronic procedures still do not evoke much trust in many citizens nowadays. Many citizens are overstrained by abstract encoding methods and digital signatures. They remain skeptical and doubt that their privacy will be protected. The abuse present in the Internet (racist ideas, pedophilia, crime, among others) frightens people off exercising their civil rights and duties over the Internet.

The eGovernment framework of the University of Fribourg (see Chap. 1) with the steps information and communication, production and participation suggests, that the highest level of participation with eCollaboration, eDemocracy and eCommunity remains one of the most challenging tasks. This is the reason why it is important to carry out successful sub-projects with eVoting and eElection, in order to reduce the citizens' fear of the unknown.

## 8.3 Process Steps for eVoting and eElection

Electronic votes and elections distinguish themselves from traditional procedures of votes and elections mainly by their succeeding and post-processing phases (see Fig. 8.3), if the advantages of electronic exchange relations are exploited. Through changed and expanded information and discussion politics in the process steps eDiscussion and ePosting, it is hoped to achieve that citizens get more involved into political issues and to further community formation. In Fig. 8.3, the following process steps are distinguished:

*Phases prior and subsequent to the election are important*

- **eDiscussion:** Prior to the vote or election, the opinion-forming process can be furthered by requesting not only information from discussion forums, but also opinions and evaluations. Furthermore, subscription services allow the citizens to draw on documents or bases of decision making, and to learn about changes and extensions in topical issues.

*Promotion of the opinion-forming process*

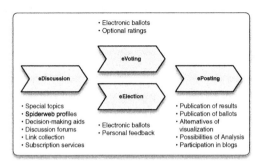

**Fig. 8.3:** eVoting and eElection as part of a process chain.

*Anonymous vote*
- **eVoting:** Within the timespan established by the authorities, the citizen could fill out his electronic ballot and send it. Before that, he must have identified himself and registered at the governmental institution; the vote afterwards is effected anonymously (see the two phases of registration and voting in Sect. 8.4). Apart from the ballot, the governmental institution can add an optional survey questionnaire on the respective topics, in order to, for example, get the citizens' feedback on questions of procedure and realization.

*Only valid ballots are accepted*
- **eElection:** By means of the published spiderweb profiles of the political candidates (Sect. 8.6) and additional information on their abilities and skills, it is easier for the voter to fill out the electronic ballot during the preceding process step of eDiscussion. Here, too, it is necessary to register previously by means of an election and checking card, and to request a valid ballot from the governmental institution, before voting electronically (Sect. 8.4). Possibly, it may be beneficial to have optional additional questions answered by the citizens.

*Increasing transparency with ePosting*
- **ePosting:** A publication of the results on the eGovernment portal of the governmental institution is not only directed at the citizens, but can also be studied and further used by other organizations or the press. To that end, suitable tools for visualizing and analyzing can be offered, so that the electoral and voting behavior, as well as the results, may be analyzed and discussed. Public blogs (see Sect. 9.6) make it possible to comment on the electronic vote or election even after the election day, and to deepen the topic. Apart from the publication of the actual voting and election results, it would be necessary to publish voting and election cards and their non-ambiguous identification numbers, respectively, in lists. By this means, every citizen has the chance to verify whether his vote has actually been registered and processed. This method is more transparent than traditional votes and elections, which help to win the citizens' trust in eVoting and eElection.

The description of the process steps eDiscussion, eVoting, eElection, and ePosting shows that the use of electronic information and exchange relations increases the citizen's involvement and stimulates the public discussion.

# 8.4 Operation of Electronic Voting and Elections

In order to carry out votes over the Internet, the established basic legal conditions of votes and elections must be met:

*Basic conditions for votes and elections*

- Only people who are entitled to vote may participate in electronic votes and elections.

- Every person who is entitled to vote has one and only one vote.

- Electronically submitted votes must not be intercepted, nor redirected or changed.

- Third parties (citizens, governmental institutions) must not become aware of the electronically submitted votes (secret vote or election).

- Data protection must be guaranteed.

- In case of a malfunction, no previously submitted vote must be lost.

The central question with electronic votes and elections is: In the electronic exchange process, how can a citizen identify and authenticate himself, and be authorized for the vote or election (see identity management in Sect. 5.3), if he wants to submit an anonymous or secret vote afterwards? With respect to the technical and legal aspect, the eVoting and eElection borrows from the absentee ballot well proven in Europe (Germany, France, and Switzerland). In analogy to it, the following two phases have to be distinguished in electronic voting and election procedures:

*Similar to familiar absentee ballot*

- **Phase I—registration:** The voter must identify and authenticate himself previously, in order to be authorized for the electronic vote.

- **Phase II—submission of vote:** In a second step, the vote is submitted anonymously, so that no third party may obtain knowledge of the voter's electoral or voting behavior.

For electronic votes and elections, a multitude of systems and procedures have been developed. In the case of electronic election machines, the citizen has his identity checked by the electoral assistant and receives a smartcard, whit which he can enter his vote electronically in the voting booth. Such systems are used in the USA,[2] but are less suitable for distant votes and elections.

*Limited application possibilities of eElection machines*

When using PIN codes (Personal Identification Number) or similar procedures, the request for anonymity depends on the integrity of the electoral organization. Apart from that, these systems usually lack a clear legal groundwork, as guaranteed for example for digital signatures and the Public Key Infrastructure in Trust Centers (see Chap. 5 on eContracting). Therefore, in the following we will outline a registration and voting procedure for eVoting and eElection, which complies with the above-mentioned requirements of correct and anonymous votes.

*Anonymity should remain guaranteed*

---

[2]After the considerable error rates in the 2000 USA presidential elections in Florida, the mechanical election machines were replaced by the majority by electronic ones, in order to avoid the emerged irregularities and to ensure recounts for control.

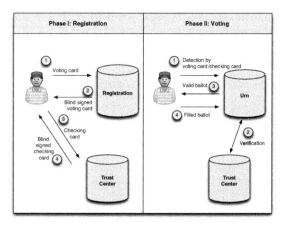

**Fig. 8.4:** Registration and submission of votes, according to Prosser & Müller-Török (2002).

*Laborious steps in registration phase*
In Fig. 8.4, the two phases of registration and submission of votes have been designed independently from each other, in order to guarantee anonymity. In the registration phase, the voter sends his encoded and signed voting card to the governmental institution and thereby is identified and authenticated (Step 1). The governmental server checks the voter's entitlement to vote based on his digital signature. In case of a positive result, the server sends back the voting card, which was signed blindly[3] (Step 2). In Step 3, the voter sends the checking card to a Trust Center and demands it back, blindly signed (Step 4). Steps 3 and 4 have the purpose to prevent that the electoral authority submits falsified votes. Now, the voter possesses an electronic voting card, and checking card, which were declared valid by the governmental institution and the Trust Center and were signed blindly.

*Submission of vote with checking card*
The second phase of voting takes place on the day of the vote or election. Then, the voter utilizes his already verified checking card. He sends both to the ballot box (step 1) for confirmation, in order to obtain a valid ballot. Before the server can return the ballot to the ballot box, the voting and checking card is verified by the Trust Center (step 2). If everything goes smoothly, the voter obtains the desired ballot in step 3. He fills out his ballot and sends it back to the ballot box, together with his proof of entitlement. After the vote terminates, the server of the ballot box publishes a list of the ballots and the voting cards.

## 8.5   Blockchain-based eVoting Systems

*Blockchain-based eVoting*
One of the bases of representative democracy is the transparency with which public elections are handled. For this reason, it is essential that the institutions in charge of these

---

[3]The blind signature is based on the encoding procedure by Rivet, Shamir, and Adleman. Indeed, the signer applies his private key to the actual document and an additional padding. When the receiver of the signature removes the padding, the signed document remains, which now can be used anonymously.

processes develop the necessary mechanisms to guarantee representative non-fraudulent elections. There are several mechanisms for the execution of votes among which we can mention the following: paper ballots, postal mail voting, public voting (i.e., *Landsgemeinde*[4] in Switzerland for public cantonal assembly with a non-secret ballot voting system), and electronic voting (e.g., electronic methods and electronic voting machines). In the context of electronic voting, there are two main approaches, centralized and decentralized .

Blockchain is a decentralized, distributed and public digital ledger used to record transactions across many nodes (computers) to guarantee that records cannot be modified without the modification of all subsequent blocks and the consensus of the network (for more details about blockchain technology, see Sect. 5.7 in Chap. 5). A common use of blockchains technology is in cryptocurrencies, with the well-known P2P system so-called *bitcoin*[5]. Blockchain technology, whose main characteristic is immutability and a decentralized architecture. Today, this technology has had a great impact on large corporations and governments. One of those possible blockchain applications for public administration services are electronic voting schemes. The main objective is to generate an open, fair and verifiable decentralized architecture independently in the processes of voting and electronic elections.

Figure 8.5 shows a high-level overview of the voting process of Agora[6], a Swiss company that provides a blockchain-based voting ecosystem. It uses a custom blockchain network developed from 2015. Agora's voting process consists of six distinct steps that are mentioned as follows:

1. *Configuration:* Election administrators create a new election event.

2. *Casting:* Voters cast their encrypted ballots to Agora's network.

3. *Anonymization:* Agora's network anonymizes all voter ballots.

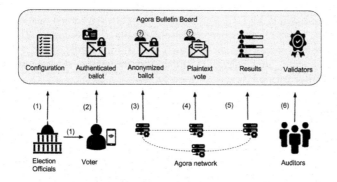

**Fig. 8.5:** Architecture of Agora blockchain-based eVoting.

---

[4]https://en.wikipedia.org/wiki/Landsgemeinde
[5]https://bitcoin.org/en/
[6]https://www.agora.vote

4. *Decryption:* Agora's network decrypts the anonymized ballots.

5. *Tallying:* All votes are counted.

6. *Auditing:* Auditors and observers post reviews confirming validity of election results.

There exist already various efforts and discussion regarding the use of blockchain to
enhance transparency and trustworthiness of eVoting processes and how it can help public administration to provide better solutions and more robust systems. An example of
the use of blockchain technologies is the trial conducted by the town of Zug in Switzerland launched a between June 25 and July 1. The trial took the form of a non-binding
questionnaire requesting the opinion of citizens in local issues, such as, whether people
would like to see fireworks at the annual town festival[7].

## 8.6  Analysis and Visualization of Multidimensional Data

In the phases of eDiscussion and ePosting, the information must be displayed and commented, so that the citizens are able to obtain a clearer picture on topical issues or political profiles of the politicians. With multidimensional visualization techniques, it is
possible to illustrate complex factual connections. For example, at the Geographical Institute of the University of Zurich, cartography methods are used to display Switzerland
as a space of different ideologies (Fig. 8.6).

*Example of a*
*multidimen-*
*sional space of*
*ideologies*
The results of all Swiss popular votes in the years 1981—1999 served as a basis
for the illustration. In Switzerland, popular votes are referendums on political issues, in
which the citizens can either respond yes or no. The percentage of "yes" votes, given on
the propositions in 3021 municipalities, was subjected to an explorative factor analysis.
The factors constitute the dimensions of the ideology space, a two-dimensional draft
of which is shown in Fig. 8.6. The political goals, derived from a qualitative content
analysis and located in the space, are displayed with circle diagrams. The surface of
the diagram corresponds with the frequency with which the goal appeared in the votes.
Colors (here: gray scale) indicate the affiliation of the goals to the categories evaluated
analytically by content.

Suitably chosen projections of multidimensional spaces or other methods of data
mining (see Sect. 10.3 on the use of knowledge based databases) make it possible to
illustrate complex political interrelations. With them, political standpoints and behavioral patterns of governments, parties or interest groups can be revealed. Additionally,
in regular time lags it can be analyzed whether the members of the government or com-
missioned bodies follow the strategies given by the people, the parliament or the government and carry out the corresponding programs (political controlling, see Sect. 8.7).

The discussed visualization methods serve to form opinions and prepare decisions
in the line of eDemocracy politics. For example, at the time of election of political

---

[7]https://www.swissinfo.ch/eng/politics/crypto-valley_swiss-blockchain
-voting-platform-begins-trial/44215246

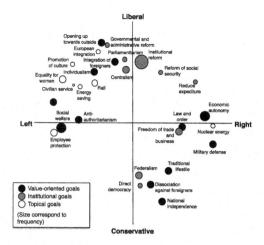

**Fig. 8.6:** Visualization of position and frequency of political goals, according to Hermann & Leuthold (2000).

delegates for the parliament, it is possible to show their profile, based on the political behavior during the past legislative periods (see Fig. 8.7, depicted in the graphic as a black, altered polygon). Groups of politicians, parliamentary groups or whole parties can also be positioned in the spiderweb of different goals, based on their behavior (dashed polygon in Fig. 8.7).

In Switzerland, political spiderweb profiles are published in the run-up to the parliamentary elections ("Nationalratswahlen") on a corresponding Web platform and in the media (see case study smartvote in this chapter). Apart from the presentation of the

*Implementation of spiderweb profiles in parliamentary elections*

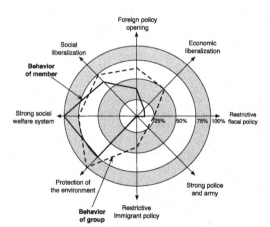

**Fig. 8.7:** Spiderweb profile of a delegate or associated parliamentary group, adapted from the research work by Sotomo (2015), University of Zurich.

candidates and further information on their political orientation and ability profile, the spiderweb profiles constitute an additional criterion for evaluation. Respective information portals in votes and elections add to the position the parliamentarians themselves have declared, and uncover whether opportunistic programs were offered, which were mainly tailored to the voters' mood, or whether the personal program aligns with the parliamentarian's actual behavior.

*Rating politics*      The rating of parliamentarians by systematically interpreting their voting behavior, constitutes a concentration of information. It can be seen as one possible type of political controlling. In the case study, this topic is deepened by the example of smartvote. Smartvote is a web-based information platform for the Swiss population in the national parliamentary elections.

## 8.7   Steps to Public Memory

*Building a public and cultural memory*      The historian John Bodnar characterized public memory as "A body of beliefs and ideas about the past that help a public or society understand both its past, present, and by implication, its future." This public or cultural memory of a society can be provided to the public by digitalizing important works, documents, images, speeches, movies, television or radio recordings, governmental programs and resolutions, citizens' initiatives, etc. in web-based libraries or digital archives. Thereby, not only jurists, historians or other experts gain access to the digitalized original documents and images, but all inhabitants.

*Subjective values and factual interests are important*      The sociologist Luhmann (2000), as a trained jurist and public official in Lüneburg experienced in administrative procedures, dedicates a whole chapter of his book "Die Politik der Gesellschaft" (The politics of society) to the memory of politics. He transfers the memory research theories influenced by neurobiology and mental systems to the collective memory. For political systems[8] and the political memory, he declares "Werte" (values) and "Interessen" (interests) important factors. Whereas subjective values constitute a moral instance in the political memory, interests are factual circumstances of each citizen. The political memory is situated in an area of conflict between values and interests, and selects what to forget and what to memorize. Luhman states that every political system reacts by distinguishing values and interests, this is "values, which facilitate the claim for memory and support it by legitimation of desiderata,[9] and interests, which, if they are heard and politically relevant, supply the communicative update" (transl. W.H.).

*Increasing transparency in the eGovernment portal*      The government and the administration have the mandate to publish strategies, programs and activities and the corresponding bills and ordinances on the eGovernment portal, providing manifold information and thereby furthering transparency. An information and knowledge society (see Chap. 10 on the Knowledge Society) is not viable without the use of computer-aided expert systems and knowledge databases.

- **Knowledge management:** A society can improve the access to politically relevant knowledge by means of suitable eGovernment programs and public memory initiatives. The World Bank, e.g., employs several hundred knowledge workers

---

[8]Luhmann's system theory is based on the evolution of communication and the evolution of society (Luhmann (2000)).

[9]A desideratum is a missed book or document that was proposed for purchase in libraries.

(see Sect. 10.4 on knowledge workers in eTeams), because it has realized that the transfer of know-how and knowledge is more important than granting money.

- **Effect-oriented administration:** Governmental offices and administrative units can increase the efficiency and effectiveness of their activities, if they make use of Web-based information and workflow management systems (see collaborative working environment in Sect. 7.5). Such systems support virtual forms of organization and collaboration (Chap. 7 on eCollaboration) and make it possible to manage the complexity of public products and services.

- **Organizational knowledge:** A learning organization or public tries to recognize and preserve structural perceptions and know-how as a collective commodity, using administrative and relationship processes between themselves and the citizens. Primarily, not individual needs or value systems are focused on, but organizational decision making procedures and collective experience (see learning organizations in Sect. 10.4).

An eGovernment portal not only offers the governmental services for citizens and companies discussed in Chap. 4, but apart from that can also comprehend procedures and knowledge databases for eDemocracy. The way to a public memory is a long and winding road, as important topics like protection of the citizens' privacy, copyright issues for digital objects and archiving concepts and periods have to be resolved continuously when using digital storage devices, etc., and they have to be implemented with suitable methods and techniques. If nothing else, a public memory, implemented in a publicly accessible eGovernment portal, offers a democratic political controlling and smoothes the way to an information and knowledge society.

*A public memory supports the political controlling*

## 8.8  Bibliographical Notes

A considerable part of the chapter at hand is retrieved from an article by Meier (2009) on electronic votes and elections. In western countries, first electronic votes and elections have been held (Krimmer (2006); Prosser & Krimmer (2004)). Different procedures with their respective advantages and disadvantages are quite known and have been deepened in research work (Brandt & Volkert (2002); Nurmi et al. (1991); Prosser et al. (2002)). Prosser & Müller-Török (2002) propose to separate the registration phase from the electronic voting phase and thereby guarantee the anonymity of electronic votes and elections.

*Literature on electronic votes and elections*

Data protection and data security are special challenges in eVoting and eElection. Manipulation should be ruled out, although it occurs with certain frequency when using voting computers (Kurz & Rieger, 2007).

In the run-up to votes and elections, the citizens must be indicated to the eGovernment portal and documented on it, in order to increase participation (Kirsch, 2004). After the successful electronic vote or election, the results and other information are to be published. To that end, visualization techniques for multidimensional data are applied (Hermann & Leuthold (2000); Jeitziner (2004); smartvote (2015); Sotomo (2015)),

*Participation and visualization*

like for example the display of ideologies as a space diagram or spiderweb profiles for politicians or political groups.

*Literature on*
*public memory*

Bodnar (1992) , Luhmann (2000), and Luhmann & Baecker (2005) make an argument for a cultural and political memory (public memory), in order to maintain the "claiming memory" and the "communicative update" (Luhmann 2000; transl. W.H.) in the information and knowledge society over the generations. In (Terán & Mancera, 2019) the authors present an extension of a VAA, implemented in within the project *Participa Inteligente* (PI), a social-network platform designed for the 2017 Ecuadorian national elections. This work concentrates on the implementation of dynamic candidate profiling using Twitter data and sentiment analysis as an additional element to the static profile generation of VAAs.

*Blockchain-*
*based*
*eVoting*

Agora published a white paper on the implementation of blockchain-based eVoting ecosystems as a decentralized method of generating cryptographically secure records (Agora (2018)). In the work of Kshetri & Voas (2018); Rubtcova & Pavenkov (2018), the authors highlight some Blockchain-enabled e-voting implementations and the approach's potential benefits and challenges.

# 8.9   Case Study—What Voting Advice Applications can Tell us About Voters

## 8.9.1   Background

Voting Advice Applications (VAAs) are online questionnaires, typically deployed before critical elections, that consist of a set of policy statements (usually between 30 and 40) to which users express agreement or disagreement. The aim of a VAA is to help voters identify parties or candidates that share a similar policy orientation to themselves. The positions of parties or candidates with respect to the policy statements are coded, either by academic experts or by the parties and/or candidates themselves. After navigating to the VAA website, citizens are able to fill in the same questionnaire and the system then produces a rank ordering of candidates/parties according to the degree of overlap with the user's own preferences.

Jonathan Wheatley, *Oxford Brookes University*

Fernando Mendez, *Centre for Democracy Studies Aarau (ZDA)*

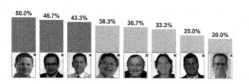 

**Fig. 8.8:** Histogram comparing congruence between users and candidates (EcuadorVota).

The first VAA to be used was the *StemWijzer* application in the Netherlands in 1989 (de Graaf 2010). It was first introduced as a paper and pencil test, a digital edition first appeared on diskette in 1994 and it first appeared online in 1998. From the beginning of the twenty-first century, virtually all VAAs have been online applications. Users are presented with different forms of digital display in order to illustrate how their own preferences relate to the policy positions of parties or candidates (for a recent, comprehensive review see Garzia and Marshall (2014)). The most common displays include a bar chart or histogram displaying the degree of congruence between party (or candidate) and user in descending order (see Fig. 8.8) and often also a map in which both user and party/candidate are plotted on a multi-dimensional space. Most commonly, a two dimensional map is used whereby users can compare themselves with parties or candidates with respect to an economic Left-Right axis and a second axis that separates social conservatives and traditionalists from social liberals and progressives (see Fig. 8.9, for an example drawn from the EcuadorVota VAA[10]).).

Uwe Serdült, *Ritsumeikan University*

---

[10]See: http://www.ecuadorvota.com

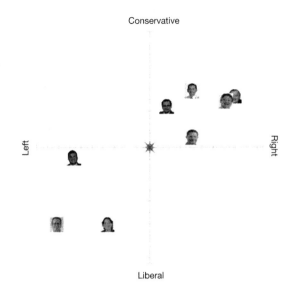

Conservative

Left                                    Right

Liberal

**Fig. 8.9:** Bidimensional Map (EcuadorVota).

VAAs are now a major feature of the election campaign in many countries in Europe prior to national elections (Marshall and Garzia (2014)). Table 8.1 shows how many users appear to have accessed the application in those countries in which they are most commonly used. While the numbers shown in Table 8.1 may overestimate the actual number of users who fill in the application, as many users may fill in it twice, or simply click on it without bothering to fill it in, we can see that in a number of countries such as the Netherlands, Finland and Germany, VAAs have already become institutionalised as a significant proportion of the electorate use these devices.

**Table 8.1:** Ten most used VAAs in Europe.

| País | Nombre del VAA | Primer uso del VAA | Usuarios (año) | % del electorado |
|---|---|---|---|---|
| Países Bajos | StemWijzer | 1989 | 4.9m (2012) | 39.8 |
| Finlandia | Vaalikone | 1996 | 1m (2007) | 22.7 |
| Alemania | Wahl-O-Mat | 2002 | 13.2m (2013) | 21.3 |
| Bélgica | Doe de Stemtest | 2002 | 840,000 (2004) | 20.0 |
| Austria | Wahlkabine | 2002 | 1m (2013) | 15.7 |
| Estonia | Valijakompass | 2011 | 111,535 (2011) | 12.3 |
| Países Bajos | Kieskompass | 2006 | 1.5m (2010) | 12.2 |
| Suiza | Smartvote | 2003 | 437,000 (2011) | 8.6 |
| Luxemburgo | Smartvote.lu | 2009 | 15,100 (2009) | 6.7 |
| Lituania | Mano Balsas | 2008 | 100,000 (2008) | 3.7 |

Source: Marschall (2014: 96)

However, it is not only in the European continent that VAAs have the potential to take off. Since 2010, VAAs have begun to be introduced into Latin America, mainly by the Preference Matcher consortium. Meuvoto 2010/Questão Pública was deployed prior to the Brazilian elections for the presidency and to the Senate in 2010 (Marzuca Perera et al. 2011), which generated over 20,000 users, to be followed by Peru Escoge for the Peruvian presidential elections the following year (50,000 users) and Ecuador Vota (see below) for the Ecuadorian presidential elections in 2013.

### 8.9.2   State of the Art

As the aim of a VAA is to help voters decide which party/candidate most closely matches their policy preferences, probably the largest body of literature relates to issues involving VAA design. Louwerse and Rosema (2011) explore the effects of the spatial models and metrics used in VAAs on the advice given to voters, while Mendez (2012) compares the extent to which the advices offered by VAAs correspond to the users' own vote intention when different metrics are used. Walgrave et al (2009) look at the effects of statement selection, arguing that different choices of issue statements within a VAA produce different advices for users, while Costa Lobo, Vink and Lisi (2010) explore the relevance of ideological dimensions such as Left versus Right for statement selection. Trechsel and Mair (2011) compare different methods for coding parties and candidates, focussing particularly on the methods used in the EU Profiler VAA. Finally, Baka, Figgou and Triga (2012) consider the relevance of the different answer categories used in VAAs, specifically the middle category of "Neither Agree nor Disagree".

Another prominent strand of literature focusses on the effects of VAAs on politics. Fivaz, Pianzola and Ladner (2010) explore the potential impact of VAAs on voting behaviour, while Marschall and Schultze (2012) consider whether or not VAAs have any impact on voter turnout. RRamonait? (2010) takes a critical look at how parties may adapt to the use VAAs, suggesting that populist parties without a clear ideological identity may exploit the tool by adapting to the policy positions of the average voter.

A third strand of the literature draws from the data provided by VAA users. As we have seen, VAAs can attract many users and thereby generate very large datasets. Moreover, most contain supplementary questions in which users are asked to provide demographic data such as age, gender and education, as well as data relating to their political orientation, such as party loyalty, previous voting behaviour and vote intention, and this data can also be accessed by the researcher. VAA-generated data can be used both to improve the design of the VAA itself and to investigate some of the "old" questions of political science. Many of the above-mentioned authors (such as Louwerse and Rosema (2011) and Costa Lobo, Vink and Lisi (2010), see above) exploit the data for the first of these goals. In terms of addressing more fundamental questions of political science that do not relate directly to VAAs, Wheatley and Mendez have taken user response data from VAAs to identify latent ideological dimensions and to map party supporters on an ideological space (Wheatley et al 2012; Wheatley 2015a; Wheatley 2015b). VAA-generated data can also be used to test the so-called directional and proximity models of voting (Mendez 2012).

**Fig. 8.10:** Example of a Political Declaration (EcuadorVota).

From a social network perspective users of a VAA can be traced to their online friends via an invitation link they share on Facebook or other social media. This network strand of VAA research is still in an embryonic phase and is bound by restrictions to data access from often proprietary social media devices that are used for sharing. Privacy issues also have to be respected in terms of obtaining network data. However, to a certain degree VAA generated data allow us to investigate whether social phenomena such as homophily hold up in the online world and more particularly amongst VAA users (see: Manavopoulos et al. 2015).

### 8.9.3   A Brief Look at Data from Ecuador

As an example of how VAA-generated data can help researchers address some of the fundamental questions of political science, let us look at the case of a VAA that was recently deployed in Ecuador. The EcuadorVota VAA was deployed by the Preference Matcher consortium in the run-up to the Ecuadorian presidential elections of February 2013 and data generated from this VAA was used to explore the dimensionality of the Ecuadorian political space. EcuadorVota provided its users with a five-point scale from "completely agree" to "completely disagree" (as well as a sixth, residual "no opinion" category) to express their opinions on thirty policy statements, based on critical election issues such as economic policy, security, social policy, constitutional affairs and the role of the Church. An example of a policy statement is provided in Fig. 8.10. After users had expressed their political preferences on the thirty policy statements, EcuadorVota then matched them with the presidential candidate that best corresponded with their views. It also requested from users certain personal details such as age, gender, education, political interest, vote intention and party identification. An example of a webpage in which users provided supplementary information regarding socio-demographics and political interest variables is shown in Fig. 8.11. A relatively large dataset containing 14,092 entries was generated, but after extensive cleaning 11,146 entries remained.

To test if any underlying trait (such as left versus right) drives voters' responses to the thirty issues, Mokken Scale Analysis was applied to the dataset generated by Ecuador-

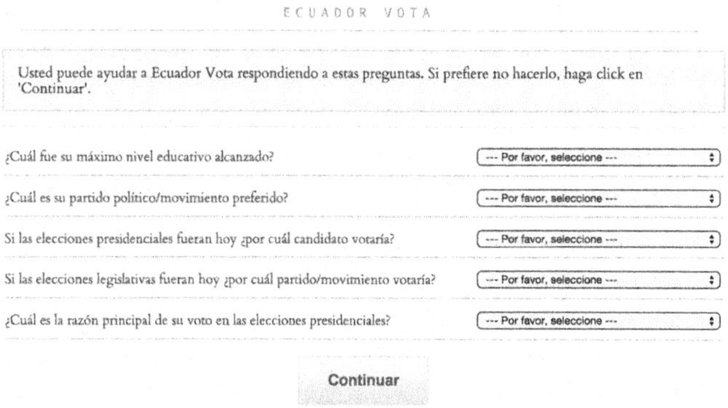

**Fig. 8.11:** Example of Supplementary Questions (EcuadorVota).

Vota in order to identify latent scales (or "dimensions") from users' responses. To form a scale, user responses for items within that scale must correlate closely with one another and vary unidirectionally with the latent trait as measured by the rest score (the summed responses to other items in the scale). Two clear and distinct scales emerged: one broad Left/Right dimension that encompasses most economic items, foreign policy, the Constitution as well as a couple of items that relate specifically to the policies of the government of President Rafael Correa (on control of the media and on appointment of the Prosecutor and auditor); and another liberal/conservative dimension on law and order, the role of religion, abortion, gay marriage and the legalization of drugs.

Having identified latent dimensions, it was then possible to map users who self-identify as party supporters with respect to these dimensions. Party supporters were identified as those who a) named a preferred political party or movement, and b) intended to vote for the same party or movement in elections to the National Assembly (which took place simultaneously with the presidential elections). Each group of party supporters was then mapped in such a way that both the mean position of each party's supporters as well the associated contour lines that enclose 50 per cent of them were plotted. The results are shown in Fig. 8.12.

Plotted in Fig. 8.12 are the mean positions and contour lines for three national parties: President Rafael Correa's Allianza País (APAIS, which won 52.3 percent of the vote), the centre-right Creating Opportunities (Creando Oportunidades, CREO, 11.4 percent), the Social Christian Party (Partido Social Cristiano, PSC, 9.0 percent), the Plurinational Unity of the Lefts (Unidad Plurinacional de las Izquierdas, UPI, 4.7 percent) and the Societal Movement for More United Action (Movimeinto Sociedad Unida Más Acción, SUMA, 3.2 percent).

Overall, party supporters tend to be distributed along a diagonal line from the left-liberal quadrant of the map to the right-conservative quadrant. There are two clearly left-liberal movements: APAIS and the UPI, although the UPI distinguishes itself from APAIS by being both slightly more liberal and slightly less leftist. This is consistent with the fact that the two movements that form the UPI—Pachakutik and the Demo-

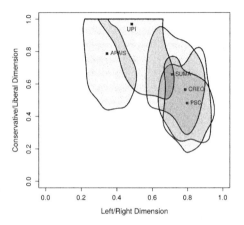

**Fig. 8.12:** Map of Party Supporters, EcuadorVota.

cratic People's Movement (Movimiento Popular Democrático, MPD)—were formerly allied with APAIS, but broke away in 2009. There are also two clearly right-conservative parties, whose supporters occupy almost identical positions on the map: CREO and the PSC. Finally SUMA is closer to the conservative-right parties, but is somewhat more left-leaning and significantly more liberal.

### 8.9.4  Summary

The example of Ecuador provides a short illustration of how VAAs can be used to tell us something about the voting population. The drawback of using VAAs for this purpose is that our sample is necessarily self-selected and tends to draw from younger, more well-educated and more politically interested citizens. This problem is particularly marked in many parts of Latin America (such as Ecuador), where the differences, especially in educational levels, between a relatively small population of "netizens" and the rest of the population is quite large.

The "holy grail" in terms of the research potential of VAAs would be to reach a point where VAA-generated data could be used as a substitute for survey data. While the lack of representativeness of the sample would pose a problem, a number of mechanisms could be used to overcome this. Further research needs to be carried out to explore to what extent post-stratification weighting techniques, such as raking, could be used to balance samples of VAA respondents. An alternative approach would be to use techniques such as propensity score matching to "match" VAA responses to responses observed from a representative survey, providing both questionnaires have a number of items in common. These techniques may be particularly promising given the very large datasets that VAAs typically generate.

Given recent criticisms directed against pre-electoral polls, especially that reluctant respondents in telephone surveys may engage in "satisfying" to get rid of the interviewer, rather than answering the questions honestly, the use of online tools such as VAAs in pre-election surveys is likely to become more attractive. A number of polling companies are already beginning to use online panels as the basis for their surveys. It is the task of VAA-designers to rise to the challenge and explore how VAAs and VAA-type surveys can contribute to this field.

## Further Readings

- Baka, A., Figgou, L., and Triga, V. (2012). *'Neither Agree, nor Disagree': A Critical Analysis of the Middle Answer Category in Voting Advice Applications*. International Journal of Electronic Governance, 5(3), pp. 244-263.

- Costa Lobo, M., Vink, M. and Lisi, M. (2010). *Mapping the political landscape: a vote advice application in Portugal*. In Cedroni, L. and Garzia, D. (eds), Voting Advisors in Europe: Perspectives from Political Science (Naples Scriptaweb), pp.139–167.

- Fivaz, J., Pianzola J. and Ladner A. (2010). *More than Toys: A First Assessment of Voting Advice Applications' Impact on the Electoral Decision of Voters*. Working Paper No. 48, National Centre of Competence in Research (NCCR), Challenges to Democracy in the 21st Century. Descargado 11-05-2014: `http://www.nccr-democracy.uzh.ch/publications/workingpaper/pdf/WP_48.pdf`.

- Garzia, D, and Marschall, S. (eds) (2014). *Matching Voters with Parties and Candidates: Voting Advice Applications in Comparative Perspective*. Colchester, ECPR Press.

- de Graaf, J (2010). *The Irresistible Rise of Stemwijzer*. In Cedroni, L. and Garzia, D. (eds), Voting Advisors in Europe: Perspectives from Political Science (Naples Scriptaweb), pp.35-46.

- Louwerse, T. and Rosema, M. (2013). *The Design Effects of Voting Advice Applications: Comparing Methods of Calculating Matches*. Acta Politica (advance online publication 18 October 2013; doi: 10.1057/ap.2013.30).

- Manavopoulos, Vasilis; Mendez, Fernando and Serdült, Uwe (2015). *Homophily Among VAA Users: the case of Ecuador*, in: Terán, Luis and Andreas Meier, ICEDEG 2015: Second International Conference on eDemocracy & eGovernment, Quito, Ecuador, 8-10 April 2015, IEEE Xplore CFP1527Y-PRT, pp. 61-66. (`http://dx.doi.org/10.1109/ICEDEG.2015.7114487`)

- Marschall, S. and Schultze, M. (2012). *Voting Advice Applications and their Effect on Voter Turnout: The Case of the German Wahl-O-Mat*. International Journal of Electronic Governance, 5(3), pp. 349-366.

182

8   eDemocracy

- Marschall, S. and Garzia, D. (2014). *Voting Advice Applications in a Comparative Perspective*. In Garzia, D, and Marschall, S. (eds) (2014) Matching Voters with Parties and Candidates: Voting Advice Applications in Comparative Perspective. Colchester, ECPR Press, pp. 1-31.

- Marschall, S. (2014). *Profiling Users*. In Garzia, D, and Marschall, S. (eds) (2014) Matching Voters with Parties and Candidates: Voting Advice Applications in Comparative Perspective. Colchester, ECPR Press, 93-104.

- Marzuca Perera, Alejandra, Serdült, Uwe and Welp, Yanina (2011). *Questão Pública: First Voting Advice Application in Latin America*, in: Tambouris, Efthimios; Macintosh, Ann; de Bruijn, Hans (Eds.) Electronic Participation: Third IFIP WG 8.5 International Conference, ePart 2011, Delft, The Netherlands, August 29 – September 1, 2011 Proceedings [Lecture Notes in Computer Science 6847]. Heidelberg, Springer, pp. 216-227.

- Mendez, F. (2012). *Matching voters with political parties and candidates: an empirical test of four algorithms*. International Journal of Electronic Governance, 5(3), pp. 264-278.

- Ramonaite, A. (2010). *Voting Advice Applications in Lithuania: Promoting Programmatic Competition or Breeding Populism?*. Policy and Internet, 2(1), pp. 117–147.

- Trechsel, A.H., and Mair P. (2011). *When parties (also) position themselves: an introduction to the EU profiler*. Journal of Information Technology & Politics, 8(1), pp.1–20.

- Wheatley, J. (2015a). *Restructuring the Policy Space in England: The End of the Left-Right Paradigm?*, British Politics, 10(3): 268-285.

- Wheatley, J. (2015b). *Identifying Latent Policy Dimensions from Public Opinion Data: An Inductive Approach*. Journal of Elections, Public Opinion & Parties, 25(2): 215-233.

- Wheatley, J., Carman, C., Mendez, F., Mitchell, J. (2014). *The Dimensionality of the Scottish Political Space: Results from an Experiment on the 2011 Holyrood Elections*. Party Politics, 20(6): 864-878.

## Contact Details

**Centre for Democracy Studies Aarau (ZDA), University of Zurich**
Küttigerstr. 21
CH - 5000 Aarau
Switzerland
eMail: {jonathan.wheatley,fernando.mendez, uwe.serdult}@zda.uzh.ch
Sitio Web del proyecto: http://www.preferencematcher.org/

# Profile of Authors

### Jonathan Wheatley

Jonathan Wheatley is a senior researcher at the Centre for Democracy Studies Aarau (ZDA). He is also lecturer at the University of Zurich and the Swiss Federal Institute of Technology at Zurich (ETH). He wrote his PhD in Political Science at the European University Institute in Florence, Italy, with a focus on post-communist transition. His research interests include democratization, state-building, parties and party systems, and the use and application of voting advice applications (VAAs) in both established and developing democracies.

### Fernando Méndez

Fernando Méndez is lecturer in Comparative Politics and the topics I have taught include democratisation, nationalism and state-building in a comparative perspective. In terms of research, my main interests are: comparative democratisation; European party systems and voter allignments in an age of globalisation; the use of online voting guidance tools (also known as Voting Advice Applications or VAAs) and their exploitation for research purposes; and politics and society the former Soviet Union. He has a grounding both in qualitative research methods and in some quantitative methods; in terms of the latter, He has experience using psychometric techniques (factor analysis and Mokken Scale Analysis) for analysing survey data. Fernando is also a founding member of the Preference Matcher consortium (`www.preferencematcher.org`), which unites academics from a number of European universities and has deployed VAAs in more than thirty countries in Europe and beyond.

### Uwe Serdült

Professor at the College of Information Science and Engineering, Ritsumeikan University, Japan, and principle investigator at the Centre for Democracy Studies Aarau (ZDA), Switzerland. Within electronic democracy he is interested in internet voting, social networks, digital divide, and the long term effects of e-democracy on political systems. Ongoing research in the field of e-democracy includes the development of internet based platforms and tools for citizens, public administrations as well as academia in order to enhance transparency and deliberation in an information society.

## 8.10    Case Study—Technical and Procedural Mechanisms to Enhance Transparency and Trust in Internet Voting for Swiss Elections and Votes

Jordi Puiggalí-
Allepúz,

*Scytl Secure
Electronic
Voting, S.A.*

Adrià
Rodríguez-
Pérez,

*Scytl Secure
Electronic
Voting, S.A.*

### 8.10.1    Background – Internet Voting in Switzerland

Switzerland has been using internet voting for politically binding elections since 2003. Initially, these trials took place during the holding of votes[11], not elections. To limit the risks associated to the introduction of a new voting technology, trials were limited to up to 30 per cent of the cantonal electorate. The first trials during a binding vote were conducted in the canton of Geneva, in the commune of Arnières, on 19 January 2013. Shortly after, Zurich and Neuchâtel also followed, each canton with its own internet voting system. Geneva's system was developed by the cantonal administration in partnership with Hewlett Packard and Wisekey. The system used by Zurich was similar to Geneva's and had been developed by Unisys. On their side, the Neuchâtel model is quite different, its internet voting solution being firmly integrated into an e-government portal that allows citizens to conduct other transactions with the administration, such as filling tax reports (Serdült et al., 2015: 127). In this context, Neuchâtel integrated in its e-government portal the cryptographic part of the internet voting system developed by Scytl Secure Electronic Voting, S.A. (Scytl).

This first trial phase was initially conceived for the period 2003-2005 and later extended to 2007. Following, a second trial phase allowed extending the internet voting franchise to the Swiss voters living abroad. As a result, additional cantons also started adopting internet voting, either using Geneva's system or the one provided by Zurich, this latter also known as the Consortium system. Up to fourteen[12] out of the twenty-six Swiss cantons ended up offering internet voting for their Swiss citizens living abroad between 2008 and 2013.

With the adoption of a new regulation in 2013, a new phase for internet voting in Switzerland has started, allowing Cantons to bypass the initial limitation of the 30 per cent of the electorate, depending on the security of the voting systems they use. In which follows, we will describe what are the Swiss requirements for internet voting during this third new phase and how Scytl's Swiss internet voting solution, developed in partnership with Swiss Post, meets them.

---

[11]By votes we generally refer to different forms of direct democracy, such as referendums, popular votes on legislation (at all levels), total or partial revisions of the Federal and/or cantonal constitutions, international treaties, or agreements on accession to international organisations. The characteristic of votes against elections is that they are simpler (since they are limited to a yes or no option), while the electoral system in Switzerland may be far more complex.

[12]Aargau, Basel-City, Berne, Fribourg, Geneva, Glarus, Grisons, Lucerne, Neuchâtel, Schaffhausen, Solothurn, St. Gallen, Thurgau and Zurich.

### 8.10.2   Scytl and Swiss Post's Online Voting Solution for Swiss Elections

In 2013, the Federal Council (the seven-member executive body of the Swiss Confederation) published its third report on internet voting, providing an evaluation of the pilot schemes conducted between 2006 and 2012 and defining its future strategy. Tacking stock of such experiences, in 2013 the Federal Ordinance on Political Rights (FOPP) was amended and a specific regulation for internet voting adopted, the Federal Chancellery Ordinance on Electronic Voting (VEleS). Both entered into force in 1 January 2014.

Among other novelties, the FOPP stablishes a set of new levels authorising a certain percentage of the cantonal electoral roll to use internet voting for federal elections (art. 27f Limits FOPP) at: a) 30 per cent; b) 50 per cent; and c) the entire cantonal electorate[13]. At the same time, limits at a) and b) cannot exceed a limit of 10 per cent and 30 per cent of the entire Swiss electorate, respectively. In turn, VEleS stipulates the requirements that an electronic vote casting system and its operation must meet to reach each level, namely:

a) General requirements for the authorisation of electronic voting per ballot[14] (art. 2) and by means of a risk assessment, the canton documents in detailed and understandable terms that any risks are within adequate limits (art. 3);

b) Voters must be able to ascertain whether their vote has been manipulated or intercepted on the user platform or during transmission (individual verifiability) (art. 4);

c) Voters and auditors are able, subject to compliance with voting secrecy, to identify any manipulation that leads to falsification of the result (complete verifiability). Complete verifiability is achieved if additional requirements for individual verifiability and requirements for universal verifiability are met (art. 5).

Following the adoption of the new legislation, the Consortium system developed by the canton of Zurich was declined authorisation in its nine cantons for the Federal Assembly Elections of 18 October 2015 because of security reasons (OSCE/ODIHR 2016). On their side, Geneva's and Neuchâtel's authorisations were renewed for its use by up to 30 per cent of the cantonal electorate. In 2016, and in partnership with Scytl, Swiss Post implemented a voting system with individual verifiability (based on the same technology used in Neuchâtel) and started the authorisation process to achieve the second limit authorisation (50 per cent of the cantonal electorate). They achieved this authorisation by summer 2017. Currently, they plan to expand to certification for all voters by the end of 2018. On their side, Geneva also announced plans to redesign its voting

---

[13]These limits do not include expatriate Swiss citizens who are eligible to vote (art. 27f .2 Limits FOPP)

[14]Such requirements include: a) that the system for electronic voting is implemented and operated so as to guarantee secure and trustworthy vote casting; b) the system must be easy to use for the voters. Account must be taken of the special needs of all voters wherever possible; and c) the system and the operational procedures shall be documented so as to enable the details of all security-relevant technical and organisation procedures to be understood.

system to achieve the limit of the entire cantonal electorate. In what follows, we detail the characteristics of the system implemented by Scytl and Swiss Post.

**Individual verifiability.**   Individual verifiability can be understood as the property of an internet voting system which enables a voter to validate that their encrypted vote accurately contains their selections (cast-as-intended verifiability) and that their vote has properly reached the ballot box and, in some cases, that it has been included in the final tally (recorded-as-cast verifiability). It is provided as a mechanism to ensure that the voting device that a voter is using to cast their vote is not infected, and that the vote has not been intercepted nor manipulated in the voting channel. In the new Swiss legislation (art.4.2 VEleS), for a system to be authorised to cover more than 30 per cent of the cantonal electorate, it is required that it provides voters with a proof that the server system has registered the vote as it was entered by the voter on the user platform (cast-as-intended verifiability). Proof of correct registration must be also provided (recorded-as-cast verifiability).

In several internet voting experiences, individual verifiability has been provided by different means. The first implementation of this property took place in Norway in 2011, during the first set of pilots with internet voting conducted in the country. In this election, cast-as-intended verifiability was implemented using a mechanism known as Return Codes. The Norwegian Return Codes worked as follows (Puiggalí and Guasch 2012): before the voting process started, voters received a voting card with the voting instructions and a set of four-digit codes (the so-called Return Codes), one per each possible voting option. The set of Return Codes was different for each voter. Therefore, the same Return Code could mean different options for different voters, making impossible to guess the candidate for a Return Code without the voting card (i.e., Return Codes do not compromise the secrecy of the vote). When the Norwegian voters cast their vote, they received an SMS with a four-digit code which had been computed by the server over its encrypted ballot. If the contents of the encrypted votes were modified, the operation would not return the correct Return Code. Since Norwegian voters were allowed to vote multiple times, they could cast a new vote from a different computer in case the four digits did not match their selected candidate.

The Swiss systems (both the Neuchâtel and the Geneva ones) also provide cast-as-intended verifiability using Return Codes. However, since multiple voting is not allowed in Switzerland, there are important differences between these mechanism as used in Norway. In order to support single vote casting, Scytl and Swiss Post added a confirmation step at the end of the voting phase to validate the vote after checking the Return Codes. In a first step, the vote is encrypted and sent to the voting server, which calculates the Return Codes, stores the vote as provisional and communicates the Return Codes to the voter. In a second step, the voter, after validation of the Return Codes, sends a confirmation code to the voting server, that stores it together with the ballot as a proof that the vote has been confirmed by the voter (Galindo et al. 2015). If the voter disagrees with the Return Codes, the vote remains unconfirmed. In this scenario, the internet voting channel cannot be used again, but voters can still use another voting channel for contingency (by post or at the polling station) because their vote casting status in the electoral roll has not been updated (Puiggalí et al. 2017).

Yet, Return Codes are not the only mechanisms which allows for providing cast-as-intended verifiability. On their side, the Estonian and Australian (New South Wales) systems, for instance, allow voters to decrypt their votes, thus showing whether it has been properly encrypted.

The other dimension of individual verifiability, recorded-as-cast verifiability, is usually provided by means of a receipt, that allows voters to check whether their vote has been received unmodified by the server. In the case of Scytl's system, a Voting Receipt is provided together with a fingerprint of the encrypted and digitally signed vote during the voting phase, once the vote has been confirmed (Puiggalí et al. 2017). If the list of the fingerprints of the votes present in the Ballot Box is published after the voting period ends, voters can check whether their Voting Receipt is included in the list as a mean to verify that their vote was also included in the final tally.

**Universal verifiability.**   Universal verifiability, by contrast, consists in allowing any third-party (i.e. election observers and auditors) to ensure that all election processes have been conducted in a proper manner. Its most common implementation allows any third party to validate that the votes decrypted and included in the tally are those valid votes received by the voting server (counted-as-recorded verifiability). In Switzerland, the new federal regulation requires systems to provide proof to auditors that the result has been ascertained correctly (Art. 5.4 VEleS). This proof must confirm that the results ascertained: a) take account of all votes cast in conformity with the system that were registered by the trustworthy part of the system; b) take account only of votes cast in conformity with the system; c) take account of all partial votes.

The first implementation of universal verifiability also took place in Norway. Counted-as-recorded verifiability in Norway was implemented by using a verifiable re-encryption mix-net. In order to audit this process, the implemented mix-net generated cryptographic proofs of content equivalence that allowed to detect any manipulation of the votes during its execution (Puiggalí and Guasch 2010). Since 2015, Neuchâtel also uses a verifiable mix-net. Until recently, only Norway and Neuchâtel's systems provided for universal verifiability. As of October 2017, the Estonian system also uses a verifiable mix-net, starting with the last municipal elections.

### 8.10.3   Discussion and Evaluation

In addition to technical guarantees, several procedural safeguards have been designed over time to provide more transparency to internet voting. The main example can be traced back to the internet voting pilots that took place in Norway in 2011, and that are known as "decryption ceremonies". These events consist in the conduct of the decryption and counting phases of the system in front of local and international experts and transmitted in live streaming, who can validate their proper conduct. In Switzerland, however, Federal legislation does not contain explicit provisions for international or citizen election observation. As a matter of fact, before the update in 2013, the Federal regulation did foresee that voters' representatives should, upon request, be allowed to observe internet voting counting (Driza Maurer 2016). As of 2014, such regulations only require that all important official procedures relating to electronic vote casting and the corresponding documentation be made available to voter's representatives (art. 27m.1 Information for the voters FOPP). In this regard, in March 2018 a motion was presented at the National Council (the lower house of the Federal Assembly of Switzerland) requesting that the Federal Act on Political Rights (FAPR) is amended in order to require that voting and counting procedures are open to public scrutiny.

Another alternative which is said to provide transparency and trust to internet voting is the publication of the system's source code. In June 2018, the Swiss Federal Council modified VEleS to request the publication of source code for systems providing complete verifiability (art.7 VEleS). This new requirement came into force already in July 2018. Previously, some cantons like Geneva had already taken steps in this direction. In September 2012, the authorities in Geneva announced that they had granted access to the source code of their internet voting application to a Geneva citizen, who was a representative of the Pirate Party. The Chancellery of the canton also announced a call for tenders to conduct an audit of the source code. After the audit, the authorities published the report, and Geneva became the first canton to publish such information (Driza Maurer 2016). Previously (2011), also Norway had full disclosure of the source code. And, more recently, Estonia published the source code of their system (2013), but just the server and mobile applications part (not the voting client) (Puiggalí et al. 2017).

Additionally, engagement of all electoral stakeholders is key to ensure trust. In Norway, for instance, and being the first election in which verifiability was provided, the government required the involvement of cryptographic experts from Trondheim University to evaluate the properties of the cryptographic protocols proposed. These experts published a security proof of the protocol of the final selected system for academic evaluation. The government also involved security, usability and IT experts to define the other secure voting system requirements and evaluate the compliance of the different technology providers' proposals. Nowadays, Swiss cantons willing to introduce internet voting are also required to follow a similar procedure.

Since 2014, the Swiss federal legislation requires a peer-evaluation (art. 27l Evaluation of the system and the operation modalities FOPP) when a canton adopts a new voting system or makes substantial changes to their previous system (accompanying group). They are also expected to successfully conduct audits if they want to offer the option to vote online to more than 30 per cent of their cantonal electorate, including with validation of the system by cryptography experts (art. 7 VEleS). Specifically, and in order to obtain a certification for use by more than 30 per cent of the cantonal electorate, the following criteria are used for review: a) cryptographic records; b) functionality; c) security of infrastructure and operation; d) protection against attempts to infiltrate the infrastructure; and e) requirements for printing offices.

For the case of Scytl and Swiss Post, prior to certification, the system underwent a certification process by third parties.[15]

---

[15]https://www.post.ch/en/business/a-z-of-subjects/industry-solutions/swiss-post-e-voting?shortcut=evoting

## Further Readings

- Driza Maurer A (2016) Internet voting and federalism: the Swiss case. In: Barrat i Esteve J (coord). El voto electrónico y sus dimensiones jurídicas: entre la ingenua complacencia y el rechazo precipitado. Iustel, Madrid, pp 261-288

- Driza Maurer A, Spycher O, Taglioni G, Weber A (2012) E-voting for Swiss Abroad: A Joint Project between the Confederation and the Cantons. In: Kripp MJ, Volkamer M, Grimm R (eds) Proceedings of the 5th Conference on Electronic Voting (EVOTE2012), LNI GI Series, Bregenz, Austria, July 11-14, pp 173 - 188

- Galindo D, Sandra G, Puiggalí J (2015) 2015 Neuchâtel Cast-as-Intended Verification Mechanism. In: E-Voting and Identity. 5th International Conference, VoteID, Bern, Switzerland, September 2-4, pp 3-18

- Gharadaghy R, Volkamer M (2010) Verifiability in Electronic Voting - Explanations for Non- Security Experts. In: Krimmer R, Grimm R (eds) Proceedings of the 4th Conference on Electronic Voting, LNI GI Series, Bregenz, Austria, July 21-24, pp 151 - 162

- Markussen R, Ronquillo L, Schürmann C (2014) Trust in internet election observing the Norwegian decryption and counting ceremony. In: Krimmer R, Volkamer M: Proceedings of the 6th Conference on Electronic Voting (EVOTE 2014), TUT Press, Lochau/Bregenz, Austria, October 28-31, pp 75-82

- Mendez F, Serdült U (2014) From Initial Idea to Piecemeal Implementation: Switzerland's First Decade of Internet Voting Reviewed. In: Zissis D et al. Design, Development, and Use of Secure Electronic Voting Systems. Hershey, PA: IGI Global, pp 115-127

- OSCE/ODIHR (2011) Swiss Confederation, Federal Elections of 23 October 2011. Needs Assessment Mission Report.

- OSCE/ODIHR (2012) Swiss Confederation, Federal Assembly Elections of 23 October 2011. Election Assessment Mission Report.

- OSCE/ODIHR (2015) Swiss Confederation, Federal Assembly Elections of 18 October 2015. Needs Assessment Mission Report.

- OSCE/ODIHR (2016) Swiss Confederation, Federal Assembly Elections of 18 October 2015. Election Expert Team Final Report.

- Puiggalí J, Cucurull J, Guasch S, Krimmer R (2017) Verifiability Experiences in Government Online Voting Systems. In: Krimmer R, Volkamer M, Braun Binder N, Kersting N, Pereira O, Schürmann C (eds): Electronic Voting. E-Vote-ID, Lochau, Austria, October 24-27, pp 248-263

- Puiggalí J, Guasch S (2010) Universally Verifiable Efficient Re-encryption Mixnet. In: Krimmer R, Grimm R (eds) Proceedings of the 4th Conference on Electronic Voting, LNI GI Series, Bregenz, Austria, July 21-24, pp 241 - 254

- Puiggalí J, Guasch S (2012) Cast-as-Intended Verification in Norway. In: Kripp MJ, Volkamer M, Grimm R (eds) Proceedings of the 5th Conference on Electronic Voting (EVOTE2012), LNI GI Series, Bregenz, Austria, July 11-14, pp 49 - 64

- Serdült U, Germann M, Mendez F, Portenier A, Wellig C (2015) Fifteen Years of Internet Voting in Switzerland: History, Governance and Use. In: Teran L, Meier A: ICEDEG 2015: Second International Conference on eDemocracy & eGovernment. Red Hook, NY: IEEE, pp 149-156

- Spycher O, Volkamer M, Koenig RE (2011) Transparency and Technical Measures to Establish Trust in Norwegian Internet Voting. In: Kiayias A, Lipmaa H (eds) E-Voting and Identity. Third International Conference, VoteID, Tallinn, Estonia, September 28-20, pp 19-35

## Contact Details

**Scytl Secure Electronic Voting, S.A.**
C/ Enric Granados 84
08008 Barcelona, Spain
Tel: +34 934 230 324
Fax: +34 933 251 028
eMail: {jordi.puiggali, adria.rodriguez}@scytl.com
Web: https://www.scytl.com/en/

## Profile of Authors

### Jordi Puiggalí-Allepúz

Jordi Puiggalí has headed Scytl's Research & Security Department since the formation of the company. He has been instrumental in the development of Scytl's technology and intellectual property, co-authoring numerous international patents on application-level cryptography and e-voting security. Prior to joining Scytl, Jordi was the Technical Director for PKI and security projects at the IT department of the Autonomous University of Barcelona. he has also actively collaborated with the cryptographic research group of the Department of Computer Science at the Autonomous University of Barcelona where he co-directed research projects on PKI and applied cryptography. Jordi is a security expert and has participated as a speaker and lecturer in numerous international conferences on computer security and applied cryptography. He has a bachelor's degree in computer engineering from the Universitat Autònoma de Barcelona.

## Adrià Rodríguez-Pérez

Adrià Rodríguez-Pérez is a Political Analyst specialising in Information and Communication Technologies for Development (ICT4D). He currently holds the position of Project Manager and Researcher (Electoral Law and Policy) at Scytl's Research & Security Department. Prior to joining Scytl, Adrià secured several years of professional experience in the international public sector (Council of Europe, Spanish Ministry of Foreign Affairs and Cooperation, AECID) as well as research and academic institutions (Pompeu Fabra University). In his previous experience, he played an instrumental role during the update of the Council of Europe's Recommendation Rec(2004)11 on legal, operation and technical standards for e-voting. Adrià graduated with Highest Honours in Political Science and Public Administration from Pompeu Fabra University and holds a master's degree in International Relations. Currently, he is a PhD candidate in Electoral Law at Universitat Rovira i Virgili, with a research project under the topic of "Secret Suffrage and Digital Electoral Technologies".

# Chapter 9
# eCommunity

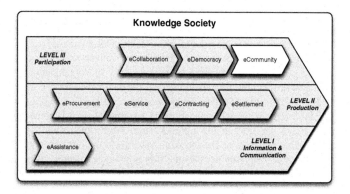

*In Chap. 9, we will discuss alternatives of communication and Web-based tools for community formation. Section 9.1 deals with communication strategies for the citizens. Another challenge is handling the different communication channels and contact media in the multi-channel management (Sect. 9.2). The performance chain in administrative communication can be carried out by a call center or a more comprehensive communication center (Sect. 9.3). A development model for online citizens is presented in Sect. 9.4. With the help of this development model, the governmental institution can estimate the degree of popularity, the capability to communicate and the personal involvement of the citizens (Sect. 9.5). Further tools for community formation, like civic network systems, buddy or recommender systems, as well as corporate blogs, are introduced in Sect. 9.6. Section 9.8 contains bibliographical notes. The case studies Participa Inteligente and the Swiss center for telemedicine, are presented at the end of this chapter.*

© Springer Nature Switzerland AG 2019
A. Meier, L. Terán, *eDemocracy & eGovernment*, Progress in IS,
https://doi.org/10.1007/978-3-030-17585-6_9

# 9.1   Push vs. Pull Communication Strategies

*Push strategy in distribution marketing*

The terms push and pull originally come from marketing terminology and stand for two important alternatives for stimulating the distribution. A push strategy in distribution marketing means that the products are "pushed" through the distribution system by a distribution organization. The producer practices an intensive sales promotion and creates a "selling pressure" in the wholesale trade, which in turn puts the same pressure on the retail trade, up to the end consumer. This distribution strategy is advisable, if the clients have little brand loyalty and the choice of brands and a possible purchase are rather spontaneous.

*Explanation of the pull strategy*

On the contrary, the pull strategy puts the effort on sales promotion to the end consumer (mostly advertising). Here, the product is "pulled" through the distribution network. In other words, a "demand pull" is created: The client demands the product in retail trade, the retail trade demands it from wholesale trade and they from the producer. In the pull strategy, it is necessary that the client perceives differences between the brands, chooses one brand and demands the product.

Push and pull strategies can be applied to communication media, specifically to the Internet and WWW. According to Fig. 9.1, an administrative unit can use push or pull for their communication policy, or a combination of both alternatives.

*Alternatives of communication: push and customized push*

In the push strategy, information and services are arranged according to topics and delivered automatically to the companies or citizens by the organizational unit. The activity originates at the administrative unit, and the Internet users can hardly defend themselves against it (setup of spam filters, see Sect. 10.5). This traditional form of mass advertising makes not much sense in the eGovernment, as it is counterproductive and hardly increases the trust in the administration. More interesting, therefore, is a service with which companies or citizens can subscribe to the push channels. Here, the Internet user can enter his preferences for the supply with information, as to say, we are dealing with a push strategy that is adapted to the person or company (customized push).

*Pull alternative*

In the pull strategy, the Internet users decide which information or offers they want to draw from the Internet or an eGovernment portal, respectively. The initiative for the information supply or utilization of services originates from the citizen. He selects in-

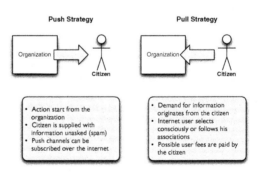

**Fig. 9.1:** Differences of pull and push strategies in the Internet.

formation and offers as he wishes and decides autonomously, which offers he wants to draw on. If applicable, he pays a user fee for services.

An administrative unit can, e.g., launch a Weblog on an important vote or a project idea. Citizens could subscribe to it with an RSS feed, in order to stay up-to-date with events or recent developments. With such a customized push, citizens would not have to visit the often-extensive Web sites of the administration or an eGovernment portal, in order to stay up to date. In contrast to the sending of e-mails, the initiative lies with the receiver and not the sender. The receiver of such information services can change his subscription anytime or revoke it, by making the corresponding adjustments in his RSS aggregator.

*Use of Weblogs*

Another news format for public administration is instant messaging (see also Fig. 7.6 and Sect. 7.4, respectively). This refers to immediate transmission of messages. With such a service, members of an administrative unit (police, firemen, civil defense, and others) or citizens can be informed about events in real-time. Short messages are distributed with the push strategy over a communication network or the Internet, respectively, and the receivers can answer immediately. Increasingly often, instant messaging systems offer audio and video conferences, as well. Such more developed forms of communication are suitable for emergency services, in which it is necessary to make quick and competent decisions.

*Instant messaging*

It is the responsibility of the administrative unit to use suitable push or pull strategies or to apply a combination in form of a customized push.

Furthermore, it is of great importance that the different administrative units on local and regional level agree on how to implement a suitable communication policy. What immediately comes to mind are eGovernment portals with Weblogs or instant messaging subscriptions, in order to bundle information and news services on national level, as well as on regional and municipality level.

## 9.2 Multi-Channel Management

In the literature, the term multi-channel management is not well established yet. Mostly, it is about managing different channels, but it is not always clear whether they are contact channels and/or distribution channels. Additionally, there is unclarity about the use of the term in the eGovernment. For example, it can be used for communication or interchange of services between administration and citizen, between different administrative units or between administration and companies/suppliers.

Here, the term multi-channel management or collaborative citizen relationship management (see Sect. 9.3) is understood as the management of parallel used contact channels on the citizens' side. It is useful to distinguish between contact and distribution channels, as distribution and communication channels have different characteristics and are operated by different information systems.

*The term multi-channel management*

When using electronic platforms for the eGovernment, different informational and communicational needs are created. If the citizen reaches the administration, regardless over which contact channel and with what intention, we speak of inbound communication. In outbound communication, on the other hand, the organization directs itself to the citizens, using adequate contact channels.

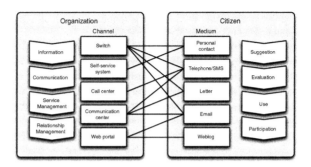

**Fig. 9.2:** Diversity of contact channels and contact media.

*What is a medium?*   By medium, we understand a means of communication, e.g., a mobile device, an interaction platform or another technical or electronic solution for information interchange. Direct media are e.g., telephone, e-mail or Weblog. With such media, the citizen is addressed directly and personally. In case that these media allow the dialog with the citizens, we are dealing with interactive media.

*Co-action of channels and media*   On the contrary to direct media, there exist indirect media, in which information gets to the citizens indirectly. The indirect media comprise radio, television, newspapers, bulletins, commercials, or placards.

Figure 9.2 shows some contact channels and direct media for information interchange between administration and citizens. The contact channel on the side of the administration is not limited to the choice of an organizational unit. Rather, a contact channel is composed of different roles and capabilities of the collaborators, activities at the counter and processes, supported by information and communication systems.

*Personal contact*   The personal contact can be effective from the point of view of the administration, especially when the members of the administration are trained and advanced accordingly. However, the costs for this kind of communication are high and are only justified for certain concerns or services. Enhancing the personal contact with electronic means can increase efficiency.

*Use of telephones*   Using telephones is promising, if the members of administration are trained and prepared for the calls. As in many organizations the phone calls are often redirected, until the citizen's concern is concluded, some administrations are introducing call or communication centers (see Sect. 9.3 and case study in this chapter). Apart from the conventional use of telephony, asynchronous alternatives of connection can be used. For example, some administrative institutions make use of the possibility to send election results via short message service.

Even in times of the Internet, traditional mail with respective supplements can be sent to the citizens in need or to interested groups. This medium is usually costly, which is why it only pays off for legally required tasks.

*E-mail*   The advantages of e-mail against conventional correspondence lie in the velocity of transmission and the fact that the information are presented in electronic form and can be further used. It is possible to attach additional documents and graphics in an easy

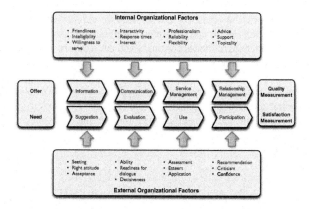

**Fig. 9.3:** Process chain in administrative communication, adapted from Bruhn (2002).

way. Legally binding attachments must be secured with a digital signature (see Chap. 5 on eContracting). When using e-mails, there is the danger that the citizens get too much material and are annoyed.

Web portals have the advantage that they can offer information and possible citizen-specific concerns anonymously. If wished, users can subscribe to Weblogs on important administrative projects. Depending on how the technology is used, expert opinions can be asked for online.                    *Web portals*

Figure 9.3 shows the process chain in case that either information or a service are requested in the eGovernment. The alignment of administrative units towards the citizens consists of internal and external goals, which have to be viewed separately. Goals with external focus are those, which have to be reached by a portal or information system with regard to the claim groups. Among them are openness, acceptance, utilization, satisfaction with the service and the offer of communication, respectively. Some internal organizational factors of the effect relationship are openness and friendliness of the members of the administration, professionalism during processing, handling of complaints and cooperativeness.

When using Web-based portals and communication systems, it is necessary to check and evaluate the achievement of objectives, the citizens' satisfaction and the quality of the offers regularly. With regard to the multitude of contact and communication channels and media, the administration has to choose and offer those channels which comply with the legal regulations and the citizens' preferences, and which justify the financial and personal investment.                    *Quality measurement in communication*

## 9.3   Establishment of a Citizen Communication Center

Call centers are organizational units of administrations, which contact the citizens by telephone. The call center can handle the contact actively (outbound), or the call center is passive and is called (inbound). A call center makes it possible for people to request                    *Definition of call center* information in elections and votes, for tax declaration, to order ID cards or passports, when changing residence, etc. It can disburden different administrative units, if the employees of the call center are trained accordingly and get access to important information systems of the administration.

*Automatic call distribution*    A call center disposes of an automatic call distribution function, in order to distribute the incoming calls to the available employees (agents). Usually, a citizen who calls is attended according to the first in, first out principle, that is, whoever calls first is attended first. If several calls come in at the same time, waiting loops are created. As soon as agents are available, they are connected to the callers in the waiting loop. Waiting citizens are informed about the approximate holding time and maybe are served with music.

*Automatic allocation*    It is possible to redirect calls with more challenging tasks to agents with expert knowledge. The call center supports these allocations and keeps the agents informed anytime about the length of the waiting line and the occupation of expert agents. So-called interactive voice response functions make it possible to free the agents from giving routine information. Apart from the recorded address of welcome, it could be the choice of language. Additionally, the caller is asked about his concern (emergency, information, service) and redirected to the corresponding expert group.

The citizens can be connected to the information system of the administration by the incoming telephone number or by stating their citizen's ID (social security number). At the beginning of the phone call, the agent knows about earlier contacts or concerns and does not have to ask the caller again nor consult with colleagues. However, this means that in recurring calls, the individual actions are documented and a history of the citizen's contact is logged electronically until the concern is resolved.

*Key figures in Call Center*    Call centers register the time of starting and ending of the incoming call and the time of mediation to the agent. Thereby, different key figures are generated:

- Total number of incoming calls on weekdays or at certain times of the day

- Holding times and interrupted calls, respectively

- Answered calls and workload of agents

- Duration of calls and distribution.

With this information it is intended to plan the amount of agents needed and their formation or specialization. Additionally, it is possible to estimate on which days of the week and at what times there are high workloads (analysis of holding times, interruptions, etc.). Both the reachability and the degree of service of the call center, and the workload of the attending agents, can calculated with this data, in order to develop suitable measures for the future.

*From call to communication center*    Over the past years, the call centers more and more changed into communication centers. This has to do with the fact that the citizens increasingly prefer e-mail or other electronic forms of contact apart from telephony. The communication center is a continuation of the call center and supports different contact channels and contact media (see multi-channel management in Sect. 9.2). It is a particular challenge to switch between different communication channels for one and the same concern. For example, a citizen can request first information on the order of an ID card by phone, place the order by e-mail and later ask about the shipping status by phone. Thus, each communication center must have a powerful multi-channel management, in order that the agents have an overview of the respective status of services anytime.

In the case study in this chapter, the special characteristics of a medical communication center are explained, which is at public disposal around the clock and even reachable from outside the country.

## 9.4   Development Model for Online Citizen

A development model for the eGovernment was proposed, which typifies the visitors of a Web platform or a portal. At the same time, this model makes it possible to evaluate the quality of a Web site and plan respective corrections or changes to it. Section 9.5 discusses key figures for measuring the success of both the typification of the visitors and the quality measurement of a Web site. With them, it is possible to analyze the communication and interaction behavior of the online citizens and to adapt the Web platform step by step to the citizens' needs. *What is the use of a development model?*

If a citizen accesses the Web, he passes through a number of phases in his communication and interaction behavior. The more experienced he becomes, the more sharpened will his power of judgment in electronic services become. At the same time, supposing that the dialog control and support are professional, the trust in the administration increases; the chances become higher that an online citizen is won or that a service is handled electronically.

Figure 9.4 illustrates the four user groups in the eGovernment, that is online surfer, online communicator, online community member and online citizen. In the following, we will characterize the four user groups. Additionally, we will indicate how the administration can influence the behavior of the online user.

**The Online Surfer.**   He acts according to the motto: I'll drop by. For example, he wants to consult the results of the latest votes in the parliament or simply be entertained. Online surfers often browse through the Web at random and jump from one Web site to the next. They use the offers passively, consume information by chance and move rather emotionally than cognitively. *Passive use of offers*

**Fig. 9.4:** Development model for online citizen according to Meier (2009).

In order to win online surfers for eGovernment concerns and services, the addresses of the Web site or portal must be known or reachable by different links. The governmental institution should assume a marketing point of view when giving the name and register important Web addresses early; e.g., a governmental office can launch a Web site under the name of a promising public project. With regard to the legal aspects of filing a Web address, and the problems with already taken domain names, we refer to the literature.

After choosing and registering the Web address, it is made public. To do so, classic advertising means like print media, television and radio may be used, or online advertising. Of course, public authorities will rarely use television broadcasts for their marketing purposes. Public institutions should however aim to place their Web addresses in highly frequented portals, search engines or Web sites of NPOs or NGOs as banner advertisement. Additionally, it is necessary to have them enlisted in online indices and to get high priority in popular search services.

**The Online Communicator.**   The surfer develops into an online communicator, if the governmental institution succeeds in establishing target-oriented and repeated contact with the citizens. The online communicator keeps the Web address in his bookmarks and clicks on the Web site for governmental services and information.

*Dialog offer is important*   The online communicator is not only appealed by the service offers of the governmental institutions, but also by the dialog offered by them. It is decisive how the informational content is presented and how the dialog is led. Naturally, the advantages of the services must be pointed out and commented on. The effect of transparent processes with corresponding help offers is not to be underestimated. For example, with the graphic capabilities of modern computers, it is possible to visualize all the necessary steps of a change of residence on the Internet and comment on it. Thus, the online communicator obtains a clearer picture of public services and their dependencies.

Some examples of the activities of an online communicator are ordering tendering texts for public construction projects, or downloading bus schedules of public busses and trolley lines. By retrieving target-oriented information, he shows higher interest than a passive surfer. In the case of an online communicator, the governmental institution has the chance to win an active online user or to arouse interest for a public project. Targeted interactive applications get the online communicator more involved and cause him to become more active.

*Advantages of membership*   **The Online Community Member.**   The online community member manifests his interest by a membership of a public program, is active and gets personally involved. For example, he is willing to give his opinion on the new district maps of the municipality. In case of specific knowledge, e.g., if he is a geologist, an environmental economist, a botanist or an urban and regional planner, he indicates deficiencies and problems or gives qualified propositions for improvement. In case the governmental institution makes corresponding arrangements on its Web site, it maintains an exchange of experiences with further members.

*Declaration of user profile*   When the online community member has come to trust the Web site, he is willing to specify his user profile in detail, if needed. He may do so especially if additional services are linked to it; e.g., the interested member should receive the respectively newest versions of the district map. Now, the member does not stand helpless against a stream of information, but rather selects the information himself by means of the submitted profile of interests (see customized push in Sect. 9.1).

Online community members of a Web site can contact each other and exchange their requests and experiences in discussion forums. Depending on the progressiveness of the governmental institutions, such communities are actively endorsed. However, it requires courage and openness to further specific member platforms, and password-secured areas have to be implemented. Many governmental institutions still hesitate to create online clubs, because they fear a bundling of critical voices or an increased influence of the citizens.

**The Online Citizen.** The online citizen is valuable, as he has great confidence in the institution and puts his skills or connections at disposal of the governmental office, if required. The governmental institution must strive to keep the online citizens with them, as satisfied and recurrent citizens. Once the trust is established, the online community members or online citizens perform Web-based administrative processes in especially delicate areas like taxation or health care. To that end, the governmental institution has to provide suitable cryptographic procedures and digital signatures (see Sects. 5.4 and 5.5). *Nurture of online citizens*

The fourth development step is critical, because the design of the Web site or portal is put to a test. If the user guidance or communications are cumbersome or even faulty, the confidence of the online citizens will quickly decrease. Any violation or abuse of privacy, e.g., during eVoting, must be prevented from the beginning by adequate measures (see Sect. 6.4 on data protection and case study in Chap. 6 on eSettlement).

The online citizen distinguishes himself from the online community member by the frequency and regularity of his visits. As the interactivity usually decreases in following transactions of visitors, the governmental office must come up with ideas to maintain the Web site attractive for online citizens. Only by targeted disclosure of significant information, optionally complemented by internal administrative surveys and policy documents, as well as the possibility to exercise influence, can the governmental institution improve their image and widen their range of influence. In Corfu,[1] e.g., a Web platform is used with which the governmental institution gathers public opinions on construction projects, watering systems and social programs. By involving the citizens at an early stage of public projects, new forms of collaboration are established. *Keeping the Web site attractive*

In the user group of online citizen, the citizens' satisfaction should be surveyed and evaluated periodically. Furthermore, the relationship must be nurtured and activated. This can be done for example by making additional offers exclusively to the online citizens. An approach considered promising is the promotion of personal communication by contact lists, forums or team building processes (see Chap. 7 on eCollaboration).

---

[1] On this topic, see the quote by Bouras et al. (2000) in the bibliographical notes in Sect. 9.8.

## 9.5   Performance Review for Public Web Platforms and Portals

*Browsing and searching*

Electronic platforms distinguish themselves by the fact that they log all citizens' interactions, including the chosen search strategy; hopefully with respective notification of the online citizen. The behavior on Web sites usually follows associative criteria, this is, the visitor lets himself be guided by the display and linking of information. All these processes of searching and browsing through individual sites of a Web site can be analyzed. This variety of information results into potential process control and checks. In particular, the design of the proper Web platform can be evaluated and, if necessary, be adapted.

It is an advantage for the governmental institution that it can record the factual contact in electronic services for citizens; depending on the sensitivity of the clientele, these records should be kept anonymously and only be used to improve the Web site and the dialog control.

*Clickstream analysis*

The system keeps a protocol of every access to a screen page and further content of the page with date, time, page, data name etc. and the address of the inquiring server. With the aim to make it possible to compare and evaluate future protocols, different propositions where made about the gathering of the most important parameters. For example, number of site accesses, clicks, and number of visits or contacts were counted. Especially insightful is the session length, as it can give hints on the attractiveness of individual sites.

*Anonymous survey*

Next to these technical parameters, it is of interest to take minutes of the online citizen's behavior. The governmental institution can and should afford to carry out these surveys anonymously and to inform the public about it: What are the citizens' searching habits? What kind of dialog control is preferred? Where and when is the visitor motivated to state personal information and his information requirements? Which online visitors are willing to give their feedback on the nature of a service or a public project?

Here, key figures are discussed which capture and evaluate the process of the citizens' development. These key figures are geared to the above mentioned visitor groups, as to say the online surfer, online communicator, online community member, and online citizen. In Fig. 9.5, the system of key figures for the development process is drawn schematically.

The term online surfer comprises both active and passive users. Active users are interested in the online offers of the institution and hope to satisfy particular needs; they are willing to make active requests (active search for information). Passive users, on the other hand, get to the Web site by chance and are willing to try out the online offer (passive search for information), if there is a respective incentive.

*Key figure degree of popularity*

The first key figure K1 refers to the noticeability of an online measure and expresses the effectiveness of the promulgation of a Web site through the media, including traditional media. As a way to calculate the key figure K1, the number X1 of online surfers can be compared to the size of the desired target group M1 (estimated number, or number of citizens).

For the purpose of a small sample calculation, realistic numbers X1–X4 are chosen for the different user groups, to indicate the size of each group in a measuring period.

As measuring periods can serve time units like day, week, quarter, or year. Apart from that, it is assumed that an average of M1 Internet users visits the Web site or the portal in a given report period. It is also possible to use the number of citizens in a catchment area as M1. In case of the first key figure K1 (degree of popularity), the potential user group M1 with 1,000, and the actual measured surfer group X1 with 30, result into an indicator of 0.03 or 3%. In other words, an average of 0.03 or 3% of the population visits the Web site or portal per day (or week or month etc.).

The next challenge of the governmental institution consists in turning the online surfer into an online communicator by an attractive dialog control. The required group of citizens X2 can be determined by counting the visits of the site. However, it is important that more than the just the homepage is accessed. An online surfer who only visits the first page of an Internet presence (calling card), is not yet an online communicator. That's why the criterion for picking out the group of citizens X2 should be based on the access of three or more pages, or correspond to a session length of more than three minutes. Hence, the second key figure K2 results from the number X2 of those willing to communicate, compared to the number X1 of the surfers.   *Key figure ability to communicate*

In Fig. 9.5, the sample calculation for 10 people willing to communicate (X2), compared to 30 surfers (X1), results into a key figure K2 of 0.33 or 33%; so approximately a third part of all visitors is willing to utilize the interactive possibilities of the Web site and to enter communication with the governmental institution.

Apart from the access of Web sites or content by the user, interaction processes are also an interesting topic. These discover whether an active dialog between the user and the governmental institution or a software agent, respectively, is taking place. If the online communicator is willing to utter suggestions and wishes and to back up his interest with a membership (subscription), he becomes an online community member. The key figure K3 expresses the degree of interaction, by comparing the number X3 of citizens, which perform the interaction process with the number X1 of visitors. The   *Key figure membership*

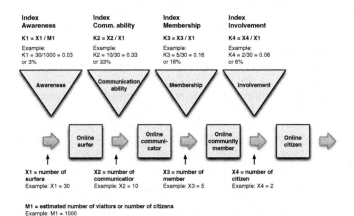

**Fig. 9.5:** Key figures for measuring success, adapted from Meier (2009).

small sample calculation shows that a 16% of the Internet visitors store a profile (or have already stored one) or take up a subscription.

*Key figure loyalty*

We can only speak of loyalty or commitment, when a user visits several times and engages actively in the activities of the governmental institution. This user group X4, compared to the number of surfers X1, results into the key figure K4, being an indicator for the citizens' loyalty and the personal involvement, respectively. In the sample calculation, we are talking about a 6% of the Internet users who participate actively in governmental projects or draw on services.

In the key figure of loyalty K4, we presuppose identifiable users. In order to recognize an online citizen, he is asked to either log in with a passport or to become a member. In addition to that, more sophisticated Web platforms require a user profile in order to cover the online citizens' preferences better.

*Deducing procedure recommendations*

With the discussed key figures, procedure recommendations can be developed, to optimize the online marketing for the governmental institution. With the help of these key figures, changes in the design of the Web site, in the maintenance of the portal, in the dialog control or in content management (see Sect. 7.2) can be measured and evaluated better.

When comparing the development of the key figures over a longer period of time, it is possible to measure the success or failure of the communication and interaction programs or other Web-based initiatives of the governmental institution. Call ups and special campaigns help to counteract the online citizens' lack of interest. Additionally, it is easier to calculate investments or disinvestments in the electronic communication and distribution channel.

## 9.6   Tools for Community Building

In recent times, the Internet is developing into an environment in which the citizens display themselves, meet with others, exchange information and services, promote common projects and overcome language and cultural boundaries (see keyword Web 2.0 and social software, respectively, in Sect. 2.2).

*Community formation in cyberspace*

Computers and communication channels not only serve the collaborators in the administration to handle their workload, but they also make encounters and communities possible. In the same way that street cafes, markets or exhibitions appear as points of encounter in real life, besides family and work, the network of networks develops into a virtual location. Topic-specific, cultural or scientific meeting points on the Internet create a new kind of community formation.

Computer networks are populated by citizens and avatars.[2] The Internet or cyberspace, respectively, can amplify one's living environment. Like in real living environments, infrastructures are developed for the virtual space, platforms for exchange are supplied and services offered. In addition, rules of conduct and protective measures intend to maintain the proper privacy and to fend off misuses. Among the communities created on the Internet, we can distinguish between two kinds:

---

[2] In Hinduism, avatars are the embodiment of a god on earth; and in today's information society they are persons displayed on the Internet who adopt a fictional identity.

- **Communities of interest**: This comprises citizens who are interested in a common thing or share a hobby.

- **Communities of practice**: This comprises groups of citizens who participate in a common project of a governmental institution and invest time and knowledge.

Both kinds of communities can be furthered by information and communication systems. Community support systems serve the members as a meeting point, or to exchange know-how and knowledge and to master tasks or challenges. Web-based platforms not only reveal the existence of communities, but also make it possible to meet other members of the community and to utilize the know-how and expertise of this community.

Web-based platforms and the corresponding software systems for community formation can be characterized as follows:

**Civic Network Systems.**   Civic networks or community networks are electronic meeting points for citizens whose common ground is a place or living environment they have in common. This may be, e.g., a city or a mountain area, whose inhabitants want to meet with their cohabitants in the virtual space. Apart from designing and moderating discussion forums, the focus lies on projects that concern the community or on improved and extended possibilities of training and further education.

*Electronic meeting points*

**Buddy Systems.**   Based on the everyday meaning of the word buddy, the buddy system shows where colleagues or friends are currently located and how they can be reached electronically. The social or task-oriented perception of group members (awareness) makes it possible to meet virtually or exchange experiences; apart from that, the system indicates it if a participant does not want to be disturbed. For actual reunions, the systems can establish audio or video connections, so that the spatial distance is overcome (media space). Recent developments admit to create three-dimensional worlds and to replace real areas of encounter with virtual ones (virtual reality).

*Perception of group membership*

**Matchmaking Systems.**   The term matchmaking originally refers to marriage bureaus, but is conceived as a wider concept in cyberspace. It is about exchanging relations for economy and society. The systems promote contacts and activities in a commonly used environment for proper purposes. For example, networks of acquaintances are utilized to make new contacts, based on an already existing mutual trust, and to exchange information.

*Networking service*

**Recommender Systems.**   These systems are about finding out the Internet users' preferences and making them suggestions for their further development. Special procedures (collaborative filtering) make it possible to categorize the participants' preferences and to pass on those suggestions for activities and further education that are important for a certain group. For example, if someone wishes to become acquainted with a new subject area, such systems recommend suitable literature, possibly complemented by an expert evaluation.

*Use of recommender systems*

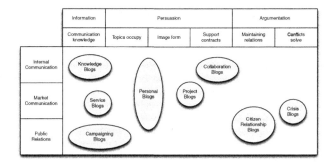

**Fig. 9.6:** Possible applications of corporate blogs, adapted from Zerfass (2007).

*Utility of corporate blogs*

**Corporate Blog Systems.**    Corporate Weblogs are up-to-date digital journals of groups of people or organizational units (see Sect. 7.4). The systems or platforms make it possible to mediate knowledge, occupy topics or nurture relationships. Corporate blogs serve to support the organizational goals and usually can be subscribed to by all interest groups. In order to deepen the topic, the applications of corporate blogs shall be discussed, as they take over different functions in an organization. Figure 9.6 gives an overview over the most important corporate blogs including their intended use.

*Classification approach*

Zerfass[3] classifies corporate blogs according to their field of application and distinguishes those, which can be attributed to internal communication, market communication, or public relations. The corporate blogs can also be used to mediate information or knowledge, persuasion (influencing or convincing) or relationship issues (argumentation).

## 9.7    Impact of Social Networks in Public Administration

*The Use of Social Networks*

In the latest years, a number of citizen movements and protests has spread across the world. One of the characteristics of such events is that demonstrations have been aroused by the use of social networking channels such as *Twitter*, *Facebook*, and *Whatsapp*, among others. Different scholars are currently analyzing this phenomenon to better understand its impact on societies. Furthermore, the use of the Internet as a driver or tool of organizing different groups and demonstrations leaves traces of social changes that have been addressed by technology.

*Impact of Social Networks*

The use of social networks for social participation and social mobilization of offline demonstrations is having a big impact on society. Researchers have found evidence that social media affects citizens' political participation (Comunello & Anzera (2012); Gil de Zúñiga et al. (2010)). Various offline demonstrations have been studied. An example is illustrated in the work of Segerberg & Bennett (2011).

The use of social networks for political participation and demonstrations is a new and evolving phenomenon. However, it plays a key role in organizing and diffusing public

---

[3] See bibliographical notes in Sect. 9.8 and the article by Zerfass (2007).

protests. While some works have focused on the structures of social networks and/or information propagation given a politically defined hashtag or group of hashtags (Conover et al. (2011); Ausserhofer & Maireder (2013)), the academic literature contains a number of case studies related to the adoption of these alternative communication channels to promote mobilizations and demonstrations around the globe (Segerberg & Bennett (2011); Passini (2012); Enjolras et al. (2013)).

Varnali & Gorgulu (2015) analyze the case of the Gezi Park protests (#OccupyGezi) in their work. In the same way, Gil Ramírez & Guilleumas (2015) present quantitative research in which they analyze the trends of tweets related to the 15M movement (May 15, 2011). In the work of Recuero et al. (2015), the authors analyze the citizens' communication through hashtags during protests that took place in Brazil in June 2013 and describe the different kinds of political hashtags (emotive, conative, and metalingual). The researchers found that hashtags containing information about streets and other places for demonstrations (referential hashtags) was a distinct behavior in the dataset. *Social Movements*

Contemporary social movements today use social networks to generate a new experience and empowerment of public space. In this sense, some of the questions that remain open for the public administrator include the different types of public demonstrations and the strategic and emotional use of social networks, as well as the sustainability of contemporary social movements.

## 9.8 Bibliographical Notes

In the marketing literature, push and pull techniques are dealt with, primarily for distribution (Kotler et al., 2007). The differences between push and pull also plays a role in communication and can be transferred to online marketing (Tiedtke & Link, 2013). The application of different communication channels and contact media (Mock, 2006) leads to multi-channel management. *Literature on communication*

The analysis of customer relations and the evaluation of the client capital (Blattberg et al., 2001) lead to the customer relationship management (Bruhn, 2002). Some parts of it can be used for nurturing the relationships with the citizens, other parts have to be adapted (Daum (2002); Raab & Werner (2009)). In particular, a development model for the online citizen can be applied with concrete key figures for the citizen relationship management (Meier, 2004). *Citizen relationship management*

Web platforms are proper for public administration and make it possible to organize communication and services electronically (Bouras et al. (2000); Priddat & Jansen (2001); Meier (2001)). To that end, community support systems (Koch, 2001) give new possibilities for information exchange and collaboration. The development of corporate blogs (Zerfass, 2007) constitutes another opportunity for the eGovernment, because it helps to further develop Web-based communication, market communication and public relations. In this matter, the rules of online law (Strömer, 1997) have to be taken into account. The particularities of medical communication centers using data warehouse technologies are displayed in the doctoral thesis by Ionas (2008). In (Terán, 2014) a fuzzy-based recommender system architecture for stimulating political participation and collaboration is proposed. It showcases the "Smart Participation" project, which uses the *Community formation*

database of (smartvote, 2015), a well-known voting advice application (VAA) for local, cantonal and national elections in Switzerland.

*Impact of Social Networks*    Section 5.7.3 is based on the work of Recalde et al. (2017) about employing wordembeddings to identify groups of interest and hijackers in political demonstrations. In the work of Gerbaudo (2018), the author analyses the culture of the new protest movements of the 21st century from the Arab Spring to the "indignados" protests in Spain and the Occupy movement. Dwivedi et al. (2017) presents a literature review of the articles on the use of social media for getting access to e-government websites from the perspective of citizens.

# 9.9 Case Study—Medical Communication Center supported by the Swiss Center for Telemedicine

Reto M. Zurflüh,
*Swiss Center for Telemedicine*

## 9.9.1 Background

England, 1879: A grandmother is woken up at night by her wretchedly coughing grandson. The little child does not stop, is short of breath and is terribly anxious. The grandmother cannot think of a remedy and calls the doctor, who lives many miles away. He diagnoses a pseudo croup via telephone and gives the concerned woman instructions on how to proceed. The child soon recovers and the grandmother is thankful for the good medical advice in the emergency.

Soon after that day, the medical journal "The Lancet" covered this medical counseling via telephone, which made history as the first documented teleconsultation. Today, this episode would hardly be worth mentioning, as such or similar stories happen every day. Modern hospitals or the day-to-day medical business is not to be thought without telemedicine. It is essential for overcoming local and temporal distances.

Telemedicine is defined as an interaction between patient and doctor (teleconsultation) or between doctors (telecounsel) in indirect connection with a medical treatment, while the involved are not in direct physical contact with each other. Virtually every medical practitioner uses telemedical methods, whether consciously or unconsciously. The patients are often glad to receive competent advice in a short telephone call. They accept the call as a legitimate and comfortable kind of contact with their doctor.

This is where the Swiss Center for Telemedicine MEDGATE comes into play. Starting form the desire to increase quality and efficiency in the health care system, the 1999 founded company offers distance medical counseling. Today, there are about 50 physicians and 25 medical specialists standing by to attend worried patients around the clock, by telephone, Internet, and video connection.

## 9.9.2 Case Medgate

Running a medical communication center or teleconsultation center is challenging. In contrast to usual medical call centers, in which health counselors distribute the patients into the different physical services, in the sense of a supply control, with the help of computer systems, a teleconsultation center is more like doctor's office. In order to meet the requirements of this broad medical service offering and the increased responsibility, Medgate disposes of a special permit by the medical police and stay under strict governmental control.

The basis of the work in the teleconsultation center is internationally recognized best practices. Some of the most important of these binding process definitions, kept by all employees, are standardized telemedical procedures for training and exams, quality circles and the support of processes by modern knowledge management systems.

In Fig. 9.7, it is shown how triage is conducted in the medical teleconsultation center by Medgate, and which part results into telediagnostics, telecare and teletherapy. This analysis is based on the experiences with proper evaluations and shows today's potential of applying medical communication centers.

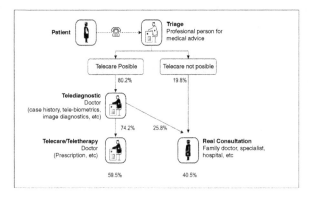

**Fig. 9.7:** Potential benefits of telediagnosis and telecare.

## The Person—Central Factor

Medgate invests a lot into the training of telephysicians. Apart from the above-average medical qualification, in the teleconsultation center it is particularly important that the counselors have sharpened senses and the ability to explain complicated topics in a simple way.

Modern information and communication technology makes the teleconsultation center particularly flexible. Ample medical knowledge and patient records can be displayed electronically and administered centrally. This flexibility requires special attention to data protection, security, and availability. However, although the standards in the teleconsultation center are very high, it is rarely the technical feasibility that sets the boundaries. Rather, it is the human resource, the elaborate testing and the trans disciplinary project management that are the limiting factors in the development cycle. Additionally, there are political and legal basic conditions, which often cannot keep up with the fast and dynamically growing needs of different claim groups.

## The Patient—Focus on the Client

The teleconsultation center unites a vast knowledge and experience from many medical specialties. Additionally, there is know-how from the areas of technology, networking, and communication. Thus, it suggests itself that the existing resources are used as varied and profitable as possible. For example, even the standard service activity goes far beyond the simple telephone call with the physician: Patients send photos of skin conditions to the doctor for evaluation, Medgate sends prescriptions directly to the pharmacy and the physician can even instruct family members to exercise cardiopulmonary resuscitation and save lives, while an ambulance is alarmed in the background.

If there are still doubts after the teleconsultation, the Medgate physician can consult a specialist through telecounsel, refer the patient to a medical specialist or give him the addresses of general practitioners near him. The patients appreciate the feeling of safety after calling the teleconsultation center and stick to the medical advice. This effect is already being used by health insurance companies and governmental institutions—e.g., during big international events—in order to control the medical care supply efficiently and thereby optimize quality and costs.

### The Hotline—Reachable at All Times

Governmental institutions have discovered telemedicine for themselves and make use of the Swiss Center for Telemedicine Medgate in the context of emergency measure plans and in pandemics. For example, at a nationally available hotline, worried citizens ask for medical advice about SARS, bird flu or radioactive hazards. The continuous analysis of requests gives the crisis management group relevant information as to how to further handle the situation.

Especially large companies count on medical hotlines in their continuous management projects, in order to counsel their concerned employees in case of emergency. Precisely multinational enterprises profit from the local independence of the teleconsultation center, which is reachable around the clock from any extension worldwide.

### The Mobile Phone—Available Worldwide

Numerous business and leisure travelers, as well as Swiss citizens in other countries, already today appreciate the advice of a Swiss physician. Not only the common language and trust play an important role, but Medgate also performs logistic services in foreign countries up to case management, including information supply and negotiations with local care providers. The networking and interdisciplinary cooperation makes the so-called medical assistance possible.

The idea of prevention, as the Federal Office of Public Health in Switzerland sees it, starts at an even earlier stage. The office offers a free consulting service for vaccination and traveling, operated by Medgate. This service enjoys strong public confidence, not only because of its independence, and is frequently drawn upon by citizens of all age groups.

### The Care Programs—Close-Meshed and Customized

Remote patient monitoring is mainly meant to improve the quality of life of people with chronic diseases. Thanks to the application of telemedical support, the patient himself can oversee the treatment independently in his familiar environment and request medical advice when needed. Medgate, together with general and specialized practitioners, applies remote patient monitoring for the therapy of high blood pressure, diabetes mellitus, heart failure, asthma, or chronic obstructive pulmonary disease.

Such care programs, called disease management, are based on standardized processes. In these processes, medical professionals and technology complement each other to a maximum degree: As the relevant health data is transferred to a central telebiomonitoring platform, called tele-laboratory, immediately after obtaining it, the caregivers have access to reliable information on the course of disease and the success of therapy.

### 9.9.3   Chances and Risks

The teleconsultation center is able to lower the overall costs in the long-term, while continually improving the quality of health care. Therefore, it suggests itself that also general practitioners, specialists, and hospitals use telemedical methods more often in the future and to look for cooperation with established teleconsultation centers.

This is the case, for example, in tele-biomonitoring. Disease management programs are becoming more and more popular. The patient improves his quality of life, while the attending doctor can retrieve the test results easily and comfortably via Internet, has an even better control of the course of treatment and can initiate changes in medication. In the future, tele-biometrics will be applied more often for prevention and thusly be used as a tool for customer retention in the health care system.

Telemedicine is, in the way it is practiced today in a professionally run teleconsultation center, a comparatively young discipline. While a great part of the patients have already discovered this form of medical care for themselves and use it without problems, in the coming months the acceptance among more conservative physicians will still increase.

The technological and medical feasibility is confronted with rapidly growing demands. Our modern society requests mobility, independence and unlimited availability, while there are challenges like unhealthy lifestyle, increased average age and cost explosion that have to be tackled.

Therefore, the task at hand is to create the groundwork and standards, which facilitate sensible applications without having to make compromises regarding quality, security and costs. To that end, all involved parties should work together, especially the legislative authorities, telemedicine providers, patients' organizations, but also medical professional societies, insurance companies, and representatives of science and research. This effort is necessary, because experience with other sectors teaches us that the development cannot be stopped anyway. But there is still time to guide it in a sensible direction.

### Further Reading

- Reichlin, S.: Remote patient monitoring - Welche Technologien sind vorhanden, um Patienten in telemedizinischen Disease-Management-Programmen zu betreuen? Patient und Umfeld, 11 p. (2007)

- Schäfer, S.: Ärztliches Informations- und Beratungszentrum in der Schweiz - Zwei Jahre Erfahrungen mit dem medizinischen Beratungsgespräch am Telefon. Doctoral thesis, Medical Faculty of the University of Basel (2005)

- Steinmann, A.: Evaluation der Evidenz von Triage am Telefon - Eine qualitative Literaturanalyse. Doctoral thesis, Medical Faculty of the University of Basel (2005)

- Von Overbeck, J.: Die Rolle der Telemedizin in der ambulaten Versorgung. Arztpraxis der Zukunft, 9 p. (2007)

## Contact Details

Swiss Center for Telemedicine Medgate
Gellerstrasse 150
CH-4052 Basel
Internet: http://www.medgate.ch
e-mail: info@medgate.ch


## Profile of Author

### Reto M. Zurflüh

Reto M. Zurflüh is a marketing specialist in the Swiss Center for Telemedicine Medgate. He supervises the services of Medgate in the consumers' market and occupies himself with tele-biometrics. Before, he was involved in marketing, PR and communication in the IT and telecommunication sector, as well as in different consumer goods markets. As head of an agency, he served clients from the nonprofit and industrial sector.

## 9.10  Case Study—Participa Inteligente: A Social Network Platform for Citizens' Discussion and Participation

### 9.10.1  Background

Luis Terán,
*University of Fribourg and Universidad de las Fuerzas Armadas ESPE*

Recommender systems (RSs) are computer-based techniques used in an attempt to present information about products that are likely to be of interest to a user. Other applications make use of RSs, such as social networks and community-building processes, among others. Electronic participation (*eParticipation*) has been addressed more often in academia and is an emerging and growing research area that makes use of internet solutions to enhance citizens' participation, providing a fair and efficient society with the use of cutting-edge technology (Macintosh, 2008). Social networks and communities have become an important environment for exchanging information about products, services, music, and movies, among others. In an information and knowledge society, such technologies could also improve democratic processes, increase citizens' interest in political issues, enhance participation, and renew civic engagement. However, the difficulty of finding other citizens or groups that share common interests is still a barrier to overcome. Informed citizens are one of the key elements of a representative democracy. The availability of reliable information has dramatically changed over time, posing major challenges to citizens who desire to make informed decisions. Just a few years ago, for example, the main information-related obstacle was the scarcity of information. People either watched TV news or read newspapers. Discussions of topics were minimal among friends, colleagues, or family members. Over time, however, the rise and spread of the internet has caused the scarcity problem to turn into a problem of abundant information. Citizens now face an enormous amount of information that cannot be processed easily. The sources are unlimited, making it very difficult to find reliable information.

In this context, the *Participa Inteligente* platform was used—under the leadership of the applicant of this grant in cooperation with academics from different universities in Europe and Latin America—to collect data from users, apply new methods and algorithms, and evaluate usability and impact. *Participa Inteligente* is a social network, the first version of which was designed for the 2017 Ecuador national elections to prove the concepts and methods developed, which include a number of tools such as RSs, a voting advice application (VAA), community fact-checks, and visualizations, among others, for different purposes. These tools are intended to allow citizens to generate spaces for discussion and participation in topics of interest in society.

### 9.10.2  Current State of Research in the Field

In the context of the 2017 Ecuador general elections, the *Participa Inteligente* platform was introduced as an alternative for citizens/voters to discuss public policy issues. This project is the first of its type to include the dynamic profile generation for a VAA that Terán and Mancera (2017) propose within a social network designed to enhance citizens' participation and discussion. *Participa Inteligente* is a research project under the leadership of Dr. Luis Terán, principal investigator (PI) from the University of Fribourg,

**Fig. 9.8:** Dynamic Profile Elements - *Participa Inteligente*.

in cooperation with the University of Zurich, *Preference Matcher* consortium, Pompeu Fabra University, Universidad de las Fuerzas Armadas (ESPE), Escuela Politécnica Superior del Litoral (ESPOL), Universidad Casa Grande, and Universidad de las Américas[4]. It uses a dynamic profile generation approach introduced in the work of Terán and Mancera (2017).

Unlike other VAA projects, the profile generation that *Participa Inteligente* uses includes three elements: (i) candidate answers, (ii) expert opinions, and (iii) candidates' *Twitter* feeds. These elements are presented inFig. 9.8. In this study, we believe that the pillar of a VAA design should be based on a resistant or resilient candidate profile model that can tolerate the answer or user manipulations to represent the most accurate information, ideas, and political orientations of candidates or political parties. The definition of a candidate profile model is crucial during elections, as it reflects the political parties'/candidates' orientations and their goals as a whole.

In the classical VAA, neither the candidates nor the voters can generate content (i.e., questions, answers, comments), but in the VAA 2.0 that *Participa Inteligente* proposed, both candidates and voters could create different types of content. With the inclusion of so-called dynamic profiles, and by allowing users to become content generators (Terán and Kasina, 2016), the intent of the RS approach described in this work is to improve the profile generation of candidates requiring that their profiles be constructed based on expert opinions. In a classic VAA, the data collection interface is designed as a navigation system, allowing users to move forward and back from different questions. Once the questionnaire is completed, each user receives through his or her user profile a set of graphical recommendations regarding different parties and candidates and their proximity. *Participa Inteligente* includes a number of tools, such as the following: recommendations of candidates (VAA), user account management (e.g., privacy settings, vote intentions, and reputation), the creation of thematic groups, posts, questions to the community, private messages, and articles, among others. The recommendations that the platform has provided are defined as a personalized RS.

The social platform was developed using the design principles similar to Facebook social network. The reason to do so was to reduce the learning curve of users using a familiar environment. Six blocks are designed for the social platform and are shown

---

[4]Participa Inteligente Team: `https://participacioninteligente.org/quienes-somos`

**Fig. 9.9:** Landing page for registered users - *Participa Inteligente*.

in Fig. 9.9. As mentioned in the previous section, the datasets used in this work were generated by the Twitter social network during the campaign period of the 2017 Ecuador elections. The datasets of Tweets (available at Participa Inteligente, 2017) were collected from each of the Twitter accounts of all presidential and vice presidential candidates.

*Participa Inteligente* was officially launched in the three main cities of Ecuador (Quito, Guayaquil, and Cuenca), as part of a communication campaign in different Universities (ESPOL, 2016; UDLA, 2016; Universidad de Cuenca, 2016). The communication group of *Participa Inteligente* contacted all candidates to join the platform and to answer the questions proposed in the VAA. Some of the candidates provided their answers and used the platform's different tools. Additionally, and as was mentioned in previous section, *Participa Inteligente* included also the experts' answers, using a 'Delphi' iterative expert survey, as was proposed by Geminis et al. (2014).

*Participa Inteligente* includes a number of tools such as: recommendations of candidates (VAA), user account management (e.g., privacy settings, vote intentions, and reputation), creation of thematic groups, posts, questions for the community, private

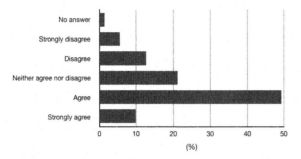

**Fig. 9.10:** Do you consider that the platform was easy to use?

messages, and articles, among others. The recommendations provided by the platform are defined as a personalized RS.

This project represents the first of its type to present a so-called dynamic VAA 2.0 implementation, which provides personal recommendations to users instead of providing a general one. The platform included several sections and features to provide information to users (e.g., discussion forums, statistics, candidate's *Tweets*, and personalized recommender systems). Not only the Ecuador academic community but also general users welcomed the platform. Based on the evaluation, most users are willing to continue to use the platform and would recommend it to others. Users have also declared that they did not find the platform to be difficult to use. In terms of the SA block, different improvements can be suggested, such as the consideration of emoticons to identify the sentiments of the *Tweets*, and the implementation of a more complete Spanish SA dictionary.

### 9.10.3   Impact Evaluation

Both improvements should be taken into account as a future version of dynamic profile generation on the VAA module. To analyze and evaluate the impact of the *Participa Inteligente* platform, a survey was conducted after the 2017 Ecuador national election commission declared the official results. The survey was developed to understand the perceptions of and user satisfaction for the different tools implemented in the platform. A total of 602 users were contacted for the evaluation, and 63 answers were collected in a period of five weeks (from 04-06-2017 to 10-07-2017). The complete evaluation included a total of 28 questions divided into six different categories: impact, user perception, VAA usability, *eCollaboration*, privacy, and user satisfaction. Partial results regarding the evaluation conducted are presented in Figs. 9.10 and 9.11 regarding the platform usability and user satisfaction.

The platform offered meaningful results and new insights regarding the relationships of voters and candidates. Nevertheless, new questions were raised that can be part of future studies: What is the right level of granularity for survey questions? Could SA block be more effective if more parameters were considered? What are the potential

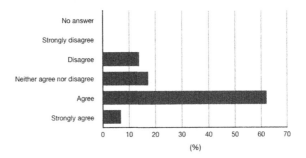

**Fig. 9.11:** Would you recommend the platform to other users?

changes in perception when adding more elements to the candidate profile? This work provides an ideal basis for future research in the area of RSs for *eParticipation*. Further development should take into consideration additional levels of participation to engage users and politicians. One of the most ambitious goals of VAA 2.0 is that the platform could also include *eVoting* and *eElections* capabilities; nevertheless, this is outside of the scope of this project.

### 9.10.4   Outlook

In addition to the various solutions developed for the *Participa Inteligente* project, many ideas have been proposed and other questions remain open. Additionally, two perspectives exist for scaling the project. The first one is technological and includes the following: the implementation of mobile applications, the enhancement of existing modules, visualizations, feedback from users, and performance evaluations in the case of user scaling. The second perspective is regional, which includes running the platform in different regions and contexts; it involves cooperation with other research groups and stakeholders in using the *Participa Inteligente* platform (e.g., research groups, NGOs, and public institutions). The implementations made will be analyzed and will become the basis of publications to be submitted to conferences and journals. At the end of this phase, the PI will present a report of activities.

Future woks should focus on the following elements: (i) analysis and the state of the art of graph-based RSs, (ii) the design and implementation of RSs, (iii) the impact of RSs for eParticipation on media and society, and (iv) how to integrate RSs for eParticipation into a new, more interactive form of online communication (Democracy 2.0).

### Further Reading

- A. Macintosh. *E-democracy and e-participation research in europe. Digital Government*, pages 85–102, 2008.

- ESPOL (2016). Participa Inteligente, red social para un voto más informado. [Online] Available at http://noticias.espol.edu.ec/

`article/academicos-desarrollan-participa-inteligente`
`-plataforma-para-fortalecer-la-democracia-en`,       [Accessed
22-June-2017].

- Geminis, D., Wheatley & Mendez (2014). *Euvox 2014: Party coding instructions.*
  University of Zurich, University of Twente and Cyprus University of Technology.

- L. Terán and J. Mancera. *Applying Dynamic Profiles on Voting Advice Applications*, pages 153–175. Springer Fachmedien Wiesbaden, Wiesbaden, 2017.

- L. Terán and A. Kaskina. *Enhancing voting advice applications with dynamic profiles*. In Proceedings of the 9th International Conference on Theory and Practice
  of Electronic Governance. ACM, 2016.

- Participa Inteligente (2017). Datasets of Twitter activity - Ecuador Elections 2017.
  [Online] Available at `https://participacioninteligente.org/`
  `docs/RAW-Tweet-Candidate-President-Ecuador-2017.zip`,
  [Accessed 22- June-2017].

- UDLA (2016). Se Lanzó la Plataforma Participa Inteligente. [Online] Available at
  `http://www.udla.edu.ec/2016/12/02/se-lanzo-en-la-udla`
  `-plataforma-para-voto-inteligente/`, [Accessed 22-June-2017].

- Universidad de Cuenca (2016). Plataforma "Participa Inteligente". [Online] Available at `https://www.ucuenca.edu.ec/la-oferta-academica/`
  `oferta-de-grado/facultad-de-filosofia/encuentro-de`
  `-literatura-ecuatoriana/28-cat-recursos-servicios/cat`
  `-prensa/3759-plataforma-participa-inteligente`, [Accessed
  22-June- 2017].

## Contact Details

University of Fribourg
Boulevard de Pérolles 90
1700 Fribourg
Internet: `http://diuf.unifr.ch/main/is/members/luis-teran`
e-mail: `luis.teran@unifr.ch` ∣ `lfteran1@espe.edu.ec`

## Profile of Author

### Luis Terán

Luis Terán (1979) is currently working as a senior researcher in cognitive computing at
the Human-IST Institute, University of Fribourg, Switzerland and academic guest at the
Department of Political Science at the University of Zurich. He is also appointed full
professor at Universidad de Las Fuerzas Armadas (ESPE), Ecuador. He earned a Ph.D.
and habilitation in computer science at the University of Fribourg. In 2009, he finished

a M.Sc. in communication systems from the Federal Institute of Technology (EPFL), Lausanne, Switzerland. In 2004, he received a B.Sc. in electronics and telecommunications from Escuela Politécnica Nacional, Quito, Ecuador. His research interests include eGovernment, eParticipation, eCollaboration, eDemocracy, eElection, eVoting, eCommunities, ePassports, recommender systems, and fuzzy classification. He is currently a board member for the IEEE e-Government Special Technical Community, the program chair and main organizer for the International Conference on eDemocracy and eGovernment (ICEDEG), an instructor in the International Seminar on eDemocracy and eGovernment (ISEDEG), and distinguished exhibitor at IEEE Ecuador Section.

# Chapter 10

# Knowledge Society

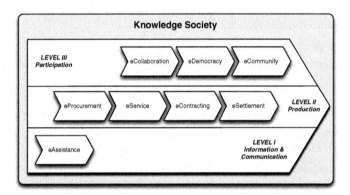

*Chapter 10 deals with the Information and Knowledge Society. First, we will discuss the dimensions of decentralization efforts in the New Public Management (Sect. 10.1), which are brought forward with the help of eGovernment projects. Changes on the market, progress in the information and communication technology and social transformations demand for setting out in the direction of an Information and Knowledge Society (Sect. 10.2). A Knowledge Society distinguishes itself by the fact that it organizes the acquisition, assurance, utilization, and distribution of knowledge, and that it allows institutions and citizens to access knowledge-based systems (Sect. 10.3). Administrative organizations and societies are asked to acquire procedures and techniques of a learning organization (Sect. 10.4). In that process, the digital divide must be avoided, that is the division of society into those citizens who have Internet access and capacities, and those without such means and knowledge (Sect. 10.5). Without ethic rules (Sect. 10.6), a knowledge society is not viable. Section 10.7 contains bibliographical notes for further studies. At the end of this chapter, a case study on the so-called cognitive cities is presented.*

© Springer Nature Switzerland AG 2019
A. Meier, L. Terán, *eDemocracy & eGovernment*, Progress in IS,
https://doi.org/10.1007/978-3-030-17585-6_10

# 10.1   Decentralization in the New Public Management

*Effect-oriented action in administration*

Until now, managerial and organizational structures in public administration have been aimed at high security and balance of risks. Many decisions and instructions were issued centrally, according to the structures and target specifications. Nevertheless, decentralization of responsibilities and aiming at effect-oriented actions are becoming more important in governmental institutions.

*Possibilities of change in the New Public Management*

The New Public Management is marked out by a real shift in paradigms. The changes in leadership and organization can be summarized according to Schedler & Proeller (2000) (see Fig. 10.1) as follows:

- **Structure:** Central structures are built, in order to work more efficiently and effectively in decentral units. At the same time, it is intended to keep the number of organizational units and offices as low as possible.

- **Orientation:** The administrational work is oriented toward the citizens' needs. The main emphasis lies on service-oriented processes, in order to overcome bureaucratic limitations better.

- **Role allocations:** Capacities are divided into the three levels financing of services, suppliers of services and demanders of services. According roles are determined for each administrative unit.

- **Leadership:** Task areas, service processes, and target groups are bundled in clearly arranged organizational units with responsibility for results. The leading cadre is given extensive authorities and is motivated by monetary and non-monetary incentives.

- **Responsibility:** Personal responsibility replaces other directed responsibility; decentralized administrative units are given the responsibility to make their own decisions and to obtain results.

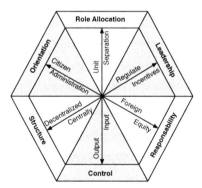

**Fig. 10.1:** Dimensions of decentralization in the New Public Management according to Schedler & Proeller (2000).

- **Control:** The control is handled by performance agreements, called service level agreements, and lump sum budgeting. Information systems, that measure performance and effects, admit to control processes and services. The quality control is part of the service level agreement.

By dividing the administrative work into the levels of financing of services (parliament, majority of government), the suppliers of services (public and private organizations) and demanders of services (citizens, companies), the traditional administration is transformed into a guarantee administration (an administration that delegates part of its tasks to private companies, but uses regulatory measures to ensure that the basic public services are upheld at all times [translator's note]). The guarantee administration distinguishes itself by a dichotomy of administrative organization into one area of commissioning and one of accepting orders. The area of commissioning, the political direction, guarantees that the requested services are provided to the agreed standards. As contractors serve not only internal administrative units, but also independent organizations and companies. This division creates an internal and external market of suppliers and demanders of services. *Financing, suppliers, and demanders of services*

The eGovernment encourages the development toward a guarantee administration in many ways: *Keystones of a guarantee administration*

- **Enhancing democratic processes:** On administration-related portals, citizens and company representatives obtain information and transparency on the administrative work (eAssistance). They participate in projects and plans or give their opinion (eCollaboration), if needed. They network and build communities (eCommunity), which take on their democratic tasks and duties (eDemocracy).

- **Acquisition and handling of electronic services:** Demanders of public services make more and more use of Web-based solutions (eProduction), in which they make agreements by electronic contracts (eContracting) and draw on immaterial services electronically (eDistribution). Administrative units tender public projects, award contracts to internal units or to third parties and procure parts of their services over procurement portals (eProcurement).

Methods and procedures of New Public Management can be realized more effect-oriented with the help of the eGovernment and can be customized better to the needs of the citizens. Governmental offices and institutions are now requested to confront the changes toward an Information and Knowledge Society and to make use of the respective tools and methods for their governmental and administrative work, as well as for the collaboration with the citizens.

## 10.2  Toward the Information and Knowledge Society

The Western industrial countries are undergoing a profound value shift in their societies and working environments. Insecurity and unemployment shape modern lives, and at the same time, requirements and expectations toward work and leisure time are increasing. People want a working environment in which they preserve their independence and *Value shift in society* which allows them to combine the working and private life better. Esteem and the possibility to leave a mark are important motivational factors, especially for employees with high qualifications. Figure 10.2 shows three areas that influence the nature of work and organizations:

*Sectoral change in structure*

- **Market changes:** The globalization of market and competition relations results into a globalization of working types and work contacts. This requires collaboration despite big spatial distance and different time zones. Linguistic and cultural boundaries must be overcome. Apart from globalization, the sectoral change in structure takes place. The long-term shift of employment from the area of agriculture (primary sector), over the sector of production (secondary sector) to services and the Information Society (tertiary sector) changes the fields of activity and the working environment. Despite occasional fluctuations, in the industrial countries the information-related professions dominate by far; this type of job comprises all activities of producing, processing and distributing information.

*Trend to miniaturization in information technology*

- **Technological progress:** The collapse of costs in computer processors and storage media, combined with increased performance, lead to a wide availability of information and communication infrastructure. Computer technology and telecommunication grow together and digitalize big parts of the economy. Even today, computer and network functions are miniaturized and disappear behind the surfaces of buildings and objects. Ubiquitous computing makes it possible to transform everyday objects into intelligent devices with the help of sensor technology and microprocessors.

*Development toward a multi-option society*

- **Social changes:** With the above mentioned value shift, lifestyles and household structures change as well. For example, the number of working single mothers or

**Fig. 10.2:** Economical, technological, and social transformation, adapted from Reichwald et al. (2013).

fathers or single households is continuously increasing. For that reason, companies and organizations have to consider changed lifestyles and newly originated needs of their employees. The society develops into a multi-option society, in which everyone fills out several functions at the same time: One offers one's skills to different companies (employee) and is an entrepreneur (employer) at the same time.

Local and temporal dependencies of activities and processes in economy and politics are dissolved step by step through the application of information and communication technologies. This produces dangers and risks and requests both organizational innovations and social adjustments.

*Education and training offensive*

The European Union and most of the Western countries have launched development plans for an Information Society in the nineties of the twentieth century. In order to smooth the way into an Information and Knowledge Society, several projects have already been started: With education offensives it is tried to bring the Internet into schools and to complement further training with multi-medial methods and techniques. Museums, archives and cultural sites go into the Internet, host discussion forums and create Web-based meeting places. Governmental institutions and political circles debate about electronic services for the population and launch eGovernment programs. Legal experts and governmental institutions are required to draft and extend regulations for the electronic information exchange and business transactions (Law on Electronic Signatures, copyright, protection of privacy, and so on). The application of information and communication technology is conceived as a chance for amplifying the capacity of individuals and organizations to act and for strengthening cross-border relations.

*Circuit in knowledge management*

An Information and Knowledge Society distinguishes itself by using existing knowledge efficiently, by accessing information and knowledge databases (see Sect. 10.3). To that end, knowledge must be acquired, renewed and made available, for example, through public and private universities and research facilities. Important factors are the distribution of knowledge and free access to knowledge databases, in order to avoid the digital divide (see ethical rules in Sect. 10.6). The necessary steps of acquisition, storage, use and distribution are shown schematically in Fig. 10.3.

**Fig. 10.3:** Processes in knowledge management.

*Utilization of*
*explicit*
*knowledge*

Explicit knowledge can be displayed and communicated. It is rooted in rationality, is gained for a specific purpose and is patented or published, if appropriate. Implicit knowledge, on the other hand, is intuitive knowledge, which is based on experience. Mental models and personal perception count among it; implicit knowledge is difficult to gather and to communicate.

*Transforming*
*implicit into*
*explicit*
*knowledge*

The knowledge management must not only utilize the explicit knowledge, but also the implicit. In order to do so, during socialization, it is tried to collect implicit knowledge from the organization or society and to concentrate it. Additionally, it is related to explicit knowledge, in order to widen the knowledge base. Shared experiences, creative ideas, meaningful perceptions, or productive behavior help to transfer implicit into explicit knowledge.

## 10.3   Use of Knowledge-Based Databases

*Value creation*
*chain requires*
*knowledge*

An Information and Knowledge Society creates value primarily by building, processing and imparting information (digital products and digital services) and knowledge (intelligent products and knowledge services), respectively. Products and services, enriched with intelligence, increase the availability and security. For example, monitoring systems in eHealth help to supervise physiological parameters of a patient and, in case of a worsening health status, can trigger alarm and emergency signals to the health care personnel and physicians.

Explicit knowledge is digitizable, it can be stored and passed on. Implicit knowledge (often called tacit knowledge) is more difficult to identify and to communicate. It comprises mental models of reality and experiences (know-how).

*No knowledge*
*management*
*without directive*
*concept*

The knowledge management needs a directive concept, so that the knowledge within a governmental institution, community or society can be gathered systematically with adequate methods and techniques (knowledge identification, knowledge acquisition), processed (knowledge development, knowledge evaluation), imparted and utilized (see Fig. 10.3 in the previous section). The knowledge management unlocks internal and external knowledge for future applications and further development. The internal knowledge of a governmental institution concerns technical details, innovative procedures, best practices, experiences and decision-making processes, among other things. The external knowledge adds to that the knowledge about the preferences of particular social strata, about important development trends in a society, strong and weak sides of the education in different scholar systems or changed lifestyles and behaviors of citizens.

Adequate tools for knowledge management are knowledge based information systems or expert systems (see Fig. 10.4). An expert system is a software system that stores knowledge about a field of application and offers solution proposals on the basis of this knowledge database.

*Knowledge basis*
*with facts and*
*rules*

The knowledge basis comprehends facts (case data) and rules. In the simplest case, the component of knowledge acquisition consists in collecting data. This can be analyzed and interlinked by human experts, optionally with additional support of adequate procedures (machine learning, data mining, etc.). The actual problem-solving component (inference machine) takes the facts and rules and generates new or more profound,

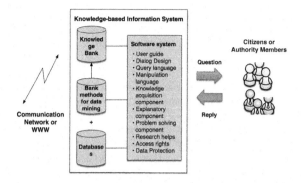

**Fig. 10.4:** Development and use of expert systems.

until then unknown, findings. Similar to a human expert, the software system can explain the previously generated recommendations on how to act (explanation component).

Expert systems are able to bundle knowledge from limited areas of application and to contribute it in a problem-focused way to the processes in the administration. Troubleshooting procedures use data mining or online analytical processing (OLAP). With their help, it is possible to extend substantial service areas of organizations with computer-aided tools, and to partially improve them.

*Use of expert systems*

Data mining refers to exploring and digging for valuable information in data stocks. Mining, a term originally used in the mining industry, means to process high quantities of rocks with technological procedures in order to produce precious stones or metals. To phrase it more precisely, data mining means to apply algorithms for extraction and display of patterns in data. For example, cluster development and deviation analysis make it possible to evaluate the citizens' behavior with respect to different criteria and to develop processes of community formation and enhancement. Neuronal nets are not only utilized for pattern recognition in data mining, but also for speech analysis or in image processing (search for criminals, recognition of pedophiles, conviction of suspects of murderer). Although some of these data mining procedures are only scarcely applied in administrations (e.g., criminology), they will help on the way to an efficient and effective citizen support, like it is demanded in the New Public Management.

*Data mining*

## 10.4   Development of a Knowledge Society

The capability to learn is often associated with individuals, but can be transferred to groups of citizens, communities, or organizations as a whole. By organizational learning, we understand the process of enriching the knowledge basis of a community or organization, improving problem-solving competences and responsibilities and increasing the exchange of experience and knowledge among the members of the community or organization.

*Organizational learning*

It is beyond dispute that individuals can learn. But, what about communities or organizations? How does the connection between individual learning and organizational learning work? Is the organizational learning more than the sum of individual learning, and if so, how is it done?

*Difference between individual and collective learning*
The main difference between individual and organizational learning has to do with the fact that knowledge, values, experiences and procedure recommendations belong to the processes of the community or organization, and are recorded there. Thus, over time the community or organization gains a knowledge basis that can exist independently of an individual. It is kept in a knowledge database, which remains property of the community or organization, even when individual members leave the organization.

*Gathering and reusing collective experiences*
In Fig. 10.5, we can see that learning in organizations or communities is not the same as the sum of the individual learning processes. The individual learning is characterized by individual rationality, personal experiences, cognitive values and changes in behavior. On the contrary, organizational learning distinguishes itself by a collective rationality and a collective frame of reference. Thus, not individual needs or value systems are focused on, but organizational decision-making procedures and collective experience.

*Balance between diversity and consensus*
The knowledge basis is accessible to all members of the community and is extended by them. This brings along contradictory phenomena, like generating diversity and at the same time creating consensus. In order to find a balance between diversity and consensus, the organizational learning needs a communicative pattern.

*Elements of the transformation*
Among the conditions for transforming individual to organizational learning are communication, transparency and integration. The agreement over a consensus and the resulting behavior patterns are obtained by personal or electronic communication. Communication makes the individual knowledge available to the organization. Furthermore, communication enhances collective argumentation processes. The course of this process and its result must be made transparent to all members, which is possible because of the electronic data and knowledge basis. Apart from transparency, integration is required as well, that means that members of the organization or community must be able at any

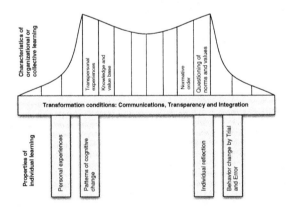

**Fig. 10.5:** Transformational bridge between individual and organizational learning, according to G. J. Probst & Büchel (1998).

times to contribute their findings and course of action into the databases. By discovering knowledge deficits, determining the knowledge reservoirs and knowledge carriers, organizational learning is furthered. In this process, it is necessary to analyze and take into consideration both the forces, which inhibit the knowledge transfer, and those, which enhance it. As inhibiting forces are considered defensive behavior patterns of the members of the organization, obsolete privileges, taboos, or disordered handling of information (information pathologies).

## 10.5   Dangers and Risks of a Knowledge Society

The Internet offers many advantages for the communication and exchange of data and information, for both citizens and administration; nevertheless, Internet services can be abused as well. The biggest dangers and risks may be resumed as follows:

- **Digital divide of the society:** The society is divided into those citizens with access to the Internet and knowledge databases, and those without (digital divide). This separation can take place within a certain group of the population or society (e.g., gender-specific, age-related, salary-dependent, etc.), or globally in the whole population. For example, citizens of developing and threshold countries until now have fewer chances to use the services and knowledge databases of the WWW; the knowledge cleft widens. *Give access to the WWW and knowledge databases*

- **Information overload:** The net of nets is growing rapidly and the Web content is developing explosively in some areas. The citizen often feels drowned by the flood of information and knows little about the means and ways to protect himself. *Tools to master the information overload*

- **Quality of information:** On the Internet and the WWW, for each topic or concern one can find a multitude of documents, reports, surveys, etc. Despite this multitude, it remains a challenge to estimate the quality of that information. Therefore, quality assurance on the Internet (see Sect. 2.6) is an important aspect. *Certifying the quality of information*

- **Violation of privacy:** The citizens leave a trace in cyberspace and there is a risk of them degrading to transparent humans. Every click in the Internet can be analyzed (clickstream analysis). Once you uttered something, it can hardly be erased or corrected. The boundaries between private and public sphere are dissolving. *Guaranteeing the protection of privacy*

- **Stomping ground for criminals:** The Web attracts criminals, who profit from the anonymity or the possibility of faked identities. Racism, pornography, pedophilia, sects, attempted blackmail, and other criminal acts can spread over the cyberspace and sometimes are hard to discover. *Curtailing crime on the Internet*

In order to illustrate a source of danger, we will discuss the distribution of junk e-mail (spam). Today, it is estimated that the mass distribution of electronic advertising constitutes over half of the worldwide e-mail amount. The costs for electronic advertising messages are minimal for the originator, but are increasing for the involuntary recipient and the operator of the server. The flood of spam not only requires the recipient's *Problem of spam*

**Fig. 10.6:** Measures to fight against spam.

time to sort out the advertising mail and to take counter-actions, but also storage and net capacity. Protective measures to fend off spam are urgently necessary (see Fig. 10.6).

*Tightening data protection*    In Europe, the distribution of unwanted e-mails and advertising messages is forbidden by the Data Protection Directive, as long as the sender hasn't asked the recipients for the anytime revocable permission before sending the e-mails (opting in). In the USA, a law regulating spam was passed, as well, which promotes the opting out. In this model, natural persons can register in a list if they want to be untroubled by spam. However, these measures are still little effective, as the spam senders are hard to catch. They can send their mass e-mails under false names or from abroad.

*Improving protective measures*    The further development of e-mail protocols aims at fighting spam effectively. Propositions range from protocols with secure authentication (see Chap. 5) to the abolition of free e-mail sending. If trifle amounts were charged for e-mails, this could help to contain mass distribution, as especially in these cases, costs would arise. In private use, a minimal fee for e-mails would carry less weight.

On the level of operators, different filtering options to fend off spam were created. For example, computers are automatically cut from the net if they send e-mails in large-scale amounts. Additionally, black lists are kept, with a register of proven spam sources. The use of spam filters on server level, in order to check content, is problematic, as in several countries the secrecy of post applies for e-mails.

## 10.6   Ethic Rules in the Knowledge Society

*How can ethical behavior be determined?*    By ethics, we understand basic principles, which limit the actions of individuals or groups of people, for the benefit of the community. Immanuel Kant asks for ethical norms, which are not derived from experience, but (a priori) before all experience claim general validity and are binding for all individuals. Hence, a sensible action, oriented at general laws, is not necessarily moral. It only is moral, according to Kant, if the internal, consenting desire, which is reflected in the attitude, adds to the action. Thus, Kant's categorical imperative states: Act only according to that maxim whereby you can at the same time will that it should become a universal law.

*Basic model on ethics in the eGovernment*    Figure 10.7 shows a basic model for ethics in the Information and Knowledge Society. The handling of information systems cannot be arbitrary, but must be controlled

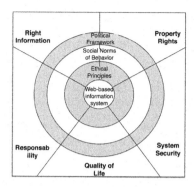

**Fig. 10.7:** The five dimensions of ethical acting, according to Laudon & Laudon (2015).

by legal regulations (political framework conditions, see outmost ring of Fig. 10.7). Additionally, social behavioral norms (middle ring) can restrict actions. Finally, the individuals orient themselves at self-imposed ethical principles (innermost ring). Such a behavioral norm is the netiquette, which refers to the behavior of communication participants in the Internet. It request that all publications on the Web are made under the correct name, or that no unwanted commercial advertising (spam) is sent. The ethical action in the Information and Knowledge Society should be geared to five dimensions, according to Laudon & Laudon (2015):

- **Right to information:** In order for the economy and society to be functional, companies, organizations, and individuals need information. At the same time, the citizens' privacy must remain protected at any time. Personal data may only be used for business purposes, and the aggrieved parties must give their consent. It is forbidden to pass on personal, and thus protection-deserving, data (see Data Protection Act). In consequence, this means: Collecting personal data on Web platforms or during Web-based activities is only allowed if the aggrieved parties give their explicit consent. The members must be informed about the purpose of data gathering, and for how long the information will be used.

  *Preventing the propagation of data*

- **Right of property:** It is a particular challenge to protect the right of property (copyright) of information and digital goods (see Chap. 5 on eContracting). Digital objects are different from paper documents, books, reports or photographs, in the sense that they can be copied and distributed easily and quickly. Apart from using digital watermarks (Sect. 6.5), cryptographic procedures and digital signatures are used in order to constrain misuse.

  *Protection of copyright*

- **Responsibility:** Both individuals and institutions are required to act responsibly. When starting a new job, employees have to sign an agreement, that they respect the rules of software use (licensing) and software distribution and those they would not use marked digital products for private purposes.

- **System security:** The availability and security of Web-based information systems must be guaranteed and supervised. The data protection laws do not only concern data protection (protection of data from abuse), but also data security (protection of data from loss or manipulation). For example, there is an obligation of disclosure for bases with personal data that means the administration has to disclose at any time which data is stored about a person. The excuse of saying the computer system were defective, is not permitted by data protection laws.

*Avoiding to leave an information trace*
- **Quality of life:** One's availability in the digital age, regarding both time and location, must not lead to a decreased quality of life for the citizens. It should, therefore, be possible for individuals to drop out of the cyberspace at any time and to maintain their privacy. The recording of all activities of all individuals in digital storage (information trace in the cyberspace) is hard to suppress.

Parting from systematic thinking, which plays a big role in information management, it is possible to develop extended ethics as an alternative to the ethic of the individual. According to this ethics, the behavior of a person, a group of people or an institution is considered good, if it causes an improvement of the higher-ranking system. A special challenge is to overcome the digital divide, which means the split of society into those citizens with access to the Internet and basic knowledge, and those who cannot afford such access or who are denied access. Here, the governmental offices and institutions must try with suitable training and elucidation initiatives to keep the obstacles for net access as small as possible. Additionally, it is tried today to provide Internet access devices in governmental meeting places, so that each interested person can visit the eGovernment portal and profit from it.

## 10.7   Bibliographical Notes

*Books on New Public Management*

Works on the New Public Management were written by Schedler & Proeller (2000), as well as Norbert & Adrian (2006). A work on the changes on distributed forms of work and organization was created by Reichwald et al. (2013). The authors illustrate the most important aspects of tele-cooperation and explore the necessary leading questions. They describe barriers and aspects of application on the performance level, on the level of overall organization and on the level of market and society.

*Learning organization and knowledge management*

Basic principles and practical examples on learning organizations are described in the book by Argyris & Schön (2018). In order to characterize the basis of values and knowledge, Argyris & Schön introduce action theories. These are based on models, strategies, cultural behavior, structures and distribution of power; they constitute the frame of reference of each organization. Haun (2013) wrote a reference book on knowledge management. The principles of learning organizations are discussed in the book by G. J. Probst & Büchel (1998). The authors explore the differences between individual and organizational learning, and illustrate the theoretical parts with case examples. G. Probst et al. (1999) have written a tool for knowledge management, as well.

*Works on ethics in informatics*

In their book on information management, the author team Laudon & Laudon (2015) gives a chapter on ethics in informatics. There, they display the dimensions of ethical actions in the Information Society and illustrate it by concrete examples. A book on computer ethics was created by Johnson (2004). In it, the author shows how ethical questions that arise when using information and communication technologies have to be tackled and what consequences the respective behavioral norms have for society.

## 10.8   Case Study—Cognitive Cities[*]

Edy Portmann,
*University of
Fribourg*

### 10.8.1   Today's City: Between "Smart" and "Cognitive"

The concept of the "cognitive city" has only recently been developed, in conjunction with the smart city concept on which the cognitive city approach is based (Portmann et al 2018; Finger und Portmann 2016). Nowadays, the almost omnipresent term "smart city" represents more than just a buzzword or a marketing phrase, as which it was often perceived and criticized (e.g., Greenfield 2013). It is the subject of scientific debate, with some of the ideas associated with the concept varying considerably. A universally valid, universally recognized definition does not exist so far. However, many of the concepts share the basic idea that the sustainable social, ecological and economic development of the urban space can be fostered by enriching city-relevant functions with Internet and web technologies (Metzger et al. 2018). In a smart city, information technology is linked to infrastructure, architecture, everyday objects and even our bodies in order to address social, economic and ecological problems (Townsend 2014). Smart cities rely on the availability of data resulting from the more or less systematic introduction of information and communication technologies (ICT) into urban infrastructure systems, which can be optimized and made more efficient by using the thus collected information (Portmann and Finger 2016; Finger and Razaghi 2017). By collecting, analyzing and processing high-quality data and making it available to the relevant stakeholders, cities are also becoming smarter (Hurwitz et al. 2015).

Simone
Franzelli,
*University of
Bern*

With this smart city approach, the efficiency challenges of today's cities can be addressed adequately. The resources of cities in terms of space, money, skills, energy and time are limited but must satisfy exponentially growing demands (e.g., energy, transportation, water, etc.). In order to become more economically, socially and environmentally sustainable, cities have to use existing resources in a more efficient way. To overcome this efficiency challenge, first of all, the physical infrastructure layers (energy, transport, water, etc.) must be duplicated by means of an information resp. data layer. On the basis of the data and information generated in this way, the infrastructure systems and consumption can be optimized (Finger and Razaghi 2017).

Astrid
Habenstein,
*University of
Bern*

However, this approach represents a highly technical, if not technocratic, approach to urban management and governance and it has limitations. First, urban issues cannot be reduced to efficiency issues alone sustainability and resilience constitute additional major challenges. In order to solve these issues, more and different approaches are necessary than the technical approach offered by the smart city. Secondly, urban systems are not just technical artefacts, but complex socio-technical systems in which technology, institutions, organizations and citizens unfold together. To solve problems, they must therefore be addressed collectively. Third, the smart city approach reduces the application of ICT to their use as a purely technical and optimizing tool. Their potential, however, is much greater and thus remains unused. The concept of the cognitive city offers approaches to overcome these deficits (Finger and Portmann 2016).

---

[*]This case study is an abbreviated translation of the chapter "Cognitive Cities" in A. Meier and E. Portmann, Fuzzy Leadership, Springer Nature Switzerland 2019

In short, the key feature of smart cities is the collection, analysis, and processing of data to gain information which can then be used to address specific problems or needs in the city. The higher the quality of the data, the smarter the city. The aim is therefore to build up and use the "urban intelligence", the collective intelligence of the city. Collective intelligences consist of individual intelligences. These can include humans, but also intelligent objects like artificial intelligence (AI) or electronic devices. Their coupling allows them to act smarter together than the individual, a group, or even a computer (system) could ever do alone, as Thomas Malone, director of the MIT Center for Collective Intelligence, put it (Kelly and Hamm 2013). Together, they form a network that is more than the sum of its elements and help to solve problems in a different way than they would as individual components (Malone and Bernstein 2015). The "glue" that turns individual intelligences into collective intelligence can best be described as "connectivism", based on the learning and cognition theory of the same name, which was developed by Siemens (2006).

Knowledge is built up by connecting ideas and concepts in new ways. According to Siemens (2006), this happens on three levels: The biological level is based on the network-creating processes of the brain and the neurons that form connections with each other. The next level up, which entails abstract concepts, is created by linking new ideas to what we already know. At the third level, interconnected learning by means of virtual realities is situated. Unlike conventional theories such as behaviorism, cognitivism, and constructivism, the "connected learning theories" and "incidental connectivism" (Siemens 2006) therefore understand learning as a process in which the learning subject or object connects itself with nodes and whereby networks are created. The nodes can be either other people or databases, apps, the Internet, smartphones, books, pictures, etc. Each node has its own networks, which the learning subject/object accesses by connecting to the corresponding node. The linking of the nodes occurs through interaction and communication. Informal, interconnected and technological learning can be included as well as human experiences and emotions, which are factors of creating meaning.

In the future, the survival of cities will depend on them being able to access these learning networks and knowledge ecosystems. By this means, for example, by increasing efficiency, efforts to increase sustainability can be supported. However, moreover considerable changes in the behavior of all involved actors are required. If the data and information generated by ICT are made available to those concerned, they can learn and, based on that, change their behavior. Data analytics tools (such as big data and/or business analytics) and the display of data, along with social media tools, contribute to individual and collective learning. The same is true for resilience: urban systems must become more resistant to withstand external shocks (economic crises, epidemics, water scarcity, pollution, political unrest, etc.). New forms of machine intelligence with human-machine interactions are applied to develop creative and disruptive systemic solutions. On this basis, cities and their citizens can learn and evolve, so that the city's entire socio-technical system is better able to cope with and adapt to environmental shocks.

Cognitive city concepts should not and cannot replace smart city approaches. But they complement them by focusing on a specific aspect of the smart city: interaction and communication between the actors and the city. The term cognitive city hereby refers to an exchanging network of information and communication nodes that forms the core of the cities of tomorrow (and today). In the cognitive city, the human factor is integrated into this communication loop ("humans-in-the-loop"). The technical foundations are cognitive computer systems that are able to recognize patterns in the vast amounts of data and to learn through interaction and communication with the humans who use them (Hurwitz et al. 2015). By constantly interacting with users, the systems learn more about what we feel, want and need. Cognitive city principles as well as techniques and technologies are applicable to all smart city issues that affect aspects of interaction and communication. Designing cognitive cities therefore means shaping the reciprocity of communication between urban ICT and the citizens (Tabacchi et al 2018).

The concept of connectivism addresses challenges that cities face in knowledge management activities. Its application leads to a kind of distributed cognition of a city (with knowledge that not only lies in the individual, but also in her social and physical environment). Therefore, knowledge that is also present in intelligent computer tools and systems (i.e. databases or (web) knowledge bases) has to be conveyed to the right people in the right context. To achieve this, cognitive computer systems are applied (Finger and Portman 2016).

## 10.8.2   Cognitive Systems and Cognitive Computing

Humans have the ability to express themselves in natural language. This allows them to share perceptions and experiences with each other. Computer systems, on the other hand, use not the natural, but a formal language. Therefore, people and computers are not yet able to communicate unambiguously. In a human being, an individual cognitive pattern is formed through his subjective experiences, which decisively influences his decision-making. By gaining more information, observing and acquiring new behaviors as well as through the exchange with other people, new knowledge can be built up, resulting in a continuous learning process through which individual cognitive patterns can change again (D'Onofrio et al. 2018).

Future computer systems should be able to understand the natural language and moreover develop other "human" skills (such as learning) so that they can eventually act "intelligently". They should thus become so-called cognitive systems whose functions are based on the human brain. A cognitive system must in principle fulfill three requirements (D'Onofrio et al. 2018): First, it should be able to continuously learn through dialogue with the user. Second, it should be able to understand, process and reproduce information formulated in natural language in its context. And thirdly, the system should be able to "think", draw conclusions and make recommendations. When data is collected, curated and analyzed, the cognitive system is supposed to search for patterns and associations. This iterative process allows the system to improve its understanding of the data. The adaptation of soft computing is essential for this.

The basis for soft computing methods are fuzzy sets. These are described by the membership function $\mu A : X \rightarrow [0, 1]$. Therefore, in a fuzzy set A, the membership of an element in $X$ to A is indicated by a real number in the value range [0, 1]. This assumption allows to mathematically analyze vague, uncertain and incomplete systems.

On this basis, methods have been developed that are based on human capabilities and are known under the name soft computing: They provide a kind of toolbox for dealing with fuzziness. Soft computing thus extends traditional (hard) computer science concepts, which seek to be exact, with tolerance for vagueness, uncertainty, partial truth and approximation. Unlike in traditional computer science techniques, the natural language, which is sometimes vague or ambiguous, can also be included on this basis. Human thinking and learning can therefore be better replicated in artificial cognition (Portmann 2018).

Lotfi Zadeh has argued in this regard that for the development of intelligent systems, the most important factor is the use of soft computing to mimic the ability of the human brain to effectively draw conclusions, which works rather unsubtly than accurate (Zadeh 1994, p. 77). This is especially central to urban systems: Conventional mathematical and analytical methods can only depict and analyze comparatively simple systems. When dealing with more complex systems like the city, they quickly reach their limits. So many factors are relevant for the holistic view of the city that the phenomenon of the city becomes too complex for handling it exactly (Portmann 2018). On the contrary: Our ability to make precise and significant statements about the behavior of a system with increasing complexity is limited by the openness and non-linearity of the cities (Portmann 2018). Zadeh calls this the "principle of incompatibility"': "As the complexity of a system increases, our ability to make precise and yet significant statements about its behavior diminishes until a threshold is reached, beyond which precision and significance (or relevance) become almost mutually exclusive characteristics" (Zadeh 1973, p. 28).

A fundamental theory of soft computing is fuzzy logic, which is characterized by the concepts of graduation and granulation (D'Onofrio et al. 2018). Graduation allows an object to be gradually assigned to different classes, the fuzzy sets, rather than to a single class. For example, a "smartwatch" may belong to the fuzzy sets "mobile devices" and "watch". Thus, this element can be gradually assigned to different fuzzy sets if its semantics matches the semantics of the fuzzy set to a particular degree, and they thus belong to the same context (D'Onofrio et al. 2018).

Granulation allows an object to be assigned to an information granule (i.e., collections of elements that are arranged together, for example, due to their similarity or coherence). This allows the classification of similar data and the recognition of patterns. Granulation is based on the natural concept of the human brain: for example, in the context of "electronic communication" the element "Whatsapp" can be classified in an information granule in which also elements such as "e-mail", "Skype", etc. occur. Thus, based on the context, nearby elements are collected to derive relevant information from them (D'Onofrio et al. 2018).

Also related to fuzzy logic is the theory "computing with words and perceptions". It enables the calculation with words and perceptions instead of numbers and thus the inclusion of natural language in cognitive city systems. In most cases, "fuzzy-IF-THEN-rules" are used: Assuming that the linguistic variable $U$, which has an element value $u$, is by graduation or granulation related to the linguistic variable $W$, which has the element value $w$, it follows that $f(U) \to W$, where $u \in U$ and $w \in W$. An example: A company $X$ offers its employees good opportunities to participate. It is further assumed that good participation opportunities increase the motivation of the employees. In this case the "participation possibilities" stand for the linguistic variable $U$ and "motivation" stands for $W$. At the same time "good" stands for the value $u$ and "high" for the value $w$. From this, the following relation can be concluded: $f$ : if $U$ is good then $W$ is high (D'Onofrio et al. 2018).

There exist also other application methods that are mainly based on the concept of "generalized constraint". Using this method, restrictions in the shape of $GC : X$ is $R$ are created on the basis of available information. $X$ is called a constraint variable and $R$ a constraint relation. $R$ stands for those values for which $X$ can stand. The main aspects of uncertainty can be accounted for by three modalities, probabilistic ($r = p$), possibilistic ($r = empty$), and Z-restriction ($r = z$) (D'Onofrio et al. 2018). Assuming that a company $X$ offers its employees good opportunities to participate, the following restriction can be formulated: "Participation opportunities (employees company $X$) are good." Derived from this, the following restriction can be formed: "Motivation (Employees Company $X$) is high." This allows to derive an approximate argument which is based on realistic facts. Computing with words and perceptions is about statements that often contain vague, uncertain, and imprecise information from which relevant information is to be extracted (D'Onofrio et al. 2018).

### 10.8.3    From Cognitive Computing to Cognitive Cities

One of the most important features of a cognitive city is the ability to provide the citizens, who are constantly interacting with the system and asking questions, a range of alternative responses, with a justification for each response. This initiates a communication process between the system and the citizens, which is useful for both sides (Finger and Portmann 2016). In order to connect with citizens in a more natural and seamless way, a cognitive computer system employs various tools and techniques such as machine learning, natural language processing, causal induction, and probabilistic reasoning. Semantic computing to some extent also makes it possible to extract syntax and semantics from texts. Through the expansion with cognitive computing, additionally a cognitive link should be enabled, which allows new information to be correctly incorporated into the context, to extract information relevant to the user and to draw conclusions on the basis of its meaning. Thus, cognitive systems form their own (data-related) cognitive patterns that can change over time. Consequently, cognitive computing aims to improve the exchange of information in order to facilitate the development of knowledge. For this, not only the perceptions and experiences of individuals count, but those of all actors. By constantly acquiring information and sharing it with other stakeholders, collective intelligence can emerge (D'Onofrio and Portmann 2017). In particular, soft computing techniques may be helpful for developing cognitive systems (D'Onofrio et al. 2018).

Soft computing methods can address the challenges that today's cities are facing by expanding traditional systems so that humans and computer systems can be connected in a natural way (e.g., by a biomimetic method). The networking of cognitive actors (e.g., citizens, cognitive systems, institutions, etc.) who learn from each other leads to cognitive cities that resemble superorganisms, whose characteristics mirror biological features such as emergence, learning, evolution, networks, fitness, autonomy, tolerance, etc. (Finger and Portmann 2016). This enables every single actor (including the cognitive system) in a cognitive city of ICT networks to develop autonomously, allowing the city to build resilience. The city learns as the actors connect different disciplines, ideas and concepts and thus a kind of network, the collective "urban intelligence", is created. Through a continuous cycle of perceptions, feedback and actions, a continuous learning process and an extension of the knowledge base are made possible (so-called "intelligence amplification loop"; see Kaufmann et al. 2012) (D'Onofrio and Portmann 2017; Finger and Portman 2016).

In order to develop cognitive cities, it makes sense to pursue a transdisciplinary (i.e., beyond academic disciplines and science) research approach. A combination of action research and design science research is particularly suitable for this. Action research aims to help actors (e.g., citizens, cognitive systems, government agencies, organizations, etc.) to improve their actions. The (biomimetic) design science research (Kaufmann and Portmann 2015) for its part includes the design of artifacts, as well as the analysis of the use and performance of such artifacts, with the aim to better understand and improve various aspects of the city.

## Further Reading

- D'Onofrio S, Portmann E (2017) Cognitive Computing in Smart Cities. Infomatik Spektrum 40(1):46–57.

- D'Onofrio S, Portmann E, Franzelli M, Bürki C (2018), Cognitive Computing. Theoretisch Grundlagen und Praxisbeispiele der Schweizerischen Post. Informatik Spektrum 41(2):113–122 .

- Finger M, Portmann E (2016) What Are Cognitive Cities? In: Finger M, Portmann E (eds) Towards Cognitive Cities. Advances in Cognitive Computing and Its Application to the Governance of Large Urban Systems. Springer International Publishing, Heidelberg, pp 1–11.

- Finger M, Razaghi M (2017) Conceptualizing „Smart Cities". Informatik Spektrum 40:6–13.

- Greenfield A (2013) Against the Smart City (The City Is Here For You to Use Book 1). Do Projects, New York.

- Hurwitz J, Kaufman M, Bowles A (2015) Cognitive computing and big data analytics. John Wiley & Sons, Hoboken.

- Kaufmann M, Portmann E (2015) Biomimetics in Design Oriented Information Systems Research. In: Tenth International Conference on Design Science Research in Information Systems and Technology (pp. 53-60). At the Vanguard of Design Science: First Impressions and Early Findings from Ongoing Research Research-in-Progress Papers and Poster Presentations from the 10th International Conference: DESRIST 2015.

- Kaufmann M, Portmann E, Fathi M (2012) A concept of semantics extraction from web data by induction of fuzzy ontologies. In: International Workshop on Uncertainty Reason-ing for the Semantic Web.

- Kelly JE, Hamm S (2013) Smart machines: IBM's Watson and the era of cognitive compu-ting. Columbia Business School Publishing, New York.

- Malone TW, Bernstein MS (2015) Introduction. In: Malone TW, Bernstein MS (eds) Handbook of Collective Intelligence, MIT Press, Cambridge (Mass), pp 1–13.

- Metzger S, Portmann E, Finger M, Habenstein A, Riedle A, Witschi R (2018) Human Smart City – der Mensch im Zentrum. Transforming Cities:62–67.

- Portmann E (2018) Wozu ist Soft Computing nützlich? Reflexionen anhand der Smart-City-Forschung. HDM Praxis der Wirtschaftsinformatik 55(3):496–509.

- Portmann E, Tabacchi ME, Seising R, Habenstein A (eds) (2018) Designing Cognitive Cities (in print).

- Siemens G (2006) Knowing knowledge. Lulu.com.

- Tabacchi ME, Portmann E, Seising R, Habenstein A (2018) Introduction, in: Port-mann E, Tabacchi ME, Seising R, Habenstein A (eds) Designing Cognitive Cities (in print).

- Townsend AM (2014) Smart cities: big data, civic hackers, and the quest for a new uto-pia. Norton & Company, New York.

- Zadeh LA (1973) Outline of a New Approach to the Analysis of Complex Systems and De-cision Processes. IEEE Trans. SMC, SMC-3(1):28-44.

- Zadeh LA (1994) Fuzzy Logic, Neural Networks and Soft Computing. Comm. ACM 37:77–84.

## Contact Details

**University of Fribourg**
HUMAN-IST Institute
Boulevard de Pérolles 90
1700 Fribourg, Switzerland
Internet: http://human-ist.unifr.ch
eMail: edy.portmann@unifr.chc

**University of Bern**
Transdisciplinary Research Center Smart Swiss Capital Region
Länggassstrasse 49
3012 Bern
Internet: http://www.hist.unibe.ch

eMail: simonefranzelli@bluewin.ch

**University of Bern**
Historisches Institut
Länggassstrasse 49
3012 Bern
Internet: http://www.hist.unibe.ch
eMail: astrid.habenstein@hist.unibe.ch

## Profile of Authors

### Edy Portmann

Edy is Swiss Post Professor of Computer Science at the Human-IST Institute of the University of Fribourg. His transdisciplinary research focuses on cognitive computing and its applica-tion to cities. After an apprenticeship as an electrician, he studied information systems, business as well as economics and, later, got a doctorate in computer science. Among others, he worked for Swisscom, PwC and EY. In addition, Edy Portmann was also a researcher at the universities of Singapore, Berkeley and Bern.

### Simone Franzelli

Simone received a bachelor's degree in Economics, Political Science and Linguistics from the University of Bern and studied Public Management and Policy at the University of Bern and the University of Lausanne for her master's degree. Her main research interests lie in smart and cognitive cities and smart governance.

### Astrid Habenstein

Astrid is research associate at the Transdisciplinary Research Center Smart Swiss Capital Region at the University of Bern. She studied History and Philosophy at the Universitiy of Bielefeld and obtained her PhD in Ancient History at the University of Bern. Her main inter-disciplinary and transdisciplinary research interests include Smart and Cognitive Cities, sociolo-gical theory formation and research development.

# Glossary

**Administration to Administration.** By administration to administration, or A2A, we understand relationships of information and exchange within the administration, e.g., between administrative units of one particular community level, or between administrative units of different levels.

**Administration to Business.** The alternative administration to business, or A2B, comprises all governmental services between a administrative unit and the companies. The European Union has determined eight service areas to count among them, like taxation, start-ups, statistical offices, customs declaration, environmental performance or public procurement.

**Administration to Citizen.** Administration to citizen, or A2C, are the governmental services between the governmental institution and the citizens. The twelve service areas proposed by the European Union comprise taxation, social facilities, employment service, social security, official IDs, schools and training, health services, etc. Additionally, electronic votes and elections count as A2C services.

**Asymmetric encoding.** see encoding

**Auction.** Electronic auctions are an instrument of dynamic pricing over the Internet, in order to determine prices flexibly in the interaction of supply and demand.

**Authentification.** The authentification checks the authenticity of a participant of the electronic market via digital signatures.

**Barrier free Web access.** By Web accessibility or barrier free Web access, we understand the capability of a Web site or a portal to be read and understood by all users; especially, it must be possible for the visually impaired, colorblind, hearing impaired or people with impaired motor skills to use the Web.

**Blockchain.** It refers to a type of data structure that enables identifying and tracking transactions digitally and sharing this information across a distributed network of computers, creating in a sense a distributed trust network without a central control institution.

**Call center.** The call center is a direct contact point to process the citizens´ concerns via telephone.

© Springer Nature Switzerland AG 2019
A. Meier, L. Terán, *eDemocracy & eGovernment*, Progress in IS,
https://doi.org/10.1007/978-3-030-17585-6

**Certificate.** A certificate is an electronic identification according to the ISO standard X.509 that is needed when using digital signatures.

**Certification authority.** see Public Key Infrastructure

**Citizen relationship management.** The citizen relationship management comprises the strategic, tactical–analytical and operative design of relationships and processes.

**Communication center.** By a communication center, we understand a central coordination office, which handles all incoming concerns (inbound) of the citizens, independent of the respective medium or contact channel.

**Community.** By community, we understand a collective on the Internet that is created by chats, portals or relationship programs.

**Content management system.** With the help of a content management system, digital information (text, graphics, images, audio or video) is processed in different forms of display and enabled for use.

**Data mining.** Data mining refers to exploring and digging for valuable information in data stocks or in the data warehouse. To that end, algorithms are used in order to extract unknown patterns in the data and to display them.

**Data protection.** By data protection, we understand the protection of data from unauthorized access and utilization.

**Data security.** Data security is about technical and software based arrangements against distortion, destruction or loss of data.

**Data warehouse.** A data warehouse is a database system to help decision making, which permits different analyzing options on the multi-dimensional data cube.

**Desktop purchasing system.** A desktop purchasing system allows the purchase of products and services via Internet. Such systems comprise electronic catalogs and offer support for delivery and payment.

**Digital signature.** A digital signature is a procedure that uncovers the authenticity of an electronic document or contract and the authentification of the sender.

**Discussion forums.** In a discussion forum (often called newsgroup), the participants are asked to comment on certain topics. It is possible to respond to the author of an entry via e-mail.

**Distribution.** By electronic distribution, or online distribution, we understand the distribution of digital goods and services over the Internet.

**Domain.** A domain name is the Internet address of a server, in order to identify Web sites worldwide correctly.

**eDemocracy.** By Electronic Democracy or eDemocracy, we understand the support and enhancement of civil rights and duties in the Information and Knowledge Society. In the focus of attention stand options of participation, which can be executed with the help of information and communication technologies, independently of time and place.

**eElection.** eElection refers to electronic elections of political candidates. By public information campaigns and personal profiles of the candidates, the citizen can form his opinion in the run-up to an eElection. Via ePosting, the election results are communicated and evaluated.

**eGovernment.** The phrase electronic government, or eGovernment, we understand the simplification and execution of information, communication and interchange processes within and between governmental institutions, and also between the governmental institutions and citizens or organizations.

**eHealth.** By means of eHealth, it is tried to optimize the electronic processes in patient care, increase the safety and make medical information better accessible.

**eLearning.** Web-based learning and teaching environments are summarized by the term eLearning. Test and simulation environments are utilized to apply and deepen what has been learnt.

**Electronic business.** Electronic business, or eBusiness, is defined as initiation, agreement and handling of electronic business transactions, with the help of the Internet and with the goal of adding value.

**Electronic commerce.** Electronic commerce (eCommerce) is a subarea of eBusiness and is concerned with the exchange of services business to business (B2B) or business to consumer (B2C).

**Electronic health record.** In the electronic health record, administrative and medical information is stored in a systematic order, optionally supplemented by digital X-ray images and further electronic documents.

**Encoding.** By encoding or cryptography, we understand procedures that encode and decode texts and documents with the help of symmetric or asymmetric pairs of keys. In asymmetric encoding, a public and a private key are used.

**ePass.** The ePass or electronic passport is a passport with biometric data. It contains a chip to store the passport photograph (for face recognition), as well as other biometric recognition features (fingerprints, iris patterns).

**eProcurement.** By eProcurement, we understand the Internet based procurement process, including a standardization of the procurement, selection of suppliers and products, negotiation of contracts and order and acquisition of further services.

**eVoting.** With the Internet based procedure eVoting, electronic votes are carried out. This electronic process begins with putting at public disposal Web-based information and discussion forums on proposed topics and ends with the publication of the voting results and the analysis of the voting behavior.

**Expert system.** An expert system is an information system, which facilitates specific knowledge and conclusions for a marked-off field of application.

**Firewall.** A firewall is a protective shield that prevents unauthorized accesses to Web servers and information systems.

**Hyperlink.** A hyperlink is a link from one Web site to another, which is effected automatically by the Internet browser when clicked on.

**Hypertext Markup Language.** The Hypertext Markup Language is a markup language in which Web sites are engineered by means of tags.

**Identity management.** The term identity management comprises all processes and stored data on user administration of Web-based information and communication systems. This includes the identification of users, authentification (verification of authenticity of users) and authorization (distribution of rights and obligations).

**Interoperability.** Interoperability denominates the ability of heterogeneous information and communication systems to exchange information efficiently and in a way so that no data gets lost, both within the governmental institution and between different organizations.

**Knowledge management.** The knowledge management renders implicit and explicit knowledge usable by means of acquisition, storage and distribution.

**New Public Management.** New Public Management is a form of administration with the goal to modernize the state. The reform is based on the application of management techniques and relocates the control from the input side to the output side.

**Newsgroup.** see discussion forums

**Patient health card.** The electronic patient health card is a smartcard with administrative information on the insured person and the most important medical data, like prescriptions, blood type, medication or basic clinical data.

**PGP.** Short for Pretty Good Privacy

**PKI.** Short for Public Key Infrastructure

**Portal.** In a portal, cross-departmental products and services are offered, in which value creation chains are integrated.

**Pretty Good Privacy.** Pretty Good Privacy procedure is a cryptographic procedure to encode electronic documents or data and mark them as authentic.

**Procurement process.** An electronic procurement process supports the selection of suppliers, contract negotiations and the handling of purchasing activities with the help of electronic catalogs.

**Provider.** A provider is a supplier, who, apart from e-mail, offers further Internet services.

**Public Key Infrastructure.** By Public key infrastructure, we understand the build-up and operation of certification offices (trust centers), which issue certificates and certify the attribution of public keys to natural persons.

**Public Memory.** A public memory is a digital and public memory of a society. It comprises the digitalization of important works, documents, images, speeches, movies, television or radio recordings, governmental programs and resolutions, citizens´ initiatives in Web-based libraries, which stay accessible to the public.

**Public Offering.** Public offering denominates the awarding and handling of public contracts (announcement, registration, submission, evaluation, awarding, etc.) by authorities with the help of the Internet.

**Pull.** In the pull principle, the Internet users can decide which Web sites they want to visit and which information they want to receive.

**Push.** In the push principle, information or advertising messages from different sources are separated into topics and sent to the Internet user by the supplier.

**SCOR.** Short for Supply Chain Operations Reference

**Search engine.** A search engine is a software program that lists relevant Web sites in the Internet after entering a search term.

**Social software.** By social software, we summarize Web-based information systems and services, which are used to exchange information, to communicate and to nurture relationships on the cyberspace. The users of social software are not subject to a hierarchical order and can comment on or change the entries anytime.

**Supply chain management.** By supply chain management, we summarize the planning and controlling of flows of material and information during the whole value creation chain.

**Supply Chain Operations Reference.** The Supply Chain Operations Reference, or SCOR, is a reference model for supply chains, based on the process parts planning, procurement, production and delivery.

**Trust Center.** see Public Key Infrastructure

**Virtual community.** see community

**Virtual organizations.** Virtual organizations agree to temporally limited partnerships with companies, organizations or persons, in order to bundle their core competences on the electronic market.

**Web 2.0.** Web 2.0 is a collective term, under which we subsume extended Internet technologies and applications (Weblogs, subscription services, wikis, social software), as well as a new understanding of the Internet by the users.

**Web accessibility.** see barrier free Web access

**Weblog.** A Weblog, or short blog, is a frequently updated journal, whose electronic entries are displayed in a chronologically descending way. There is a multitude of Weblogs, ranging from private diaries, over topical Weblogs to corporate blogs.

**Web site.** A Web site is an Internet presence and an information offer of a governmental office or institution, organization or a citizen on the Internet.

**Wiki.** A wiki is an online database, in which it is possible to create, edit and cross-link entries to a topic easily and quickly. The entries can be extended, changed or deleted by other users.

**Workflow management system.** A workflow management system is an active software system to control the workflow between participating parties. Such systems work according to a given process sequence.

# References

Agora. (2018). *Bringing Our Voting Systems Into the 21st Century (Whitepaper V 2.0)* (Tech. Rep.). Author.

AGS. (2002). *Eine Einführung in die wirkungsorientierte Gemeindeführung und Verwaltung* (Tech. Rep.). Amt für Gemeinden und soziale Sicherheit des Kantons Solothurn.

Alby, T. (2007). Web 2.0. *Konzepte, Anwendungen, Technologien, 2.*

Appelfeller, W., & Buchholz, W. (2005). Supplier Relationship Management: Strategie, Organisation und IT des modernen Beschaffungsmanagements, Wiesbaden 2005. *Procurement Event Monitoring.*

Argyris, C., & Schön, D. A. (2018). *Die Lernende Organisation: Grundlagen, Methode, Praxis.* Schäffer-Poeschel Verlag.

Asghari, R. (2005). *E-Government in der Praxis: Leitfaden für Politik und Verwaltung.* Software & Support Verlag.

Ausserhofer, J., & Maireder, A. (2013). National Politics on Twitter. *Information, Communication & Society, 16*(3), 291-314.

Baden-Württemberg, I. (1996). Kommunaler Produktplan Baden-Württemberg. *Schriftenreihe des Innenministeriums Baden-Württemberg zum kommunalen Haushalts-und Rechnungswesen*(2).

Bashir, I. (2017). *Mastering Blockchain.* Packt Publishing Ltd.

Bauknecht, K., Mühlherr, T., Sauter, C., & Teufel, S. (1995). Computerunterstützung für die Gruppenarbeit. *Bonn: Addison-Wesley.*

Beck, A. (2007). Web 2.0: Konzepte, Technologie, Anwendungen. *HMD Praxis der Wirtschaftsinformatik, 44*(3), 5–16.

Berentsen, A., & Schär, F. (2017). Bitcoin, Blockchain und Kryptoassets: Eine umfassende Einführung. *Aufl. Norderstedt: BoD–Books on Demand.*

Bieler, F., & Franz, A. (2007). *e-Government: Perspektiven, Probleme, Lösungsansätze.* Erich Schmidt.

Bitzer, F., & Brisch, K. M. (2013). *Digitale Signatur: Grundlagen, Funktion und Einsatz*. Springer-Verlag.

Blattberg, R. C., Getz, G., & Thomas, J. S. (2001). *Customer Equity: Building and Managing Relationships as Valuable Assets*. Harvard Business Press.

Bodnar, J. (1992). Remaking America: Public Memory. *Commemoration, and Patriotism in the Twentieth Century (Princeton, 1992), 14*.

Borghoff, U., & Schlichter, J. (1998). Rechnergestützte Gruppenarbeit–Eine Einführung. *Verteilte Anwendungen Berlin: Springer*.

Bouras, C., Kastaniotis, S., & Triantafillou, V. (2000). Citizen Information Services Using Internet Technologies. In *ECIS 2000 Proceedings* (p. 169).

Brands, G. (2013). *Verschlüsselungsalgorithmen: Angewandte Zahlentheorie rund um Sicherheitsprotokolle*. Springer-Verlag.

Brandt, M., & Volkert, B. (2002). E-Voting im Internet: Formen, Entwicklungsstand und Probleme. *Akademie für Technikfolgenabschätzung in Baden-Württemberg*.

Brenner, W., & Wilking, G. (1999). Dezentrales, Internet-basiertes Beschaffungsmanagement—Internet-basierte Einkaufsseiten aktiv Nutzen. *Beschaffung Aktuell, 8*, 54–56.

Bruhn, M. (2002). *Integrierte Kundenorientierung: Implementierung einer kundenorientierten Unternehmensführung*. Gabler Verlag.

Buchmann, J. (2010). *Einführung in die Kryptographie*. Springer-Verlag.

Büchner, H. (2001). *Web-Content-Management: Websites Professionell Betreiben*. Galileo Press.

Bullinger, H.-J., & Berres, A. (2013). *E-Business—Handbuch für den Mittelstand: Grundlagen, Rezepte, Praxisberichte*. Springer-Verlag.

Chopra, S., & Meindl, P. (2007). *Supply Chain Management. Strategy, Planning & Operation*. Springer.

Christ, O. (2013). *Content-Management in der Praxis: Erfolgreicher Aufbau und Betrieb unternehmensweiter Portale*. Springer-Verlag.

Comunello, F., & Anzera, G. (2012). Will the revolution be tweeted? A conceptual framework for understanding the social media and the Arab Spring. *Islam and Christian–Muslim Relations, 23*(4), 453–470.

Conover, M., Ratkiewicz, J., Francisco, M. R., Gonçalves, B., Menczer, F., & Flammini, A. (2011). Political Polarization on Twitter. In *ICWSM*. The AAAI Press.

Daum, R. (2002). Citizen Relationship Management und Electronic Government. *E-Government, HMD Praxis der Wirtschaftsinformatik*(226), 80–86.

Dittmann, J. (2013). *Digitale Wasserzeichen: Grundlagen, Verfahren, Anwendungsgebiete.* Springer-Verlag.

Dolmetsch, R. (2000). *eProcurement: Sparpotential im Einkauf.* Addison-Wesley.

Dolmetsch, R., Fleisch, E., & Österle, H. (1999). Desktop Purchasing: I-Net-Technologien in der Beschaffung. *HMD - Praxis der Wirtschaftsinformatik, 206,* 77–89.

Drescher, D. (2017). Blockchain Grundlagen: Ein Einführung in die elementaren Konzepte in 25 Schritten. *Husby, mitp.*

Dwivedi, Y. K., Rana, N. P., Tajvidi, M., Lal, B., Sahu, G. P., & Gupta, A. (2017). Exploring the Role of Social Media in e-Government: An Analysis of Emerging Literature. In *Proceedings of the 10th International Conference on Theory and Practice of Electronic Governance* (pp. 97–106).

Enjolras, B., Steen-Johnsen, K., & Wollebæk, D. (2013). Social Media and Mobilization to Offline Demonstrations: Transcending Participatory Divides? *New Media & Society, 15*(6), 890–908.

European Comission. (2007). *Public Services for Citizens - Public Services for Businesses.* http://ec.europa.eu/information_society/eeurope/2002/action_plan/pdf/basicpublicservices.pdf. Accessed 27 Dec 2007.

European Comission. (2016). *European eGovernment Action Plan 2016-2020.* https://ec.europa.eu/digital-single-market/en/european-egovernment-action-plan-2016-2020. Accessed 13 Jul 2015.

European Comission. (2017). eGovernment Benchmark 2017. Taking Stock of User-centric Design and Delivery of Digital Public Services in Europe. *EU Publications.*

European Comission. (2018). *2018 Reform of EU Data Protection Rules.* https://ec.europa.eu/commission/priorities/justice-and-fundamental-rights/data-protection/2018-reform-eu-data-protection-rules_en. Accessed 13 Jul 2018.

Friedhelm, G., Schinzer, H., & Tacke, A. (2002). Public E-Procurement, Netzbasierte Beschaffung für öffentliche Auftraggeber. *Verlag Vahlen. München.*

Fröschle, H.-P., & Reinheimer, S. (2007). *Serviceorientierte Architekturen.* dpunkt-Verlag.

Gadatsch, A. (2013). *Management von Geschäftsprozessen: Methoden und Werkzeuge für die IT-Praxis: Eine Einführung für Studenten und Praktiker.* Springer-Verlag.

GAZ. (2003). *Wirkungsorientierte Gemeindeverwaltung - Produkte.* http://www.gaz.zh.ch/internet/justiz_inneres/gaz/ de/gemeindefinanzen/themen_projekte/npm/grundlagen/ _jcr_content/contentPar/downloadlist/downloaditems/ 521_1282631175619.spooler.download.1303895555861.pdf/ Grundlagen.pdf. Accessed 13 Jul 2015.

Gerbaudo, P. (2018). *Tweets and the Streets: Social Media and Contemporary Activism.* Pluto Press.

Gianpietro-Zago, M. (2018, May). *50+ Examples of How Blockchains are Taking Over the World.* https://medium.com/@matteozago/50-examples-of -how-blockchains-are-taking-over-the-world-4276bf488a4b. Accessed 13 Jul 2018.

Gil de Zúñiga, H., Veenstra, A., Vraga, E., & Shah, D.-v. (2010). Digital Democracy: Reimagining Path-ways to Political Participation. *Journal of Information Technology & Politics, 7*(1), 36–51.

Gil Ramírez, H., & Guilleumas, R. (2015, 11). Communication Networks of the 15M Novement on Twitter. *Redes. Revista hispana para el análisis de redes sociales, 28.*

Gipp, B., & Beel, J. (2005). *ePass - der neue biometrische Reisepass.* Shaker.

Gisler, M., & Spahni, D. (2001). *eGovernment: Eine Standortbestimmung.* Bern-Stuttgart: Haupt-Verlag.

Gora, W., & Bauer, H. (2013). *Virtuelle Organisationen im Zeitalter von E-Business und E-Government: Einblicke und Ausblicke.* Springer-Verlag.

Götzer, K., Schneiderath, U., Maier, B., & Komke, T. (2004). Dokumenten-Management–Informationen im Unternehmen effizient nutzen. *dpunkt-Verlag.*

Griese, J., Kohler, R., Geiser, T., & Webbuild, K. (1999). Deutschschweizer Gemeinden im World Wide Web-eine Bestandesaufnahme. *Zusammenarbeit mit Webbuild, Internet Technologie.*

Gross, P. (1994). *Die Multioptionsgesellschaft* (Vol. 917). Suhrkamp Frankfurt aM.

Haas, P. (2005). *Medizinische Informationssysteme und Elektronische Krankenakten.* Springer-Verlag.

Haas, P. (2006). eHealth Verändert das Gesundheitswesen–Grundlagen, Anwendungen, Konsequenzen. *HMD Praxis der Wirtschaftsinformatik, 251,* 6–19.

Hässig, K. (2000). *Prozessmanagement: erfolgreich durch effiziente Strukturen.* Versus.

Haun, M. (2013). *Handbuch Wissensmanagement: Grundlagen und Umsetzung, Systeme und Praxisbeispiele.* Springer-Verlag.

Helmke, S., & Uebel, M. (2003). *Online-Vertrieb: erfolgreiche Konzepte für die Praxis.* Hanser.

Hermann, M., & Leuthold, H. (2000). Einsatz von kartographischen Methoden und GIS zur Analyse und Visualisierung mehrdimensionaler Strukturen in den Sozialwissenschaften. *Visualisierung Raumbezogener Daten: Methoden und Anwendungen, 3,* 77–92.

Herwig, V. (2001). *E-Government: Distribution von Leistungen öffentlicher Institutionen über das Internet.* Eul.

Hildebrand, K., & Hofmann, J. (2006). Social Software. *HMD Praxis der Wirtschaftsinformatik*(252).

Hippner, H. (2006). Bedeutung, Anwendungen und Einsatzpotenziale von Social Software. *HMD–Praxis der Wirtschaftsinformatik, 43*(252 S 6).

Hochmann, S. (2001). *Elektronische Signatur.* BoD–Books on Demand.

Hofmann, J., & Meier, A. (Eds.). (2008). *Webbasierte Geschäftsmodelle. Praxis der Wirtschaftsinformatik* (No. 261). HMD.

Hofmann, J., & Reich, S. (2008). *eGovernment: Praxis der Wirtschaftsinformatik* (No. 265). HMD.

HONCode. (1995). *Health on Net Foundation.* http://www.hon.ch. Accessed 13 Jul 2015.

Ionas, A. (2008). *Modellierung, Entwicklung und Nutzung eines Data Warehouse für medizinische Communication Centers* (Unpublished doctoral dissertation). Departement für Informatik–Universität Fribourg, Fribourg.

Jablonski, S., Böhm, M., & Schulze, W. (1997). *Workflow-Management: Entwicklung von Systemen und Anwendungen Facetten einer neuen Technologie.* dpunkt-Verlag, Heidelberg.

Jähn, K., & Nagel, E. (2003). *e-Health.* Springer.

Jain, S., & Kumar, P. (2018). Semantic Web, Ontologies and E-Government: A Review. *Mody University International Journal of Computing and Engineering Research, 2*(1), 40–44.

Jeitziner, B. (2004). Wahlen im Internetzeitalter. Informationsvermittler als politische Berater von Wählern und Politikern. *Perspektiven der Wirtschaftspolitik, 65,* 47–64.

Jiménez, C. E., Falcone, F., Solanas, A., Puyosa, H., Zoughbi, S., & González, F. (2015). Smart government: Opportunities and challenges in smart cities development. In *Handbook of Research on Democratic Strategies and Citizen-Centered E-Government Services* (pp. 1–19). IGI Global.

Johnson, D. G. (2004). Computer Ethics. In F. Luciano (Ed.), *The Blackwell Guide to the Philosophy of Computing and Information* (pp. 65–75). Blackwell.

Karlsson, J., & Taga, K. (2006). M-Payment im internationalen Kontext. In *Handbuch E-Money, E-Payment & M-Payment* (pp. 73–87). Springer.

Kaushik, A. (2007). *Web Analytics: An Hour A Day*. John Wiley & Sons.

Kirsch, G. (2004). *Neue Politische Ökonomie* (Vol. 8272). UTB.

Koch, M. (2001). Community-Support-Systeme. In *CSCW-Kompendium* (pp. 286–296). Springer.

Kollmann, T. (2010). *E-Business*. Springer-Verlag.

Kotler, P., Keller, K. L., & Bliemel, F. (2007). *Marketing-management: Strategien für wertschaffendes Handeln*. Pearson Studium.

Krallmann, H. (1989). *EDV-Sicherheitsmanagement: integrierte Sicherheitskonzepte für betriebliche Informations-und Kommunikationssysteme*. Schmidt.

Krimmer, R. (2006). Electronic voting 2006. *GI Lecture Notes in Informatics*, 86.

Kröger, D., & Gimmy, M. A. (2000). Handbuch zum Internetrecht: Electronic Commerce. *Informations-, Kommunikations-und Mediendienste, Berlin, Heidelberg ua.*

Kshetri, N., & Voas, J. (2018). Blockchain-Enabled E-Voting. *IEEE Software*, *35*(4).

Kurz, C., & Rieger, F. (2007). Nedap-Wahlcomputer–Manipulationsmethoden an Hard-und Software. *Informatik-Spektrum*, *30*(5), 313–321.

Lammer, T. (2006). *Handbuch E-money, E-payment & M-payment*. Springer-Verlag.

Laudon, K. C., & Laudon, J. P. (2015). *Management Information Systems: Managing the Digital Firm Plus MyMISLab with Pearson eText–Access Card Package*. Prentice Hall Press.

Lawrenz, O., Hildebrand, K., & Nenninger, M. (2013). *Supply Chain Management: Strategien, Konzepte und Erfahrungen auf dem Weg zu E-Business Networks*. Springer-Verlag.

Limper, W. (2001). *Dokumenten-Management: Wissen, Informationen und Medien digital verwalten*. Dt. Taschenbuch-Verlag.

Lisbon Strategy. (2008). *Lisbon Strategy: Lisbon European Council, 23 and 24 March 2000*. http://consilium.europa.eu/ueDocs/cms_Data/docs/pressData/en/ec/00100-r1.en0.htm. Accessed 13 Jul 2015.

Liu, B. (2007). *Web Data Mining: Exploring Hyperlinks, Contents, and Usage Data*. Springer.

Luhmann, N. (2000). Die Politik der Gesellschaft [The politics of society]. *Frankfurt am Main: Suhrkamp.*

Luhmann, N., & Baecker, D. (2005). *Einführung in die Theorie der Gesellschaft.* Carl-Auer-Systeme Heidelberg.

Mandl, T. (2006). *Die automatische Bewertung der Qualität von Internet-Seiten im Information Retrieval* (Unpublished doctoral dissertation). Universitätsbibliothek Hildesheim.

Mehlich, H. (2013). *Electronic Government: Die elektronische Verwaltungsreform Grundlagen-Entwicklungsstand-Zukunftsperspektiven.* Springer-Verlag.

Meier, A. (2001). *Internet & Electronic Business: Herausforderung an das Management.* Zürich: Orell Füssli.

Meier, A. (2002). eGovernment. *Praxis der Wirtschaftsinformatik* (No. 226). dpunkt-Verlag.

Meier, A. (2004). Citizen Relationship Management–Ein Online-Kommunikationsmodell für Bürgerinnen und Bürger. *HMD, 41*(2004), 235.

Meier, A. (2009). Elektronische Abstimmungen und Wahlen. *HMD Praxis der Wirtschaftsinformatik, 46*(1), 51-61.

Meier, A. (2010). *Relationale und postrelationale Datenbanken.* Springer-Verlag.

Meier, A., & Stormer, H. (2009). *eBusiness & eCommerce: Managing the Digital Value Chain.* Springer.

Meier, A., & Stormer, H. (2018, December). Blockchain = Distributed Ledger + Consensus. *HMD Praxis der Wirtschaftsinformatik, 55*(324).

Merz, M. (2002). *E-commerce und e-business: Marktmodelle, Anwendungen und Technologien.* dpunkt-Verlag.

Mezler-Andelberg, C. (2008). Identity Management–eine Einführung. *Grundlagen, Technik, wirtschaftlicher Nutzen. dpunkt-Verlag.*

Misoch, S. (2006). *Online-Kommunikation.* UVK Verlag.

Mock, T. (2006). Was ist ein Medium? *Publizistik, 51*(2), 183–200.

Müller, K.-R. (2008). *IT-Sicherheit mit System.* Springer-Verlag.

Nakamoto, S. (2008). *Bitcoin P2P e-cash paper.* https://www.mail-archive .com/cryptography@metzdowd.com/msg09959.html. Accessed 13 Jul 2018.

Nekolar, A.-P. (2013). *E-procurement: Euphorie und Realität.* Springer-Verlag.

Noizat, P. (2015). Blockchain Electronic Vote. In *Handbook of Digital Currency* (pp. 453–461). Elsevier.

Norbert, T., & Adrian, R. (2006). Public Management, Innovative Konzepte zur Führung im öffentlichen Sektor. *3, Auflage, Springer Gabler.*

Nurmi, H., Salomaa, A., & Santean, L. (1991). Secret Ballot Elections in Computer Networks. *Computers & Security, 10*(6), 553–560.

Passini, S. (2012). The Facebook and Twitter revolutions: Active participation in the 21st century. *Human Affairs, 22*(3), 301–312.

Picot, A., & Fischer, T. (2006). Weblogs professionell. *Grundlagen, Konzepte und Praxis im unternehmerischen Umfeld. dpunkt-Verlag.*

Picot, A., & Quadt, H.-P. (2001). *Verwaltung ans Netz!: Neue Medien halten Einzug in die öffentlichen Verwaltungen.* Springer.

Piller, F. T. (2004). Mass Customization: Reflections on the State of the Concept. *International Journal of Flexible Manufacturing Systems, 16*(4), 313–334.

Priddat, B. P., & Jansen, S. A. (2001). *Electronic Government: Neue Potentiale für einen modernen Staat.* Klett-Cotta Verlag.

Probst, G., Raub, S., & Romhardt, K. (1999). *Wissen managen: Wie Unternehmen ihre wertvollste Ressource optimal nutzen.* Gabler Verlag.

Probst, G. J., & Büchel, B. (1998). *Organisationales Lernen: Wettbewerbsvorteil der Zukunft.* Springer.

Prosser, A., Kofler, R., Krimmer, R., & Unger, M. K. (2002). e-Voting. at. Entwicklung eines Internet-basierten Wahlsystems für öffentliche Wahlen. *Institute of Information Processing and Information Management*(04).

Prosser, A., & Krimmer, R. (2004). *Electronic Voting in Europe-Technology, Law, Politics and Society.* Ges. für Informatik.

Prosser, A., & Müller-Török, R. (2002). E-Democracy: Eine neue Qualität im demokratischen Entscheidungsprozess. *Wirtschaftsinformatik, 44*(6), 545–556.

Przepiorka, S. (2006). Weblogs, Wikis und die dritte Dimension. *Weblogs professionell. Grundlagen, Konzepte und Praxis im unternehmerischen Umfeld, 1*, 13–27.

Qiao, L., & Nahrstedt, K. (1998). Watermarking Methods for MPEG Encoded Video: Towards Resolving Rightful Ownership. In *Multimedia Computing and Systems, 1998. Proceedings. IEEE International Conference on* (pp. 276–285).

Raab, G., & Werner, N. (2009). *Customer Relationship Management: Aufbau dauerhafter und profitabler Kundenbeziehungen; mit Tabellen.* Verlag Recht u. Wirtschaft.

Recalde, L., Mendieta, J., Boratto, L., Teran, L., Vaca, C., & Baquerizo, G. (2017). Who You Should Not Follow: Extracting Word Embeddings from Tweets to Identify Groups of Interest and Hijackers in Demonstrations. *IEEE Transactions on Emerging Topics in Computing.*

Recuero, R., Zago, G., Bastos, M. T., & Araújo, R. (2015). Hashtags Functions in the Protests Across Brazil. *SAGE Open, 5*(2).

Reichwald, R., Möslein, K., Sachenbacher, H., & Englberger, H. (2013). *Telekooperation: Verteilte Arbeits-und Organisationsformen.* Springer-Verlag.

Richardson, W. (2010). *Blogs, Wikis, Podcasts, and Other Powerful Web Tools for Classrooms.* Corwin Press.

Riesch, M., & Zugang, S. S. z. B. T. (2007). *Schweizer Accessibility-Studie 2007: Bestandesaufnahme der Zugänglichkeit von Schweizer Websites des Gemeinwesens für Menschen mit Behinderungen; eine Studie der Schweizerischen Stiftung zur Behindertengerechten Technologienutzung.* Stiftung Zugang für Alle.

Riga. (2006). *European Ministerial Declaration, Conference ICT for an Inclusive Society.* http://ec.europa.eu/information_society/activities/einclusion/events/riga_2006/index_en.htm. Accessed 13 Jul 2015.

Rubtcova, M., & Pavenkov, O. (2018). Implementation of Blockchain Technology in Electronic Election in Sierra Leone. In *2018 Conference: Re-thinking Regions in Global International Relations.* Philippines: SSRN.

Ruh, H. (1995). *Anders, aber besser - für eine solidarische und überlebensfähige Welt.* Waldgut.

Runge, A. (2000). *Die Rolle des Electronic Contracting im elektronischen Handel: eine aus betriebswirtschaftlicher Perspektive vorgenommene vertragstheoretische Analyse am Beispiel der amerikanischen Versicherungsbranche.* na.

SAGA. (2011). *SAGA 5 für die Bundesverwaltung.* https://www.cio.bund.de/Web/DE/Architekturen-und-Standards/SAGA/saga_node.html. Accessed 13 Jul 2015.

Savini, M., Stormer, H., & Meier, A. (2007). Integrating Context Information in a Mobile Environment using the eSana Framework. In *Eceh* (pp. 131–142).

Schedler, K., & Proeller, I. (2000). *New Public Management.* Haupt.

Scheer, A.-W., Kruppke, H., & Heib, R. (2013). *E-Government: Prozessoptimierung in der öffentlichen Verwaltung.* Springer-Verlag.

Schinzer, H., Thome, R., & Hepp, R. (2005). Electronic Commerce und Electronic Business–Mehrwert durch Integration und Automation, 3. *Auflage, Verlag Franz Vahlen, München.*

Schögel, M., Tomczak, T., & Belz, C. (Eds.). (2002). *Roadmap to E-Business.* St. Gallen : Verl. Thexis.

Schubert, P., & Ecademy, C. (2002). *Procurement im E-Business: Einkaufs-und Verkaufsprozesse elektronisch optimieren; Begriffe-Konzepte-Fallstudien.* Hanser.

Schwabe, G., Streitz, N., & Unland, R. (2012). *CSCW-Kompendium: Lehr-und Handbuch zum computerunterstützten kooperativen Arbeiten.* Springer-Verlag.

Schwenk, J. (2002). *Sicherheit und Kryptographie im Internet.* Springer.

SCOR. (2004). *Supply-Chain Operations Reference Model.* http://www.supply-chain.org/slides/SCOR5.0OverviewBooklet.pdf. Accessed 04 Apr 2004.

Segerberg, A., & Bennett, W. L. (2011). Social Media and the Organization of Collective Action: Using Twitter to Explore the Ecologies of Two Climate Change Protests. *The Communication Re-view, 14*(3), 197–215.

smartvote. (2015). *Webbasiertes Wahlhilfesystem für Parlamentswahlen in der Schweiz.* http://www.smartvote.ch. Accessed 13 Jul 2015.

Sotomo. (2015). *Sociotopological Modeling.* http://sotomo.geo.unizh.ch/research/. Accessed 24 Jan 2008.

Spivack, N. (2009). *Web Evolution.* https://www.slideshare.net/novaspivack/web-evolution-nova-spivack-twine. Accessed 13 Jul 2015.

Strömer, T. H. (1997). *Online-Recht: Rechtsfragen im Internet und in Mailboxnetzen.* dpunkt, Verlag für digitale Technologie.

Szugat, M., Gewehr, J. E., & Lochmann, C. (2006). Social Software–Blogs. *Wikis & Co. entwickler. Press, Frankfurt am Main.*

Taga, K., Karlsson, J., & Arthur, D. (2004). *Little Global M-Payment 2004* (Tech. Rep.). Viena, Austria: D. Little's Telecommuni-cations, IT, Media & Electronics (TIME) Practice.

Terán, L. (2014). *SmartParticipation. A Fuzzy-Based Recommender System for Political Community-Building.* Springer.

Terán, L., & Mancera, J. (2019). Dynamic Profiles Using Sentiment Analysis and Twitter Data for Voting Advice Applications. *Government Information Quarterly.*

Tiedtke, D., & Link, J. (2013). *Wettbewerbsvorteile durch Online Marketing: Die strategischen Perspektiven elektronischer Märkte.* Springer-Verlag.

Varnali, K., & Gorgulu, V. (2015). A Social Influence Perspective on Expressive Political Participation in Twitter: The Case of # OccupyGezi. *Information, Communication & Society, 18*(1), 1–16.

Warnecke, H.-J. (2013). *Revolution der Unternehmenskultur: das fraktale Unternehmen.* Springer-Verlag.

WCAG. (2007). *WVAG 2.0 - Web Content Accessibility Guidelines, Version 1.0.* http://www.w3.org/WAI/. Accessed 13 Jul 2015.

Weiber, R. (2013). *Handbuch Electronic Business: Informationstechnologien-Electronic Commerce-Geschäftsprozesse.* Springer-Verlag.

Wirth, N. (1976). *Algorithms+ Data Structures= Programs Prentice-Hall Series in Automatic Computation.* Prentice Hall.

Wirtz, B. W. (2001). *Electronic Business.* Springer-Verlag.

Wöhr, H. (2004). *Web-Technologien: Konzepte-Programmiermodelle-Architekturen.* dpunkt-Verlag.

Wüthrich, H. A., Philipp, A. F., & Frentz, M. H. (1997). *Vorsprung durch Virtualisierung: Lernen von virtuellen Pionierunternehmen.* Gabler.

Zerfass, A. (2007). *Corporate Blogs - Einsatzmöglichkeiten und Herausforderungen.* http://www.bloginitiativegermany.de. Accessed 13 Jun 2015.

# Index

Accessibility, 22, 24
Administration to administration, 4
Administration to Business, 6
Administration to business, 5
Administration to Citizen, 6
Administration to citizen, 4
Administration to Administration, 6
Auctions, 43, 47
auditability, 184
Authentication, 77, 91
Authentification, 80
Authorization, 77

Benchmarking, 62
Binding Elections, 184
Blockchain, 83, 168
Blockchain-based eVoting, 168
Buyer-side, 39

Capability maturity model, 5, 62
Catalog, 19, 38, 40, 41, 59, 76
Certificate, 82
Certification authority, 81
Cognitive Cities, 234
Communication, 5, 9, 17, 24, 60, 194
Communication center, 197, 209
Community building, 204
Community formation, 21, 61
Content management, 132
Contracts, 74
Copyright, 108

Data model, 55
Data protection, 61, 89, 107, 115, 230
Data security, 61, 89, 107
Desktop purchasing, 40, 45

Development model, 199
Digital divide, 232
Digital divide, 229
Digital signature, 89
Digital signatures, 80
Document management, 130

eAssistance, 9, 13
eBusiness, 7
eCollaboration, 10, 129
eCommerce, 7
eCommunity, 10, 193, 214
eContracting, 9, 73
eDemocracy, 3, 10, 21, 161
eElection, 163, 164, 166
eGovernment, 3
eHealth, 60, 66
Elections Ecuador, 175
Encryption, 78
ePassport, 91
eProcurement, 9, 35, 39, 41
eService, 9, 53
eSettlement, 9, 99
Ethic, 230
eVoting, 163, 164, 166, 184
Expert system, 226

GDPR, 111, 113
Governmental services, 56, 57
Groupware, 21, 139

HONCode, 25

Identification, 76
Identity management, 76
Information, 5, 9, 17, 60, 231

© Springer Nature Switzerland AG 2019
A. Meier, L. Terán, *eDemocracy & eGovernment*, Progress in IS,
https://doi.org/10.1007/978-3-030-17585-6

Intermediary, 40, 41
Internet, 14
Internet Voting, 184
Interoperability, 54

Key figure, 198, 202
Knowledge management, 172, 225
Knowledge society, 11, 221, 223, 229, 230

The Lisbon Declaration, 2

Marketplace, 40
MOOCs, 151
Multi-channel, 195

Negotiation process, 75
New public management, 222

Offline distribution, 104
Online distribution, 104

Participation, 3, 6, 60, 162
Payment system, 101
Performance review, 202
Personalization, 22
Persons with disabilities, 27
Political controlling, 170
Portal, 6, 20, 162
Pretty Good Privacy (PGP), 81
Private Key, 79
Private keys, 83
Procurement model, 38, 39
Procurement process, 36
Product plan, 58
Production, 6
Public key infrastructure, 81, 89
Public memory, 172
Public offering, 42
Pull, 194
Push, 194

Really simple syndication, 17, 137

Security, 110, 114, 121
Seller-side, 38
Smart Government, 19
Social and economic inclusion, 27

Social inclusion, 27
Social network, 16
Social software, 17, 204
Spam, 230
Supply chain, 100
Systems approach, 27

transparency, 184
trust, 184
Trust Center, 81

User profile, 38, 200
User-centric Government, 62

VAA 2.0, 214
VAAs, 175
verifiability, 184
Virtual campus, 144
Virtual organization, 140
Voting Advice Applications, 175

Watermarks, 108
Web, 15
Web 1.0, 16
Web 2.0, 16, 204
Web 3.0, 18
Web 4.0, 18
Web accessibility, 27
Web content accessibility guidelines, 23
Web mining, 26
Web services, 14
Weblog, 17, 136, 137, 206
Wiki, 134

Printed by Printforce, United Kingdom